The Beatle Myth

The Beatle Myth

The British Invasion of American Popular Music, 1956-1969

by

Michael Bryan Kelly

"DOC ROCK"

McFarland & Company, Inc., Publishers
Jefferson, North Carolina and London

British Library Cataloguing-in-Publication data are available

Library of Congress Cataloguing-in-Publication Data

Kelly, Michael Bryan.
    The Beatle myth : the British invasion of American popular music,
1956–1969 / by Michael Bryan Kelly.
      p. cm.
    Includes bibliographical references and index.
    ISBN 0-89950-579-1 (lib. bdg. : 50# alk. paper) ∞
    1. Rock music—United States—History and criticism. 2. Rock
music—Great Britain—History and criticism. 3. Beatles.
I. Title.
ML3534.K44 1991
781.66'0973'09045—dc20   90-53500
                                                      CIP
                                                      MN

"Doc Rock" ® 1978 is a registered service mark of Michael Bryan Kelly

Manufactured in the United States of America

McFarland & Company, Inc., Publishers
  Box 611, Jefferson, North Carolina 28640

To Bob Barber/The Morning Mayor, Mongo Barker, J. Walter Beethoven, Dick Biondi, Prof. J. Jazmo Bop, Johnny Canton, Charlie Christian, Jim Collinson, Johnny Dark, Dan Diamond, Rick Douglass, Bob Elliott, Richard Ward Fatherly, Sara "Rhonda Rock" Garey, Bill Hanson, Doc Holliday and Belle Star, Larry James, Phil Jay, Roger Johnson, Mr. Lee, Louie Louie, Larry Miller, Larry Neal, Bob Potter, Ricky the "K", Rock Robbin, Rockin' Robbin, Rockin' Robins, Rob Robbin, Lloyd Thaxton, Charlie Tuna, Rick Wrigley, Julie Wells, Lyle "Superjock" Wood ... and John, Paul, George and Ringo — thanks for all the music!

Acknowledgments

Special appreciation is expressed for the support of these people, without whom this volume would not have been possible:

Buzzie Kelly
Lauri Klobas
Timothy P. Kelly
Shawn A. Kelly
Steve Lardy
Mom and Pop

Table of Contents

Introduction

Are you a victim of the Beatle myth? Take the Quiz and find out.

THE BEATLE MYTH TRUE OR FALSE QUIZ

1. The "Beatle haircut" was responsible for U.S. males wearing long hair.
2. The Beatles introduced "Beatle boots" to America.
3. The Beatles created and popularized the musical lyric "Yeah Yeah Yeah!"
4.a. In 1964, the Beatles and the rest of the British invasion groups eliminated the established American artists from the American charts.
4.b. In 1964, the Beatles and the rest of the British invasion groups eliminated the established American musical styles (girl groups, surf and drag, teen idols) from the American charts.
5. British music dominated the U.S. charts in the mid-'60s.
6. The Beatles popularized the practice of artists writing their own songs.
7. Anything and everything the Beatles released in the United States became a hit.
8. The Beatles and their music were popular naturally, unlike the manufactured images and popularity of early '60s American artists, and the British invasion artists in general were more successful than the U.S. teen idols.
9. Beatle LP albums were the first played on AM radio, which had up to then played only hit 45s.
10. American rock 'n' roll was unable to compete musically with the British sound.

If you answered "true" to any of the questions, then count yourself among the victims of the Beatle myth, because all 10 statements are false.

The goal of this book is to tell the true story of the Beatles and the British invasion from one who was there and who took notes.

1

A Rock 'n' Roll Fan Is Born

When I was swimming at a lake the summer in between kindergarten and the first grade, I heard the song "Sh-Boom" on a portable radio. I don't recall now if it was the Chords' original, or the Crew Cuts' cover version. No matter, because either way it was a momentous occasion. Because even if it was the Crew Cuts, who sound very tame and bland by today's standards, in 1954 even their record was totally outrageous.

From that day on, I have been devoted to rock 'n' roll. I drove everyone crazy singing rock 'n' roll on the school bus and in the family car. In the first grade, when we were assigned to draw with Crayolas, I would use my pictures to illustrate my favorite rock 'n' roll records.

I watched television rock 'n' roll on "Red Skelton," "Ed Sullivan," "Dick Clark," "Shindig," "Hullabaloo," "Malibu U," "Action," "The Donna Reed Show" (Shelley Fabares, Paul Peterson), "The Patty Duke Show" (Chad and Jeremy, Patty herself), "Ozzie and Harriet," "The Dick Van Dyke Show" (also Chad and Jeremy), and countless other programs. One of my favorites was a public service announcement by the Everly Brothers for Savings Bonds — they sang "Bye Bye Love." When my parents and I saw Elvis on television, I was mesmerized, they were disgusted.

When the transistor radio was finally invented, I took one to school, I slept with one under my pillow, and I carried one with me at all times. I got my first reel-to-reel tape recorder in 1962 so I could tape everything off the radio with the microphone. But the sounds of my littlest brother crying got on the tapes (there were no "tape in" and "tape out" plugs in those days). So, I took the cover off my best radio, took apart the microphone, and attached the wires of the radio speaker to the wires of the microphone cable, and made direct hi-fi recordings.

I got my first stereo phonograph in 1963, the same year I saw the Beatles sing "She Loves You" on the "Jack Paar Show." That night I fell in love with the Beatles' music, months before Ed Sullivan mass-marketed it. Later, the Dave Clark Five on Ed Sullivan seemed better to me than even Elvis had. My parents offered no opinion.

In 1965, I had a battery-powered turntable balanced on the front seat of my car. I had some good times that summer, but there was a down side, too. Besides having to change the record every two and a half minutes, the big problem was that the records speeded up when I turned right, slowed down when I turned left, and skipped when I burned rubber. I also warped a lot of records in the sun that summer.

At home, there were (and are) extension speakers in the basement, kitchen, garage, shower, and under the bathroom commode.

In the '70s, I got stares as I carried one of the first huge portable stereo cassette decks when I jogged, or when I flew on airliners.

Today I have two car tape players, five cassette decks, one reel-to-reel, three turntables, two mixers, three amps, three tape recorders, 10,000 45s (I gave away 20,000 45s in 1987), a couple of thousand LPs, and uncounted songs on tape. And one CD.

Starting in 1962 and up to the present, the music has been on constantly—turned on before I wake up by clock radios and clock cassettes, and putting me to sleep with timers; running constantly through meals and in cars; keeping me company while doing junior high and high school homework, while studying for my bachelor's degree in liberal arts, my master's degree in Human Development, and my Ph.D. in Behavioral Science. The music plays even while I'm watching television sometimes.

In the '60s, I went out each week and got as many radio station Top-40 lists as I could at the record counters:

K-TOP 40	KAKC Top 50 Survey
KGGF Super 50	WREN Best Music List
KUDL Great 38	KLEO More Music Fab 40
WLS Hit Parade	WHB Silver Dollar Survey
KIMN Hit Parade	KOMA All American Survey
KRCB Music Guide	WABC All American Survey
KELI Fabulous 40	KING KAROL Top Selling Pops

and any stray list a jobber or distributor happened to leave behind when stocking the drug store record rack. I still have all those lists.

I introduced myself to every oldies DJ I could get in touch with. Since 1978, I myself have been doing weekend oldie shows as Doc Rock on a succession of radio stations. In 1987, I made for my own listening enjoyment and for background music as I wrote this book, a four-hour tape of every British invasion record to come out between "I Want to Hold Your Hand" and "Help."

Which is to say, I have lived rock 'n' roll. I was there, listening, keeping track, all the way. But unlike most writers, I was doing my listening in mid–America, which gave me a different perspective as a fan and gives me a unique perspective as a rock 'n' roll historian.

The Invasion in the Heartland

The East Coast was overrun by the Beatles British invasion. After all, the Beatles and all of the other British invasion groups physically landed on the East Coast of America, just as had the American colonists 350 years before. New York DJ Murray and the K gave progress reports on the radio as the Beatles flew across the Atlantic. All New York area rock 'n' roll radio stations played only Beatle records. Largely as a result of this publicity, huge crowds of fans, estimated at between 40,000 and 60,000 people, plus the press, met the Beatles at the airport. Some schools were let out so kids would not have to play hooky to try to get near the Beatles. Wall Street was closed and the Stock Exchange shut down early, as a quarter of a million people lined the route from the airport to the hotel. At the Plaza Hotel where the Beatles were staying, there were barricades and mounted police for security and crowd control. Local media coverage was immense, with many interviews, radio call-ins from the Beatles' hotel suite, and appearances. Beatlemania gripped the East Coast, and no doubt all record stores within screaming distance of the Beatles' route were mobbed.

I can't say first-hand what the reaction was on the West Coast to the Beatles' New York arrival, but it's safe to assume it was minimal. After all, Californians see celebrities all the time, and the Beatles' landing was thousands of miles away. Rock and roll historian Guy Zapoleon published a list of the Top 1000 Los Angeles singles of the period 1958 to 1972 in the Warner/Reprise newsletter *Circular,* Volume 4, Number 39, on October 2, 1972. Zapoleon's record-popularity survey was based on the published hit record postings in record stores of Los Angeles radio stations KHJ, KRLA, and KFWB. It revealed that the Beatles' biggest L.A. hit was "I Want to Hold Your Hand." (I bought my copy in January 1964.) Its ranking on the All-Time Top 10 was #8. Bigger hits included "All I Have to Do Is Dream" by the Everly Brothers at #7, "Hawaiian Wedding Song" by Andy Williams at #4, and "Exodus" by Ferrante and Teicher at #3. Chubby Checker's "The Twist" was the all-time #1 hit in Southern California. Also interesting to note is that the Beatles' classic "Yesterday" ranked #90. Other classic favorites, albeit of less stature compared to "Yesterday," came in as follows: #56 for "Johnny Angel" by Shelley Fabares, #29 for "Goodbye Cruel World" by James Darren, #23 for Paul Anka's "Lonely Boy," #13 for the Fleetwoods' "Mr. Blue," and #11 for Frankie Avalon's "Venus." Evidently the impact of the Beatles British invasion was dulled as it crossed the American continent.

An absolutely enchanting film called *I Want to Hold Your Hand* tells the story of hordes of Beatle fans in New York fighting parents, police, and the establishment to get a glimpse of the Fab Four the night they first appeared on "The Ed Sullivan Show." This movie recreates a wonderfully accurate feeling for the atmosphere and mood of early 1964 and Beatlemania, and I recommend it without reservation. However, it should not be taken literally, as if it were a documentary demonstrating how every teenager in America was dedicating his or her life in 1964 to Beatles music.

At the time of the Beatles British invasion, I was the ideal age to absorb and appreciate the movement. Going to high school in the Midwest, in fact at the geographic center of the 48 contiguous states, I heard Beatles music on the radio, played right along with American music. It is true that when *A Hard Day's Night* was coming to the Varsity Theater downtown, we kids bought our tickets a week or two in advance, when normally the theater never sold tickets more than a half hour before any show. Buying our tickets early did get us a round cardboard badge to wear announcing the fact, and incidentally promoted the Beatles and their film. I lost mine many years ago, but my brother, Tim Kelly, tacked his to the ceiling of his bedroom at our parents' house. It stayed in the same spot for over 25 years until today, when he, now an attorney, loaned it to me for use in this book. During the showings of *A Hard Day's Night* in 1964, little of the soundtrack could be heard over the din of the girls in the movie theater audience. They screamed in true Beatlemania fashion through the entire 85 minutes. That *was* exciting!

But, my school did not let out the day the Beatles arrived in Kansas City, Missouri, less than an hour from my home. No local record counters had runs on their Beatle discs. And when I saw the Beatles in person in Kansas City in September 1964, nearly half the tickets went begging, and before the Beatles came out, everyone in every section got to move up closer into the many empty seats. My brother, sister and I moved up very close to the stage. After watching *A Hard Day's Night*, which was and still is taken as if it were actual newsreels instead of more fictional Beatle hype, we all expected the Beatles to be literally overrun by screaming fans. That was why we were not surprised to see that the stage was being guarded by police augmented by professional football players. The extra security turned out to be excessive, although one adult woman dressed in an evening gown did get past the guards, threw herself on the (barbed?) wire fencing strung around the stage, and was carried off. As at the movie theater, screaming, in which I must admit this time I took part, was continual. The noise prevented us from identifying most songs until they were half over, although highlights were "She Loves You" and "You Can't Do That," plus their special opener, "Kansas City." Still, the sight of the half-empty stadium was a bit depressing.

Many excuses have been made since to explain the poor turnout. Some say people hated the promoter of the show, Charlie Finley; I for one had never heard of him, and could not have cared less who the promoter was anyway. The drizzle earlier that day is also blamed. But it didn't rain at the stadium before or during the show, and watching *I Want to Hold Your Hand* does not suggest a little rain would dampen a real Beatlemaniac's enthusiasm. The tickets were said to be too pricey. But to see the Beatles and all the other acts (I was there almost as much to see Jackie DeShannon as the Beatles), even box seats were only $6.50. Notice for the appearance was said to be too short, only about a month. But with all of the national hype of the previous eight months, four weeks seems to me like enough time to save up and buy a general admission ticket. Tickets were sold at the door,

The Beatle Badge, a promotional gimmick employed for the release of *A Hard Day's Night*.

and the local rock and roll station, WHB, played Beatle records exclusively leading up to the show that day. Another station, KEWI in neighboring Kansas' capital city of Topeka, even chartered a Beatles train which they promoted on the air. Fans from the Kansas cities of Manhattan, Topeka, Lawrence, Wichita, Emporia, and elsewhere could board and ride with the DJs to the show.

The bottom line was that, excuses or not, at the height of 1964's British invasion Beatlemania, a live Beatles show lost tens of thousands of dollars.

What was the real reason? Here in the "real world" of the Midwest, we and our contemporaries up north in Wisconsin and the Dakotas, down south in Arkansas and Louisiana, and out west in Utah and Oregon, were all far from Madison Avenue's publicity mill. We loved the Beatles, but that love was based on their records, not on the hype that was laying the groundwork for the Beatle myth.

A Record Collector Is Born

So, resuming developments as experienced here in the Midwest on the eve of the Beatles' American invasion, in 1963 I decided I needed records, not just tapes. So I started buying a few 45s, mostly used, off-the-juke-box five-for-a-dollar, plus any picture sleeves I wanted. When I saw the Beatles on Jack Paar in 1963, I memorized as much as I could of their sound, lyrics and appearance. Because, being as they were in England, I thought sadly (and mistakenly) that I would never hear them again. When they surfaced in 1964, I was ecstatic. I bought my first Beatles 45s and LPs in January 1964. I really liked the way so many British groups were redoing records I already owned by the original American artists, although I thought it was strange the DJs never mentioned that these Beatles and British records were remakes. I eventually gathered every Beatles British invasion record ever to make the charts, and many that did not.

All of that was the sweet part.

In 1964, the British invasion was bittersweet. I loved the music and seeing the groups on television, that was the sweet part. The bitter part was that every time in January 1964 that I heard a British song on the radio, I knew I was by definition missing an American record. This was never more clear to me than one morning early in 1964. I noticed that station KEWI (Kee Wee) was announcing songs like "Popsicles and Icicles" by the Mermaids and "Telstar" by the Tornadoes, but playing only Beatles records. All day between classes, I went to my locker to check my radio to see if they were still doing it. They were.

I finally caught a DJ apologizing on the air for making a nasty remark about the Beatles the day before. It seems the station had been deluged with complaints. So, to make amends, for 24 hours they were playing only Beatles records. It was a great day. Since the Beatles had only a few singles out so far, 24 hours of programming meant playing LP cuts as well as singles. The odd part was they still announced the regular playlist. It was weird to hear the DJ *say* "Here's the Pixies Three with the #25 song this week, '442 Glennwood Avenue'," but *play* "She Loves You!" Or to hear the jock talk over the ending of "I Saw Her Standing There," saying "There's Paul and Paula, with their big #1 song this week, 'Hey Paula'."

As much fun as a Beatles Day was, I wanted to have my cake and eat it, too. That is, I wanted to hear all the British music, but I also wanted to hear all the American music. That's when I became a serious record collector. Any American song I wanted to hear more of, I would buy.

The British invasion feeding frenzy didn't last long. There were no more Beatles Days on the radio. Gone were the days when the Fab Four held positions 1 through 5 on the Top 10. My fear that I wouldn't be able to hear American records unless I bought them myself had been unfounded. Each

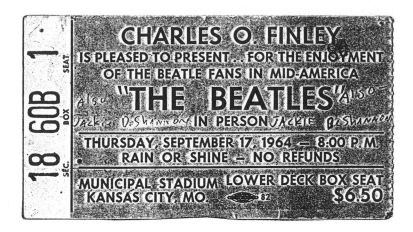

The front and back of a Beatles concert ticket.

week, fewer and fewer Beatles records were played. Finally, when I picked up my K-TOP 40 Survey for May 18, 1964, #1 was Jan and Dean's "Dead Man's Curve," and there were only five British groups listed. Why, a year before, there had been more girl group hits on the Top 40 than that.

America's passion for the Beatles British invasion was cooling off as fast as it had heated up, but I had been bitten by the record-collecting bug, and soon I started collecting British records as well as American ones. That was the lasting impact the early '60s Beatles British invasion had had on me.

In 1969–70, the rock 'n' roll revival (which is still going full tilt) began. Richard Nader began holding Madison Square Garden oldies shows with artists like Bill Haley and Gary U.S. Bonds. Sha-Na-Na began releasing songs like "Remember Then." And the first television oldies album went on the air, hosted by Chubby "The Twist" Checker, but featuring Joey Dee's "Peppermint Twist!" "The Midnight Special" began having golden oldies nights, hosted by Wolfman Jack and featuring everyone from Danny and the Juniors to the Skyliners. Some radio stations went to 24-hour oldie formats for the first time.

I thought the rock 'n' roll revival was great. I could hear all those songs without having to go to the trouble of playing them on my car turntable myself!

Then the Beatle myth happened.

How the Beatle Myth Was Born

As near as I can tell, the seeds of the Beatle myth were planted in England when Brian Epstein managed the huge publicity mill for the Beatles. It was built upon when "The Ed Sullivan Show" broke ratings records with the Beatles' appearances. Beatles Days on the radio hammered the point home that the Beatles were big. For a few weeks, every record store had so many requests for Beatles and British records that the whole system became backlogged. When the Beatles had records in each of the top five slots on *Billboard,* it was official. The Beatles had taken over.

But that was the peak. For a few weeks, the Beatles, assisted soon enough by the other British invasion groups, really had taken over. It was impressive and thrilling. But soon the Beatles' impact shrank, as did the impact of the invasion groups. Oh, sure, the Beatles were still the biggest thing since Elvis. But the Dell "Beatle" posters at Woolworth's were marked down from 25 cents to 10 cents, and still didn't sell, and thousands of Beatle dolls were left gathering dust in warehouses and stock rooms.

The lasting impact of the short-lived Beatles/British supernova explosion on me was that I became a record collector. The lasting impact on many other people was that they remembered only the supernova, not the cooling off. They remembered the amazing days when a station might play all Beatles for a day, when half the Top 10 was Beatles, when a third of the Top 40 was British. They forgot that this lasted for only a few weeks early in 1964.

In the wake of the Beatles' massive but short-lived period of supernova was left long hair, suddenly called the Beatle haircut; low-topped boots, suddenly called Beatle boots; the four-man rock band, suddenly called the Beatle band; and the collarless jacket, suddenly called the Beatle jacket. All these things and more, such as artists writing and producing their own hits, predated the Beatles, but were now *attributed* to the Beatles.

Yes, the seeds of the Beatle myth had been planted back in 1964.

People remembered the weeks of Beatlemania, and in their memories it grew. The first time I came across the myth was when I excitedly read Lillian Roxon's *Rock Encyclopedia* which I had special-ordered at the campus bookstore. This was one of the first two rock 'n' roll reference books I ever heard of, and the only time "my music" had been taken seriously by the establishment.

Unfortunately, it turned out that Roxon's book was ludicrous. It purported to be the story of rock 'n' roll. Instead, it was Lillian Roxon's personal retrospective of rock music as viewed through Beatle-colored glasses. She left out three quarters of the major stars of the '50s and '60s, presumably because she didn't like them—they weren't Beatle bands, combos who played their own instruments. In their place, she listed small-time acts which never amounted to anything. She omitted classic hitmaker Bobby Vee in favor of unknown Dave Van Ronk. She left out the Shirelles but included Silver Apples. She documented the group Kangaroo, but left out the Crows, the Flamingos and the Penguins.

Her worst crime against reason was her discussion of the Beatles and the subsequent British invasion groups. Remember, her book was the first and only rock encyclopedia. In it, she asserted that 1964 was a British-dominated time when the only American music to survive was Motown.

Everyone read what Roxon wrote.

Apparently everyone believed it.

I knew she was wrong. I had been taping off the radio, buying records, and studying the surveys for over 10 years. I knew that the Beatles and British, as huge as their impact had been, had never been more than about 10 percent of the music scene after those first few hectic weeks. I knew that no American groups or musical subtypes had been eliminated by the British invasion. But apparently I was the only one . . . except for one other person. He wrote the other rock 'n' roll reference book.

That other book was *Record Research* by Joel Whitburn, published in 1969, the same year as Roxon's book. Here were the facts, in black and white. Every song to ever hit *Billboard* was listed, in black and white, name, rank and serial number, or in this case, artist, title, record label and number, date, weeks, and chart position. I found this book fascinating. Like Joe Friday said on "Dragnet," "Just the facts." I read it from cover to cover, and saw who had what hits when, confirming my own recollection that American music had been complemented, not eradicated, by the British invasion.

I guess no one else read *Record Research,* or Roxon's cockeyed notions would never have prevailed as they have. Compared to Roxon's, Whitburn's book was boring. But that is because it was just one long list which was not meant to be read, but referred to. So, while everyone read, believed, and repeated Roxon's idiosyncratic and ill-conceived opinions, evidently no one read, cared about, or mentioned Whitburn's accurate facts.

Roxon's book said, "In America, it was still Bobby Vinton singing 'Blue Velvet' (#1 in January 1964), but not for long" because the Beatles and British invasion were on their way to save America from its music. Whitburn's book revealed that she was dead wrong. In fact, Bobby Vinton had three more Top-20 hits in 1964, including another #1 hit, and over 30 more post–Beatles hits in subsequent years! The Beatles took their share of turns being #1, but they did not quash Bobby Vinton or anyone else.

What Really Happened — The Subject of This Book

But the Beatle myth was born and evidently never to be killed thanks in large part to Lillian Roxon. Soon every writer was reporting revisionist rock 'n' roll history about how Beatles music had wiped out surf music, girl groups, and every established American artist from Lesley Gore to Roy Orbison, and how the British invasion made it impossible for American artists to have hits. This became the Beatle legend, based on fact like many legends, but going way beyond the truth, like all legends.

No argument, the Beatles had been and still are so important, they have become legendary. In considering their legend, I am reminded of the case of the father of our country, George Washington. He was great — a great man, general, and president. They wanted to make him king, but he declined. He also made the unpopular move of limiting himself to two terms in office.

Washington did not chop down a cherry tree, did not say "I cannot tell a lie," and did not skip a silver dollar across the Potomac. Who needs that Washington legend, when the real man was so great? The Washington legend is a myth, and a Washington myth is unworthy and unbecoming such an esteemed personage. But at least it is not perpetuated at the expense of other people.

The Beatle myth is also unnecessary and unbecoming. It is not needed. The Beatles' real accomplishments are so great they need not be embellished upon, especially when it is used unfairly to denigrate other artists and rock 'n' roll styles.

This book will be taken by many as a criticism of the Beatles, but it is not. The Beatles were and are the biggest and the best. Their success and quality will probably never be equalled. This book is meant as a correction for the revisionist rock writers who promulgate the Beatle myth.

This book has only one goal — to establish the facts and set the record straight about the impact in America of the greatest rock 'n' roll group to ever walk the face of the earth, the Beatles, and of the subsequent British invasion.

Chapter 1

The Beatles British Invasion Story

Without a doubt the single most identifiable event in the history of rock 'n' roll was the "British invasion," the coming to America of the music of the Beatles and other groups from Great Britain. The term "British invasion" refers to the fact that an unprecedented number of young British citizens, led by the Beatles, had rock 'n' roll hit records in the United States, beginning early in 1964. For people who lived through the Beatles British invasion, as well as for those who did not, taking in the entire invasion is a task that is beyond the scope of anyone's personal memory. Even people who lived through those exciting years don't accurately remember or never knew all the details. And of course, those fans who were in England or Europe in 1964 have no way of knowing how the invasion unfolded in the United States.

Therefore, to set the stage for an evaluation and assessment of the effects and influences of the Beatles British invasion, a comprehensive chronology of the British acts who took part in this invasion, and the dates of their hits, are necessary.

The following chronology is in three parts. The first part covers Phase I, the pre–1964 period, and introduces the artists by year and in the monthly order of their appearance on rock 'n' roll radio. The second part reviews Phase II, 1964, the year of the Beatles British invasion, and introduces the artists and their records month by month in the order of their appearance on U.S. rock 'n' roll radio. The last part covers Phase III, 1965–1969, and summarizes the remaining artists and records.

Phase I: Pre-1964

1956

March. Unlike in the United States, the youthful music of British teens in the 1950s was not rock 'n' roll, but skiffle, a sort of hillbilly/rhythm and blues/jazz style that caught up everyone from Lonnie Donegan to John

Lennon. Back in 1953, Lonnie had played banjo and was a featured vocalist in Chris Barber's Jazz Band (see 1959) using his original name, Tony Donnegan. He changed his name to Lonnie Donegan after his idol, blues guitarist Lonnie Johnson, then started the British skiffle craze with his own huge hit record, "Rock Island Line," an American folk song about an American railroad! The popularity of this one song established an entire musical movement, called skiffle, which dominated the English musical scene for almost a decade. Lonnie had over 30 hits up into 1962 — in England. In the United States, he had three hits, "Rock Island Line" and "Lost John" in 1956, and his biggest, the 1961 novelty tune "Does Your Chewing Gum Lose Its Flavor on the Bed Post Overnight?"

Skiffle was a variant of American folk music that grew out of traditional popular music in England, and was the basis for later British rock 'n' roll music, for rock music, and for the British invasion. As such, it consisted of the guitar combo setup that was to be the basis of almost all that was to follow from England.

It was fortunate for Lonnie that novelty tunes were big in the United States from 1958 to 1963. Had they not been in vogue, "Does Your Chewing Gum Lose Its Flavor on the Bed Post Overnight?" would never have been a Top-10 hit. On the other hand, that novelty song is the only example of skiffle that most U.S. kids ever heard, and that is unfortunate, in that it was not typical. It was after all, a novelty tune!

1957

May. Skiffle was very popular in England, but more because it was easy to play than because people liked hearing it. There were darn few skiffle hit records, but local skiffle groups proliferated, and a great many Beatles British invasion groups began as skiffle combos. The idea was to reproduce American, mostly Negro folk music with simple, original instruments. As such, little formal musical training or skill was required. As Cliff Richard wrote on the liner notes on one of Sire Records' two–LP sets, "Most of the groups in England started off doing skiffle because it was the easiest thing to do. You put your fingers on the chord of D and you strummed away for about half an hour."

So everyone played it, but few had hits. One artist who did was the Chas. McDivitt Skiffle Group. Early in 1957, they had their only British chart record with the American song "Freight Train," obviously a skiffle descendent of "Rock Island Line." A few months later, an American country singer from Missouri via Tulsa, Rusty Draper, released his version in America, followed immediately by the release of Chas. McDivitt's version. Draper's went Top 10 in the United States, while McDivitt's, featuring singer Nancy Whiskey, inched into the U.S. Top 40.

McDivitt had no more hits anywhere. Draper had a number of other U.S. hits, but none as big, and a lone British-only hit, "Mule Skinner Blues," in 1960. (Just for the record, the American version of "Mule Skinner Blues" was by the Fendermen in 1960, and originated by Jimmie Rodgers in 1931, making it prime skiffle-era material.)

June. The third English act to crack successfully the U.S. rock 'n' roll business was Russ Hamilton's, and the song he did it with was called "Rainbow." In the summer of 1957 Russ had a two-sided hit in England, "We Will Make Love" and "Rainbow," with "Rainbow" the lesser hit. Interestingly, the record was on the U.S. charts a month before it hit the British charts. "Rainbow" was Hamilton's only hit in the United States (he had one follow-up in England), and it was a very mild love song, in the style of Bobby Vinton's hits in the 1960s. Hitting the Top 10 in the United States, he got the British pre-invasion off to a good start!

1958

February. The third British act to have a hit on the U.S. rock 'n' roll radio stations was a boy from London, named, appropriately enough, Laurie London. He was only 13 when he recorded his famous record, "He's Got the Whole World (in His Hands)." This record was a hit in Laurie's native land late in 1957, but failed to make the Top 10 there. The song spread across Europe, finally reaching the U.S. charts and radio stations in the early spring of 1958. In the United States, it was a #1 song on most radio stations. The song was much in the style that Wayne Newton would establish a career with five years later, with a soft style and high voice that could be mistaken for a woman. While the song was hardly rock 'n' roll, in the true rock 'n' roll tradition of the one-shot artists, Laurie was never popular in the United States or England again!

1959

January. Lonnie Donegan had been in Chris Barber's Jazz Band before he slipped off to begin his own career with the record "Rock Island Line." There were no hard feelings—Barber played bass on Lonnie's hit record!

In 1959, Chris' own group hit the U.S. charts with one Top-10 hit, "Petite Fleur." The song was an oddity, mainly a clarinet solo by Monty Sunshine that was not rock 'n' roll at all. The follow-up, a Britain-only hit, was "Revival," but that was all for this strange import.

October. Cliff Richard was the fifth Britisher to hit the U.S. charts, the second for 1959, and first true rock 'n' roll act to transplant hits from British soil to the colonies. Cliff, whose real name was Harry Webb, converted his skiffle group, called the Drifters, into a rock 'n' roll group. Then he changed its name to the Shadows, presumably to avoid clashes with the popular American rhythm and blues group the Drifters.

Cliff was *the* rock 'n' roller in England, their Elvis, if you will, with well over 60 hit records starting in 1958. His fourth hit over there, and his first #1 song, was "Living Doll," which was a simultaneous hit in the United States.

On this side of the ocean, Cliff had only a half-dozen hits, and those were mostly only regionally successful (not that there is anything wrong with that). Regional success was a hallmark of early American rock 'n' roll.

In England, Cliff was credited with getting rock 'n' roll off the ground, much as Elvis received credit here, starting the trend of male rock balladeers who were all over the British charts in those days. In point of fact, in both countries it was likely that rock 'n' roll would have caught fire even without these dynamic performers, though perhaps not quite as quickly.

In the United States, Cliff is only of historical importance in the story of the British invasion. But he was significant in that he was the only one of a phalanx of young British rock 'n' rollers—Marty Wilde, Adam Faith, Billy Fury, and other lesser stars—to have any chart success in the United States.

Even for Cliff, it seemed that success was tricky at best. His '50s and '60s U.S. hits were:

1959 "Living Doll"	1964 "I'm the Lonely One"
1963 "Lucky Lips"	1964 "Bachelor Boy"
1963 "It's All in the Game"	1968 "Congratulations"

All but one ("Bachelor Boy") of these songs were also hits in England, but as to why these few made it in the United States, even on a regional basis, is not clear. They were not among Cliff's bigger successes in England, and "Bachelor Boy" was not a hit in England at all!

Cliff's style was something of a hybrid of Elvis and Bobby Rydell. His lack of major success in the United States in 1964, when British artists were so big here, can undoubtedly be attributed to one major factor. He did not look like the Beatles.

1960

January. One characteristic of early rock 'n' roll was that the songs could be hits in different parts of the country by different artists. The classic example of this was the song "Look for a Star." This song was from the movie *Circus of Horrors* and was a hit simultaneously in the United States by Gary Miles (a.k.a. Buzz Cason), Deane Hawley, and Billy Vaughan. Brit Gary Mills did an excellent job of imitating U.S. mellow rock 'n' roll when he had his only U.S. hit, a fourth version of "Look for a Star." No one knew he was British. His British chart follow-ups were "Top Teen Baby" and "I'll Step Down."

1961

In 1961 the trickle of British artists seemed to have dried up. One reason for this was undoubtedly the fact that rock 'n' roll in America had grown up, in the sense that the music was getting better, the hits getting bigger, and the Top-40 radio stations developed into a major market instead of the minor competitor with the adult stations. For whatever reason, the British stayed home.

1962

Then, in 1962, something seemed to be afoot. One after another, British artists started getting onto the U.S. charts more and more frequently. It was as if the American record companies recognized that rock 'n' roll had developed into something bigger than pabulum for 13-year-old girls. Still, as a record company, unless you had a top artist already in your corner, you generally had to take a chance on an unknown, untried, teen artist.

Such a move could be very expensive for a company, or for someone who worked for the company and made too many bad guesses about what could make it as a hit in the highly competitive teen market. For every successful record and artist of the period, there were literally hundreds of unsuccessful records and scores of artists who never got a hit.

One way to cut down the odds was to sign up an unknown established star, or at least an unheard-of hit record—in other words, import some British hits, run them up the U.S. flagpole, and see who defects. With a new U.S. artist, a company had no idea if a record would sell. But with a British hit record and singer, at least a company knew that British teenagers liked the record, and therefore U.S. kids might like it, too!

January. The first flag run up the pole in 1962 was Londoner Charlie Drake's, who with three novelty-tune hits in England in the early days of rock 'n' roll probably seemed to American record execs like a potential chart artist in the United States. In 1958, he did his own version of Bobby Darin's "Splish Splash." In fact, in England his version was Top 10, while Bobby's was only Top 20! Then in 1960 he had a hit with his own interpretation of Larry Verne's "Mr. Custer." This time, his was the only version that was on the British charts.

Had Charlie Drake continued doing his own versions of American hits, he probably would have remained strictly a British artist. But in the summer of 1961 he got weird and original, and came up with "My Boomerang Won't Come Back," another British Top-20 hit. In January, the record with its self-explanatory title about an untalented Australian aborigine made its way to the United States, where it was edited down considerably in length. Shortly after "My Boomerang Won't Come Back" appeared on the U.S. charts, civil rights–minded American record company execs censored it, changing the line, "Practiced 'til I was *black* in the face" to "Practiced 'til I was *blue* in the face."

"Boomerang" was Charlie Drake's only hit in the United States, although his follow-up, "Drake's Progress," about planting explosives(!), got fairly wide U.S. distribution. In 1972, Charlie had one more hit in England, a Top-50 oddity, "Puckwudgie." Around 1980, he recorded an LP produced by Genesis.

February. Listening to Britisher Kenny Ball's music was almost like having Chris Barber's Jazz Band back again. In fact, legend has it that Kenny Ball was discovered by none other than the old Barber alumnus, Lonnie Donnegan!

Skeptics like to argue that the only way a song like "Midnight in Moscow" by Kenny Ball and *his* jazz band could become #1 on the U.S. Top-40 stations was: (1) rock 'n' roll was so bad in this period, even this pop jazz number sounded good by comparison; (2) station managers, groping for decent records among the rock 'n' roll pap, played "Midnight in Moscow" regardless of its true popularity; or (3) it was the adult station airplay plus sales of the record to adults that got it so high on the charts.

Explanation #1 was made by fans of hard rock. Explanation #2 was the explanation of lovers of "good music." Number 3 was Mom and Dad's.

The truth was "Midnight in Moscow" *was* rock 'n' roll in 1962. If it was music, it could become a hit. There was, as yet, no elitism in rock 'n' roll. The music was for fun, and any record that was fun to listen to could be a hit, with no explanations or apologies needed. "Midnight in Moscow" was a hit because kids in the United States liked listening to it. Of course, one fun record does not a career make. After two small splashes in the spring ("March of the Siamese Children") and summer ("Green Leaves of Summer"), Kenny Ball faded into rock 'n' roll history.

But, no matter. As long as someone, somewhere, heard Kenny's songs on their station's Top-40 countdown, Kenny's music was not in vain.

March. No one knew for sure what an "Acker" was, let alone a "Bilk." So, Atco Records put a "Mr." on the label, and voilà, Mr. Acker Bilk became famous. Playing his clarinet! It was catchier than his old name, the Paramount Jazz Band, although that name had been more descriptive. Following in the grooves of Chris Barber and Kenny Ball before him, Acker went all the way to #1 in the United States with *his* jazz instrumental,

"Stranger on the Shore." Going even further in that well-worn groove, Acker had the #1 record for the entire year of 1962 with his moody instrumental!

Most of the British records which hit the U.S. charts so far had been by male artists and had been either jazz-oriented, instrumentals, skiffle, or a combination. All of that was about to change!

August. In 1961, the Springfields, a trio, began a string of about a half-dozen hits in England. Their sound was folksy—U.S. folk, that is, not skiffle. The group included a brother and sister, the brother being Tom O'Brien, his little sister being Mary Isobel Catherine O'Brien. Tom and Mary adopted their group's name as their own last name, Springfield. The threesome from Hampstead in North London was first completed by Tim Field, who originally did a duo with Tom, and at another time by Mike Pickworth, the only one of the four to never have the word "field" in his name!

It was a bit surprising that none of the Springfields' British chart records made the hit lists in the United States. Their biggest U.K. songs were "Island of Dreams" and "Say I Won't Be There." The two U.S. hits were "Silver Threads and Golden Needles" and "Dear Hearts and Gentle People." The former made a very big splash, although, again, teenagers really had no idea that this was a British group. If they had, it would not have made any difference. It was rock 'n' roll, with a bit of "hootenanny" thrown in, and that was A-OK in 1962.

One thing about the Springfields made them nearly unique—their records were released in both England and America on the same record label, Phillips. This was almost never the case with any other import artists before or since.

Other than those two good records, they were gone. Or were they?

September. Closing out the imports from 1962 was a male singer who began his career in Australia then became one of the biggest artists in England and Europe, Frank Ifield. He was a 25-year-old heartthrob teen idol in England. The U.S. folk influence was there as well, as was evidenced by the "yodel" featured in many of his hits.

The yodel was strictly squaresville in the United States in 1962. Yodeling was for Alps types in lederhosen hollering from mountaintop to mountaintop, was found in old Roy Rogers movies, or else was a part of hardcore country-western music. But in England, there were actually heated arguments over who was the best rock 'n' roll yodeler! Frank Ifield was the winner.

Frank was from Coventry, but began singing while in Australia. His first two modest hits in England were "Lucky Devil" and "Gotta Get a Date," both in 1960. Then, after a dry spell, he hit big with "I Remember You" in the summer of '62. This was his first of three consecutive #1s in

England, the next two being "Lovesick Blues" and "Wayward Wind." A small slip was "Nobody's Darlin' but Mine," still Top 10, then he was #1 again with "I'm Confessin'."

Frank continued to hit big through the end of 1966 in England. After so many British artists had done well in the United States in 1962, it was natural that Frank's management and label would look for a U.S. outlet. Since Frank's British label was Columbia, one might have expected Columbia in the United States to release Frank's hits. But it was rare for the same label to release a given artist on both sides of the Atlantic, and Frank was a case in point. Moreover, Columbia U.S. was not into rock 'n' roll that early in the decade. So in 1962 Frank's material went out on bid.

To sweeten the deal for any U.S. label that might be willing to buy Frank Ifield's contract, the British record moguls threw in as a bonus the contract of another new British group that had just begun to make the U.K. charts. The U.S. label that decided Frank was worth a try was Vee Jay. Vee Jay had long been a rhythm and blues label, but they were beginning to turn to rock 'n' roll by this time, and had just hit the big time with "Sherry" by the Four Seasons. So, they gave Frank Ifield a try.

Soon, Frank's U.K. hits were also riding the U.S. radio airwaves. His first big British hit, "I Remember You," was also a top tenner in the United States in September of 1962. The follow-up, "Lovesick Blues," carried on the yodel tradition and was up-tempo, but only received regional recognition in the United States.

After that, Frank made what probably seemed like a good move at the time, by getting his contract switched over to a big U.S. label that was just beginning to try rock 'n' roll, including "Surfin'" by the Beach Boys. Capitol released "I'm Confessin'," another regional U.S. hit, and "Please," which did not sell. Being on Capitol did not seem to help.

Goodbye, Frank. "Yodel-ay-eee-ooo!"

November. Back to the instrumentals, with a studio group called the Tornadoes that had aspirations of having their own hits. From the fall of '62 up through the fall of '63 the dream came true, in England, where Decca released their songs under the name the Tornadoes. Since Decca is also an American label, we might think that the U.S. Decca label would rush to release the Tornadoes' songs in the United States. Right? Wrong.

Ironically, in the United States it was a label called "London" that made the Tornadoes' British material available. The group consisted of five guys, Clem, Roger, Heinze, George, and Allan. In the United States, only their original U.K. hit made the national big time. The year 1962 went down in history as the year of the U.S.-U.S.S.R. space race. The United States made headway in the race by launching a communications satellite called "Telstar." Get it? "Tel" for "telephone, telegraph, telemetry," etc., and "star" for a shining light in the sky?

Well, the Tornadoes got the message, and they communicated by naming their instrumental hit "Telstar." Instrumentals from England were nothing new by then, but this song was simplicity incarnate. It featured the same simple guitar and organ riffs over and over. It was, however, one of the few British imports to employ sound effects. Supposedly the sound of a satellite launch, this was actually a recording of the noise of a British toilet being flushed and played backwards at half-speed. In spite of being unrealistic the sound effects were a good gimmick. The record worked wonderfully, rising to the top of all the U.S. charts.

The U.S. follow-up to "Telstar" was not one of the Tornadoes' several British hits. Called "Ridin' the Wind," it had regional U.S. success at best, although it was a fine reworking of the sound effects, guitar and organ formula blended so successfully in "Telstar."

The Tornadoes' records were produced by one Joe Meek, who was the producer on uncounted British hit records and had a penchant for outer space themes. He also felt he was in tune with Buddy Holly's eternal spirit, and committed suicide on the 10th anniversary of Holly's death.

1963

While the British imports practically flooded the U.S. charts in 1962 when compared to any previous year, none of the artists showed any real staying power. Perhaps for this reason, the flow was reduced to a bare trickle in 1963. Another big reason was that U.S. rock 'n' roll was developing several new trends and styles that would be around for a long time, including girl groups, surf and drag, Motown, hootenanny/folk, and combo rock 'n' roll. However, there were two more British tries, one valiant but doomed, the other very novel.

March. Remember Frank Ifield, and the sweetener to his record deal offered to Vee Jay Records? In March of 1963, Vee Jay decided to give this bonus artist a try at the U.S. market. This new British act had just made the British charts for the second time. While the first record by this artist had barely dented the British Top 20, their second had reached #1 on most lists.

Vee Jay released three U.S. records by this group. They did not catch on, and one more release on a small label (which had previously featured mostly Freddy Cannon and Danny and the Juniors) also failed to click with American kids. Only one of the songs, released in late summer, sold even a few copies. Lack of sales success in the United States must have been a big disappointment for these Britishers from Liverpool — John, Paul, George, and Ringo!

November. Much more successful than the previous artist was a duo consisting of two females. The Caravelles were two London office workers who became the first totally female imported artist group to make it on the U.S. rock 'n' roll scene. Lois Wilkinson and Andrea Simpson sang together at parties. Their break came on Decca in England and Smash Records in the United States. Their hit was a breathy number — literally, you could hear them taking breaths on the dreamy "You Don't Have to Be a Baby to Cry." Smash was a good label for the Caravelles, since the American girl group the Angels had just had a string of hits for the same company in the United States, including the legendary #1, "My Boyfriend's Back."

But the Caravelles' fame was fleeting. No other British hits were forthcoming, and a bit later their one U.S. follow-up, "Have You Ever Been Lonely," sold poorly. The Caravelles ended Phase I of the British invasion.

Phase II: 1964.
The Year of the Beatles British Invasion

What came before, in Phase I, was very small potatoes compared to what arrived in Phase II. This section will go through the first year of the Beatles British invasion, to relive in exquisite detail the sequence of the hits as they were charted in the United States. Anyone who was not around and listening back then can gain perspective; anyone who was around and listening can re-experience the invasion as the Beatles British invasion unfolds hit by hit, group by group, month by month. In addition, each group's U.S. success will be compared to how well their songs did back in England.

January — two artists. It works out very neatly, the British invasion's Second Phase beginning in the first month of the year marking the 10th anniversary of rock 'n' roll. The invasion was spearheaded by the Beatles. The first week, they fired their first shot, "I Want to Hold Your Hand," onto the U.S. Top 100. This was not really their first shot of course, since 1963 had already seen three Beatles releases that failed to sell in the United States.

The Beatles were a great sensation. Only someone who lived through the months that followed can ever know the thrill of those times, the excitement of those records, and the spell that the Beatles and the other British groups cast on American youth. But you had to be between the age of about 13 and 17 to really experience the times and be swept up by the men and their music.

For three weeks, "I Want to Hold Your Hand" was the only Beatles song on the U.S. charts, but not the only British record. Other British hits already on the charts at this time were Frank Ifield's "Please," which was on the same label as "I Want to Hold Your Hand" (Capitol); the Caravelles' "You Don't Have to Be a Baby to Cry"; and "It's All in the Game" by Cliff Richard. These three songs, however, were on the Top 40s of scattered radio stations around the United States. They were not national U.S. hits, and therefore their chart placements nationally are not impressive.

By the end of the month, the Beatles had their second U.S. hit with "She Loves You." "She Loves You" was not really new, but a Beatles "oldie" recorded and made a hit overseas back in '63. Musically, these two songs were wonderful if primitive throwbacks to the American music which began with groups like Bill Haley and the Comets. "She Loves You" was all guitars, drums, and yelling—a "rave up," to use the British term. "I Want to Hold Your Hand" featured a tight harmony style very much like the Everly Brothers' sound or the new Beach Boys' records. In fact, one American reviewer described "I Want to Hold Your Hand" as "Surf on the Thames!"

A second British artist entered the United States teen scene during the last week of January. Things would be a lot neater if Dusty Springfield hadn't popped up when she did. The entire point of the British invasion was that it was a whole bunch of groups of male mop-tops singing mostly up-tempo, driving rock 'n' roll. Now along comes Dusty, breaking the pattern into little pieces.

Dusty Springfield had been born Mary Isobel Catherine O'Brien, and was a member of the Springfields—remember "Silver Threads and Golden Needles" back in 1962? The next summer, she began a solo hit career in England with "I Only Want to Be with You," which went Top 5 in British popularity. It is debatable if we would have heard of her in 1964 had it not been for the Beatles paving the way. The Beatles' success could have inspired Phillips Records to release her material on their sister Phillips label in the United States.

Construction of such a scenario is not necessary. After all, Phillips USA had already scored a hit in '62 with her previous Phillips UK hits with the Springfields' group. "I Only Want to Be with You" was recognizable as British only if you noticed little things, like Dusty's heavy eye make-up, practically a trademark of British girls. The record was only Top 20 here, but it was very hard rocking for mid-'60s femme music and almost had a girl group sound, so perhaps that can be the explanation for its success, if one is needed.

February—three artists. "I Want to Hold Your Hand" was on Capitol Records, which had also acquired Frank Ifield by this time. Recall the package deal—buy Frank Ifield's material and we throw in the Beatles for good measure! Vee Jay once had both acts, but had now let both slip over to Capitol. "She Loves You" was on Swan Records. With these two successes on Capitol and Swan, Vee Jay dusted off the least disastrous of their three 1963 stiffs by the Beatles, "Please Please Me." In England, this had been the Fab Four's first real hit, and the title of their first LP. Now it was a U.S. hit at last.

In less than two months, disc jockeys had already gotten the hint — kids wanted to hear more Beatles music. So the DJs turned over "I Want to Hold Your Hand" and found "I Saw Her Standing There." This song was just an LP cut in England, and was on *two* LPs in the United States, one by Capitol and one by Vee Jay. At this point, the Beatles had four songs on the U.S. Top-40 playlists at the same time, a first for rock 'n' roll.

Not to be left out, someone at MGM Records remembered that in their early days, the Beatles had backed singer Tony Sheridan on some recordings. Checking the files, they discovered that John Lennon had sung lead on the ancient chestnut "My Bonnie." Naturally, they released it as a Beatles record. To everyone's or no one's surprise, depending on your point of view, this recording reached the U.S. Top 30. It was this record as much as any which started the notion that anything anyone released, as long as the Beatles had recorded it, would become a hit in the United States. Anything. Even, as the joke went, breathing.

Certainly the record moguls on both sides of the Atlantic had gotten the idea — compared to Cliff Richard and the Caravelles, this Beatles stuff was a gold mine. Between Vee Jay, Swan, and Capitol, it looked as if Beatles music was pretty well beyond the reach of other record companies. But, figured U.S. record label executives, there must be some more moptops in England who might just sound and look enough like the Fab Four to fool — 'er, to please — the American teen market!

Enter the Dave Clark Five. Oops, there are five guys in this group, and one plays an organ. Oh well, maybe no one will notice the extra guy. After all, their hair is long, so they do seem like the Beatles if you don't listen or look too closely.

Looks like we were right. About the same time that "I Saw Her Standing There" rose from the obscurity of a flip side to the status of a hit, the Dave Clark Five emerged with "Glad All Over." Leader Dave was a drummer, so the sound of the DC5, as they were soon known, was a thunderous, stomping beat that made the Beatles' sound seem melodious in comparison. And "in comparison" was not an accidental choice of words. Due to the haircuts, the combo format, and the British accents, everyone was comparing the Beatles and the DC5 from the outset. For a time, it was thought that the 5 might emerge on top. But whereas their fans in 1964 knew that Lenny Davidson played the guitar, Denis Payton played the sax, Mike Smith played the organ and sang, and Rick Huxley played the bass, today their names are forgotten, while John Lennon, Paul McCartney, George Harrison, and Ringo Starr live on, in memory if not in reality.

Meanwhile the Caravelles (remember the British girl group which was the last of Phase I of the invasion — or, the first of Phase II, depending on how you look at it) came out with their follow-up to "You Don't Have to Be a Baby to Cry" called "Have You Ever Been Lonely." Its sound was soft and its success was spotty, at best. Most record buyers at this time were girls, and they wanted to buy records performed by boys, British or otherwise!

March—four artists. March was Beatles Month Number Three, and it seemed the Fab Four dominated the charts from both the import and U.S. angle. Turn on a radio and you heard a British record as likely as not, and a Beatles record, almost surely. First was another song from Vee Jay, "From Me to You." Not an actual release intended to be a hit, this was in fact the flip side of "Please Please Me," the song released four weeks before in February in hopes of having a hit! Moreover, neither side was really new. When this song was first played on the radio in 1964, this writer took it for an "oldie but a goodie" from 1963—which as it turned out, it was.

It went like this. In the spring of 1963, American rock 'n' roller Del Shannon, best known for "Runaway" and then currently "Little Town Flirt," was touring England where he had already had over a half-dozen hits. The Beatles were also on the tour, but it was Del who was the big headliner. "From Me to You" by the Beatles was also popular at that time in England, along with "She Loves You." Between shows, Del told the Beatles (who looked up to Del as a major rock 'n' roll star) that he was going to go back to the United States and release his own version of "She Loves You." After all, it had his style of music—guitar and drums, yelling, trademark falsetto, the works.

The Beatles begged Del to lay off. The Fab Four were themselves planning to release their British hit version of "She Loves You" in the United States, but they knew that their version could not hope to compete with a version by a big rock 'n' roll star like Del Shannon. Being a nice guy, Del said okay, but when John asked Del backstage not to cut "From Me to You" either, Del ignored Lennon and proceeded to put out his version in the United States.

The Beatles were right: They could not compete with Del. When they released "She Loves You" on Swan Records in the United States in 1963, it didn't sell enough copies to pay for the shipping. But Del's version of "From Me to You" made the U.S. national charts in 1963 and the playlists of Top-40 stations in most U.S. cities. This makes Del Shannon the first artist, American or British, to have a hit in the United States, or anyplace outside of Britain, with a Beatles tune!

With some five songs on the U.S. Top-100 charts, the Beatles were having an enormous impact. Because their influence was so big, it is now constantly overemphasized. Five records hitting at once is a lot, but it is, after all, only 5 percent of the chart, hardly overwhelming U.S. rock 'n' roll as an institution. There were still over 90 other artists having Top-100 hits at the same time, and all but a handful of those were American.

Next up in March were the Swinging Blue Jeans. The core of the Blue

Jeans was made up of two veterans of skiffle days, Norman Kuhkle and Ray Ennis. In England they first hit it big with "It's Too Late Now," written by Ennis, but their real success in England and the United States was with "Hippy Hippy Shake," a tune that the Beatles had often done in their early stage act in Hamburg, West Germany, where the Blue Jeans also played. "Hippy Hippy Shake" was originally a hit in Los Angeles by its American composer, Chan Romero. But its major impact was in England, and is sometimes credited with sparking off the entire Liverpool beat movement. Certainly both the Beatles and the Blue Jeans copied Chan Romero's arrangement very closely.

The Blue Jeans' style was a long way from their skiffle origins by this time, and had been developed when they used their early transitional group name, the Bluegenes. Supposedly the winners of a Liverpool talent contest, the Swinging Blue Jeans even had their own radio show in England. The Swinging Blue Jeans had been around since 1959, originally as the Bluegenes. Over the years, their personnel would change many times. Among their many members would be Terry Sylvester, who later became a member of the British invasion group the Hollies. Their early days included many a show in Germany at the legendary Hamburg Star Club.

Before they were done, the Blue Jeans would have only two more U.S. hits and three more in the United Kingdom, failing to fulfill the promise they showed at this early stage.

The next British invasion record was from the Beatles. Capitol was releasing "official" Beatles records in a logical order. They ignored the older Beatles songs, and were releasing instead the new material that was just hitting big in England. Capitol Records did not appreciate the way that Vee Jay had been taking advantage of Capitol's gigantic promotional push for the Beatles' "I Want to Hold Your Hand" by releasing old material like "Please Please Me," or the success that Swan was having with "She Loves You." How could Capitol keep to a logical schedule of release dates with these other labels putting out all of this old stuff any time they pleased? Adding insult to injury, Vee Jay's subsidiary label, Tollie, began releasing old Beatle material as well.

Since the Beatles' manager, Brian Epstein, had been trying to get U.S. hits with Beatles songs for some time before Capitol released "I Want to Hold Your Hand," there was a great deal of older material, including audition tapes, lying around the vaults of various American labels. Tollie let loose with another old song which was already available here on a Vee Jay LP, *Introducing the Beatles*. The 45 Tollie released was a song which had already been a hit for the American Isley Brothers, "Twist and Shout," and became the next British invasion hit release.

Vee Jay, Swan, MGM, and Tollie weren't the only outsiders Capitol had to worry about. In March, Capitol of *Canada* released two Beatles records, and enough copies crossed the border to make Beatles original "All My Loving" and Chuck Berry revival "Roll Over Beethoven" fair-sized hits in the states.

Another British rock 'n' roll band appeared at this time. The Searchers were named after the 1965 John Wayne western film of the same name, although none of us kids knew it at the time. Their *British* success was sudden and big, with a national #1 and #2 right away: "Sweets for My Sweet" and "Sugar and Spice." Their next caloric ode was "Sweet Nothin's," not so big but still a hit. Two of these three songs were former U.S. hits by American artists — the Drifters' "Sweets for My Sweet" and Brenda Lee's "Sweet Nothin's" — as was their next song, another #1 in England, and their very first success in the United States — "Needles and Pins." This song was written by Sonny (of "and Cher" fame), and had been a mild stateside success by American female singer Jackie DeShannon, who served as a warm-up act for the Beatles' first U.S. tour.

The Searchers had been together since 1960, and were extremely popular in the Beatles' home territory, Liverpool. This made them prime candidates for U.S. importers of British rock 'n' roll. It worked out in terms of quantity. The Searchers had more U.S. releases than most British groups dreamed of having. But seldom were Searchers hits very near the top of the charts.

The chronology returns to the Beatles for the next invasion bull's-eye. In theory, the release of "Twist and Shout" and the other old Beatles songs should have killed the Beatles' sales. Usually, when more than one song is out by an artist, the hard core fans buy both songs, but the general public does not. This splits the sales and reduces the impact of both records. Tollie probably did not care, but they were taking quite a chance in releasing "Twist and Shout." This was the first Beatles hit in the United States that had not been on a single in England!

Capitol was justifiably concerned that Vee Jay and the others would kill the goose that was laying the golden records. Not to worry. The hard core fans of any artist always bought every 45 and LP by their idols, and it seemed that there were enough hard core Beatles fans in the United States in 1964 to make almost every release a hit! Not to be left behind though, Capitol released the chronologically correct current English Beatles hit, "Can't Buy Me Love." This was the third week of March, only some 11 weeks after "I Want to Hold Your Hand," rather soon for another release by usual standards. But Capitol could not afford to let Vee Jay and the others hog the momentum, and no one, least of all the Beatles, knew if the fad would last out the spring! The kids paid no attention at all to what label a song was on. During those 11 weeks, *five more* Beatles songs became popular on three labels, two of the songs Beatles flip sides!

"Can't Buy Me Love" was very apropos. By now the Beatles were becoming rich beyond their dreams, and were soon to learn that money is not everything. But this song was tamer than most of their previous U.S. chart songs, and very well received, going to #1.

Vee Jay was not to be outdone. Their subsidiary, Tollie, was zipping up the charts with "Twist and Shout." This emboldened them enough that they decided to let loose with another Beatles British non-hit, "Do You Want to Know a Secret." It turned out fine, hit-wise, in spite of another unique attribute: "Do You Want to Know a Secret" was a ballad, it had been a hit in England by Billy J. Kramer with the Dakotas, not the Beatles, and it was the first slow song out of the eight Beatles songs to hit the charts in the United States. Had the Beatles realized this, perhaps they would have changed their style somewhat, and sooner.

Next there was another appearance by that invasion oddity, Dusty Springfield. At the end of March, her follow-up to "I Only Want to Be with You" was released. "Stay Awhile" had proven itself Top-10 material the month before in England, so it looked like a good bet for U.S. release. It was, even though it barely made the Top 40 here.

April—six artists. Again, the Beatles. They began the month effortlessly, sliding onto the charts slick as can be with two more flip sides! One was "official"—sort of—the flip side of Capitol's "Can't Buy Me Love." It was a rocker called "You Can't Do That," about a two-timing girlfriend. It was featured on the Beatles' first U.S. tour, and marked the second time the Beatles got on the U.S. charts with a British non-hit! "You Can't Do That" featured good Beatles harmony, the best Harrison guitar licks yet, and was improved by a moral.

Meanwhile, back at Vee Jay, with kids figuratively flipping over the song "Do You Want to Know a Secret," the dee jays literally flipped over that record and played the flip side, "Thank You Girl." This song had also not been a hit in England. It was beginning to look as though any Beatles song released in the United States and played on the radio would be a hit, regardless of vintage, style, or quality.

It had been a month and a half since the Dave Clark Five's debut disc, "Glad All Over." Their U.S. label, Epic, released their current British follow-up to "Glad All Over." It was another rocker, "Bits and Pieces." If anything, and incredibly, it featured even *more* pile-driving drums and ear-shattering echo than "Glad All Over" had, and it was a smashing success in both countries. Meanwhile, a small U.S. record label, Congress, released an old DC5 record. "I Knew It All the Time" was like some of the obscure Beatles recordings dredged up by small labels now that the group was a hit. But whereas most of the old Beatles material did well, the Congress 45 did not make the U.S. Top 40. Another DC5 record on the jubilee record label didn't even make the Top 100! It was an instrumental, mostly, titled "Chaquita." A steal from the Champs' U.S. hit, "Tequila," the band played for a bit, then every once in a while, someone intoned the Spanish word, "Chaquita." It was ... interesting.

As if there were not enough Beatles songs on the charts, Tollie Records reared its head again in April. A full month after "Twist and Shout" became a hit, its flip side, "There's a Place," hit the charts. It was another semi-slow song, another British non-hit, but did it matter? Ten songs on four labels. The impact of the Beatles on U.S. radio and teenagers in the first three months of Phase II was certainly unprecedented. The impact on Tollie wasn't bad, either. They came out right away with another Vee Jay LP cut, "Love Me Do." This new song was distinctive. It was medium slow. It was the only slow song the Beatles had made the charts with yet in England. But, unbeknownst to the American teens who made it a #1 single and the fifteenth Beatles hit in four months, this had actually been the first Beatles hit in England back in '62.

No one knew it at the time, but as all devoted fans have learned since, Ringo had just recently been hired as the drummer for the Beatles when they recorded "Love Me Do." He had experience drumming for British rock 'n' roller Rory Storm, but even so, British record execs considered Ringo inexperienced at worst and an unknown quantity at best. That's why Beatles record producer George Martin hired a session drummer, Andy White, to cover for Ringo on "Love Me Do" at the recording session back in 1962. On some takes Ringo did play the drums, and supposedly did so on the version that was a hit in England in 1962. But in 1964, American Tollie Records released another version with White on drums and Ringo on tambourine. This was the first but far from last time that different versions of the same Beatles song were hits in the two countries.

April saw the return of Cliff Richard to the U.S. charts. However, he was seen as more of an oldie artist and not considered a part of the invasion. He did not look or sound like a mop-top, so all in all he was not very successful with his release, "I'm the Lonely One," in spite of the fact that it was Top 10 in England, where he continued to have tons of big hits for many more years.

The same time that Cliff was trying to hit the U.S. charts (or at least his U.S. label was trying to — it is doubtful that Cliff really considered U.S. teen rock 'n' roll fans when he went to a recording session), a group called the Bachelors was making its American debut. The Bachelors were one of many invasion artists that shared a penchant for redoing U.S. hit songs of the recent and not-so-recent past. This was a very paradoxical situation. Presumably these invasion artists were popular because they were British and provided an alternative to American rock 'n' roll. And yet nearly all of them redid old American material! At any rate, the Bachelors were not really British, but Irish. John and Declan Stokes, and Con Clusky were from Dublin. They began their career as an instrumental (nonsinging) harmonica trio, the Harmonichords. This is rather surprising, since the Bachelors had better "singing voices" than any other invasion artists! Their fourth British release got them a #1, and that was their first hit song in the United States, "Diane." By 1966, they were no longer big stateside, but in England they went to the top of the playlists in 1966 with their huge hit version of "Sounds of Silence."

American teens embraced yet another new invasion artist in April, this one also from Liverpool. At least, the lead singer was from the Beatles' hometown. But William Ashton was backed up by a group from Manchester, England, the Dakotas. William's stage name was Billy J. Kramer, and he was the most Beatle-like of all the invasion stars. This was in spite of the fact that he combed his hair back instead of forward and was almost a solo artist, backed up by a band as he was, rather than a part of a group. However, Billy J.'s manager happened to be Brian Epstein, the genius behind the Beatles. Brian had the idea of pairing Billy J. with an established band, the Dakotas, which had already hit in England once in 1963 with "The Cruel Sea." Together, Billy J. Kramer with the Dakotas released "Little Children," a very British song which made the U.S. Top 10 with ease.

An honorable mention for April went to the Beatles. They didn't really have a hit with their next record, but MGM did release another song from the Tony Sheridan session, this one called "Why." Its impact was minuscule in the United States and nonexistent in England.

May—ten artists. By now, the U.S. record companies knew that British could equal bucks, and they began importing British talent like it was going out of style—which of course it was presumably in danger of doing at any time. In May there were an unprecedented ten British acts to have hit records.

Returning to the veterans of the invasion, it had been six weeks since the Searchers had brought back a U.S. hit, "Needles and Pins." It was time for another old U.S. rock 'n' roll song, this time the Coasters' "Ain't That Just Like Me." Like Billy J., the Searchers were not mop-tops. They wore the hoody, greased-back hairdo of the American rock 'n' roll singer. But then, even in the Beatles-crazy U.S. there were only about three normal high school boys who had Beatle haircuts at this early date, and no U.S. rock 'n' roll stars had adopted the mop-top as yet! Even with normal hairstyles, the Searchers were apparently enough like the Beatles to get by.

The Dave Clark Five had done original songs for their first two American hits, "Glad All Over" and "Bits and Pieces." Now they joined the ranks of so many other imports by having a hit with an old American song by the Contours, "Do You Love Me." This song raised the booming sound of the DC5 to new decibel heights. Of all the new wave of rock 'n' rollers so far imported, the DC5 were the most hard rocking. The Swinging Blue Jeans were a close second.

It was not hard to rock, either. The Blue Jeans, for their follow-up to "Hippy Hippy Shake" on both sides of the ocean, did another old American hit, this time from a real rocker, Little Richard. "Good Golly Miss Molly" was not as big in the states as in England, but was still an important part of the invasion of imports.

Another Beatles British invasion paradox: The British invasion groups are best known for their heavy beat. Certainly the Beatles, who even used the word "beat" in their name, emphasized the beat more than the melody. Yet one of the most "beat" groups, the Blue Jeans, was not that popular in the United States, while the next invaders, Peter and Gordon, were a very harmonious duo and a smashing success.

Peter and Gordon were also known as Asher and Waller (their last names) and, originally, as Gordon and Peter! They were not managed by Brian Epstein. Better yet, Peter's sister Jane was a sweetheart of Beatle Paul McCartney, so (you guessed it) Peter and Gordon were handed Lennon-McCartney songs to record and release. The first, "World Without Love," was Top 20 in England, but #1 in the states. These two singers did affect Beatle haircuts, and Peter was probably the world's first readheaded mop-top! They sang deep in an echo chamber, and were about as well received in the United States as any group short of the Beatles themselves.

How important was it to their success that groups like Peter and Gordon and Billy J. Kramer with the Dakotas released Beatles material? Did this really make their records into hits, or would American teens have liked their records even if they had been written by someone else? We'll never know for sure.

There are clues, however: interesting insight is provided by examining a feature on U.S radio stations in the first half of the '60s called "Make It or Break It," which was played with new records. This was an audience participation feature in which no one won, but listeners could participate. The DJ would play a brand new record without revealing the artist, and ask the audience to listen to it and then call in on the telephone to vote "make it" or "break it." If the majority of callers voted "make it," then that record would be played as a hit on that radio station, even if it did not sell 10 copies in the rest of the Free World. On the other hand, if the "break it" votes outnumbered the "make it" votes, then the DJ would actually break the record in two on the air, producing an audible and satisfying "crack." That song would never be played on that station again, even should it turn out to be #1 on every other radio station in the country!

A midwestern rock 'n' roll radio station, KEWI, in Topeka, Kansas, played "Make It or Break It" regularly in the mid-'60s. One of the two rock 'n' roll stations in the capital city of Kansas, KEWI covered a large listening area. In May 1964, one of their DJs played "Make It or Break It" with Peter and Gordon's "World Without Love." Taking votes while the record was playing, the DJ announced at the close of the tune that the votes were going heavily *against* the song. At that point he gave the name of the artist, Peter and Gordon. Those names meant nothing. However, he went on to say that the song was written by the Beatles, and he was surprised that no one liked it, what with its being a Beatles song and all.

The next record played as the DJ continued to take votes in the "Make It or Break It" over the phone. His next announcement was startling. Since mentioning that the Beatles had penned "A World Without Love," every single vote was "Make It." Ultimately, the song did indeed make it. Interesting that those who voted while the song's composers were unidentified did not care for it and voted "Break It," but those voting after the composers were identified as Lennon-McCartney did like it and voted "Make It!"

Prob'ly didn't hurt a British act to get to do Beatles songs in 1964. On the other hand, the Lennon-McCartney names alone were not enough to ensure a hit. Worth noting: When "World Without Love" made #1 in the states, Peter and Gordon became the first British invasion artists besides the Beatles to reach that goal, and it happened in June, over five months after "I Want to Hold Your Hand" had become #1!

Speaking of the Beatles, May was almost the first month in 1964 not to feature a new hit by the Beatles on any record label—except for a Tollie flip side called "P.S. I Love You." This was not the same "P.S. I Love You" that had been a U.S. hit years earlier—it was a Beatle original. Nor was it a British hit. It was just the flip side of the #1 smash, "Love Me Do," and just happened to make the Top 10 as well. The Beatles were unstoppable!

It is interesting to note that May was the first month that the Rolling Stones appeared on the U.S. rock 'n' roll radio stations. Their first song was typical of much of the invasion sound, a remake of an old LP cut from an American artist, Buddy Holly. The song was "Not Fade Away," and was only a very minor hit. Also true to the style of the invasion, the flip side of "Not Fade Away" was a song called "I Wanna Be Your Man," composed by (did you guess it?) the Beatles. In England, both songs were hits for the Rolling Stones, in late 1963 and early 1964 respectively. In the United States neither song made it very far at all, although "Not Fade Away" did chart. The Rolling Stones were too radical, musically and visually, to be embraced by the teenage girls who thought Paul was cute and Billy J. was handsome.

By mid–May, the hits were coming faster than they ever had from across the pond. All at once, a whole boatload of U.S. labels began offloading the hits of Britons on the American teen market, with widely varying degrees of success.

Worthy of first mention was the first woman artist of Phase II, Millie Small, billed as the Blue Beat Girl. She wasn't actually British, but nationality was the least of her dissimilarities with the rest of the invasion artists. She was small, she was black, she was female, of course, and she was Jamaican.

In England, Millie (last name not used) was a three-hit wonder, with "My Boy Lollipop" a Top-10 hit in mid-1964, a Top-30 follow-up "Sweet William" in the fall, and one more chart song, "Bloodshot Eyes," over a year later.

In America, she was known as Millie Small, and her career was similar, but her hit list was minus "Bloodshot Eyes." She had the familiar female rock 'n' roll "little girl-big voice" larynx, à la Rosie Hamlin of Rosie and the Originals, Sue Thompson, Brenda Lee, Teresa Brewer, and others. A few years later and she might have been called female bubble-gum. In other words, she was doing good old rock 'n' roll, while it lasted. Her excellent records sounded particularly distinctive because she was one of several artists in 1964 to try the Jamaican Ska beat. Others from the states and Jamaica included Tracy Dey with "Ska Do Dee Ya," the Ska Kings with "Jamaican Ska," and the Fleetwoods with "Ska Light, Ska Bright (Jamaican Ska)."

As May progressed, the Searchers continued their hit list. They had formed back in 1960, and being from Liverpool like the Beatles, they simply imitated the Beatle approach of redoing the hits of the early '60s and became stars. However, this time they came up with an original song, "Sugar and Spice." It was a #2 follow-up in England to their original U.K. #1 hit, "Sweets for My Sweet." In the United States, "Sweets" was a big Top-40 hit in the Midwest, but failed to make the national Top 100. "Sugar and Spice," the Searchers' third stateside hit, was also only regionally successful. Before the month was out, the Searchers made the Top 20 with "Don't Throw Your Love Away," a slower number that made #1 in England. In all, the Searchers had 14 British hits, six in the Top 5 in England, and three #1s. This is compared to 13 hits in the United States, no #1s, and only one Top-5 song on the national level!

Another debut artist in May was Gerry and the Pacemakers. Most DJs called him "Gary," until they found out that Gerry is pronounced "Jerry" in England. Gerry Marsden had what it took in 1964—a winning smile, a "Beatle" haircut, and a strong accent. He wore his electric guitar very high with a short strap. And he just happened to be from Liverpool.

Gerry and the Pacemakers did well with both slow and fast songs. In England their hits had been coming for a year already, starting with three consecutive #1 records: "How Do You Do It?," "I Like It," "You'll Never Walk Alone," and "I'm the One," which was #2. Of these, the first three would be hits in the United States many months later. It was his fifth and least popular ("only" #6) British hit, "Don't Let the Sun Catch You Crying," that was his first release in the states, and almost made #1. In fact, Gerry and the Pacemakers never did make the top slot of the U.S. national charts.

"Don't Let the Sun Catch You Crying" was the first really slow ballad to come out of the British invasion. This did not prevent it from becoming a hit, but it did mislead teenagers into thinking that Gerry and the Pacemakers were not rockers. Little did they know that Gerry's many rocking U.K. hits, now oldies but goodies in England, would be released in the United States as "new" records!

With the success in early May of Capitol Records' duo, Peter and Gordon, it was almost expected, yet something of a surprise, when Capitol introduced Chad and Jeremy in late May. At first no one could tell the two — or, four — apart. In fact, the duos were so similar that Capitol put a photo of Peter and Gordon on a Chad and Jeremy LP! Or, was it vice versa? No one ever knew if it was an accident, or just someone's little joke. Chad and Jeremy's record was "Yesterday's Gone," which was simultaneously a U.S. hit by another British group, the Overlanders. Neither version was a huge hit, but at least Chad Stuart and Jeremy Clyde's version hit the Top 40.

As big as they became in America, most of the British invasion artists were even more successful in their home country, England. Some had equal popularity in both countries. A few were not popular in England at all. The Overlanders were unusual since they had exactly one hit in each country, but with different songs! In the United States, their hit was "Yesterday's Gone" in 1964, also a hit for Chad and Jeremy. It did not make the national Top 40 but had good regional popularity. The Overlanders' one hit in England was their version of the Beatles' "Michelle," which was #1 in 1966, two years later than "Yesterday's Gone"! So besides having only one hit in each country, and having the hits be different songs, each song was also a hit by some other group.

Chad and Jeremy had nearly a dozen hits on the U.S. charts between 1964 and 1967, half in the Top 40. But in Mother England, Chad and Jeremy had only the one lone hit, "Yesterday's Gone," which was only a bit more popular there than it was here.

Yet another new group, the Hollies, appeared on this side of the Atlantic for the first time in May. They began their career as the Deltas in 1962, but renamed themselves after Buddy "Holly." The Hollies contributed another of the many invasion records which were new versions of American hits from as recent as 1963. "Just One Look" (see page 73) was the Hollies' only U.S. chart record for the entire year of 1964, and it only reached the 90s on the popularity polls. It had been a very successful #2 in England when it was released as the Hollies' fourth hit there.

In the "before Beatles" days, kids paid little or no attention to the composer credits on records. But in 1963 in England and in 1964 in the United States, just the names "Lennon-McCartney" between parentheses, in fine print, under the title on a record label were sometimes sufficient to make a record a hit.

The last invasion entry of May was Billy J. Kramer with the Dakotas. Remember how Billy J.'s manager, Brian Epstein, was also the manager of the Dakotas and of the Beatles? In that latter capacity, he got Lennon and McCartney to write songs for Billy J. Kramer with the Dakotas.

Billy J. with the Dakotas came out with "Bad to Me," their second chart song and a typical entry for them. It sounded a lot like a song Carole King might have written for Bobby Vee. It started off with a short spoken introduction, then proceeded to tell a little story. It was very effective. Stateside, it was big — Top 10. In England, it was the follow-up to their big hit "Do You Want to Know a Secret," which the Beatles wrote and had as a U.S. hit. Billy J. was even more popular in England. On the British charts, "Secret" reached #2, and "Bad" was #1.

Besides being Billy J.'s second U.S. hit and his second Top-10 hit, "Bad to Me" was the flip side of "Little Children," his first U.S. hit, which was also penned by Lennon-McCartney! Billy J. Kramer with the Dakotas were quite important players in the invasion force.

June — five artists. As summer arrived, the winter of '64 was still fresh in teenagers' ears, and there were still plenty of British songs on the charts. But the importation of hits was slowing down, from 10 in May to only three British groups placing new songs on the charts in June, and the Beatles were nearly not among them.

Next best, sort of second-string Beatles, the Dave Clark Five produced "Can't You See That She's Mine" for their fourth consecutive hit. It was far less rocking than the first three, and not at all pretty. It contrasted sharply with U.S. hits of the same summer, such as Jan and Dean's "Little Old Lady (From Pasadena)," the Beach Boys' "I Get Around," Roy Orbison's "Oh! Pretty Woman," and Dean Martin's "Everybody Loves Somebody Sometime." But the kids liked it enough to push it into the Top 5.

Also less than hard rocking was the new hit by Peter and Gordon, "Nobody I Know." It was a perfect follow-up to their first hit, "World Without Love," and nearly made the national Top 10 (it did make it in England!).

Not every U.S. radio listener up to now knew about Dusty Springfield. Neither "I Only Want to Be with You" nor "Stay Awhile" had been on the national Top 10, and often songs that do not make the Top 10 are either never particularly noticed, or they are quickly forgotten. Now Dusty came up with her first U.S. top tenner, "Wishin' and Hopin'." Partly because it was her first really huge record, and partly because it was much slower than her other two songs had been, many kids thought she was a new artist that summer. While "Wishin' and Hopin'" was Dusty's biggest Phase II song in the states, in England it wasn't even on the charts.

Just how did the Beatles do in June? In mid-month they squeaked in at the edge of the U.S. Top 100 with a Capitol EP *Four By the Beatles*, with "This Boy," "Roll Over Beethoven," "All My Loving," and "Please Mr. Postman." At the end of the month, a special 45 release on Swan Records of "She Loves You," called "Sie Liebt Dich," appeared. This was one of two songs on which the Beatles recut their vocals in German, as a nod to their fans in Hamburg where they got their start. Placing in the 90s like the EP had with "Sie Liebt Dich," the notion that anything released that was by the Beatles would be a hit was shot down. (The other German recording was "Komm, Gib Mir Deine Hand," or "I Want to Hold Your Hand" on their *Something New* U.S. LP.)

The only other June addition to the ranks of Invaders records was the Bachelors' second hit. The Bachelors were the least rocking of all the invasion artists, and their song, "I Believe," characteristically a remake of a U.S. song, failed to make the Top 30 in the states, even though it had gone clear to the top of the U.K. charts.

July — six artists. In July the U.S. rock 'n' roll jungle shook once again from the roar of the British lions, as the Beatles burst forth with a banging guitar chord from their movie *A Hard Day's Night*. Both the flick and the lick were #1 *everyplace*. By now, all of the other record labels had either run out of older Beatle material to release, or had been scared out of releasing any more by Capitol Records' legal department. All but one of the future Beatles U.S. releases were "official" Capitol 45s, released in sequence as the Beatles recorded them. That odd one out was an interesting 45 that Atco came up with, "Ain't She Sweet," an old Beatles recording of a truly old American tune, from the earliest recordings of the Beatles, and it amazingly made the Top 20.

Obviously, the Beatles were still as popular as ever. Their *Hard Day's Night* movie was a great success. But there had been fewer releases and smaller sales of Beatles and British invasion records in the early summer, and that had correctly foreshadowed what was coming at this six-month point in the British invasion: The passion of U.S. teens and radio stations for the British in general and the Beatles in particular was starting to cool off.

Here is an example of that cooling off. Up to "A Hard Day's Night," the Beatles had pretty much had big, two-sided hits every time out. But this time, "I Should Have Known Better," the flip side of "A Hard Day's Night," missed the Top 40. Shortly after that, Capitol released another single from the movie, "And I Love Her," which actually missed the Top 10. The flip side of "And I Love Her," "If I Fell," missed the national Top 40 altogether. A third single from the film, "I'll Cry Instead," missed the Top 20, and the flip side, "I'm Happy Just to Dance with You," scarcely cracked the Top 100 at all.

No, you couldn't say the Beatles were no longer hot. With a movie and seven songs on the Top 100 pretty much simultaneously, they were still the biggest thing in music. They just were no longer *white* hot.

Billy J. Kramer with the Dakotas popped up again in July. While their first two-sided smash ("Little Children" and "Bad to Me") was still being played nearly constantly, Imperial Records decided to flood the market with old Billy J. British hits, after the fashion of the Beatles earlier in the year. The new one was "I'll Keep You Satisfied," which had been a British 1963 top tenner, and made the Top 30 here in '64. Since it was another Lennon-McCartney composition, its less-than-strong showing represented either a further cooling off of the Beatle magic, or another great composing triumph for the Beatles, depending on whether you see a glass as half full or half empty. It was produced by George Martin, the Beatles' producer, but it was not a two-sided hit.

Gerry (pronounced Jerry, remember?) and the Pacemakers got a rocker off for their follow-up to the ballad "Don't Let the Sun Catch You Crying." "How Do You Do It" had been their original hit in England over a year earlier, and #1 at that, and now sold well in the United States. Laurie Records next tried the trick that had worked for Imperial with Billy J., and for Capitol with the Beatles: getting the British backlog released in the United States as quickly as practical. Could this approach work for just every Tom, Dick, and Gerry? Yes. Laurie Records released another Gerry Marsden British chart topper/oldie the same month. But "I'm the One" barely placed in the U.S. So much for the unstoppable magic of the invasion. American teens, while still in love with the British, were becoming progressively more selective and beginning to value quality over mere tonnage.

Apparently teenagers didn't find what they were looking for during the rest of July. The Rolling Stones tried again, this time with "Tell Me" and "It's All Over Now." This was the month that London Records thought it would be neat to start releasing more than one Stones record at a time. These two songs were hits but failed to make the Top 20, probably a shock to the group and the label; while "Tell Me" had not been a hit in England, "It's All Over Now" had been their first #1.

A new woman came over at this time. When the British invasion is mentioned, the image conjured up is four (or maybe two or five) boys with shaggy hair, wearing suits and playing guitars, drums, and perhaps an organ or piano. Fans of the invasion like to point out (with questionable justification) that British rock 'n' roll, because it was performed by self-contained bands, was greater than U.S. rock 'n' roll. One of many things that they fail to realize is that we never did embrace the full range of the British rock 'n' roll spectrum. First we got the Beatles, then we got any other group of four (or two to five) shaggy boys that a U.S. record company could sign up before anyone else could! But in England, rock 'n' roll was more than groups of mop-tops and combo bands. It was every bit as diverse as was American rock 'n' roll, with instrumentals (Sounds, Inc., the Shadows, and others), solo male vocalists (Matt Monroe, Frank Ifield, Cliff Richard, Tommy Steele) and female vocalists (Helen Shapiro, Sandie Shaw, and Cilla Black).

Cilla's real name was, believe it or not, Priscilla White. But as Cilla Black she had some two dozen hits in England, beginning in 1963. Every single one of her records made the British Top 40, and she had three British #1's and nine British Top-10 hits. Her hit songs included "You're My World" (#1 in the spring of 1964) and "You've Lost That Lovin' Feelin'" (#2 in 1965). The American version of "Lovin' Feeling,'" by the Righteous Brothers, didn't phase her popularity in England, even though the Brothers' version was also #1 on the British charts around the same time as Cilla's.

Cilla Black was the next July invader. Cilla got her start and her name by accident. She worked in the Cavern Club, since she lived in Liverpool, but not as a performer. She was invited on stage one night by Rory Storm's group and sang "Fever" as a lark. A favorable *Mersey Beat* reviewer called her Miss Black by mistake, and she decided to stick with the new name. Her manager was Brian Epstein, same as the Beatles'. Black's first U.S. release was "You're My World," but unlike its #1 success in England, it was just Top 30 here.

Last for July was Cliff Richard. This Phase I invasion star, who was still so very popular in England, made a very minor appearance in July with a song almost no Americans remember today, "Bachelor Boy."

June and July were not as spectacular as a Beatles British invasion month in 1964 could have been. With five and six artists each, they fell short of the springtime month of May which had more new artists than any other, with 10. August would continue the summer's comparative lull.

August — four artists. Summer did end with some good stuff. True, the Beatles skipped August, but they were riding high on the charts with four sides of two records from previous months. Meanwhile, the DC5 surprised everyone by continuing to slow down the pace of their music with "Because." Even with the slower pace, the song was still a huge hit. "Because" was not even a single in England, where "Thinking of You Baby" was the DC5's current U.K. hit. This song was not even a single in the states.

Billy J. Kramer with the Dakotas did it again in July with a third Lennon-McCartney composition, "From a Window," produced by the Beatles' producer, George Martin. That made four hit songs on three records, all in the same summer for Billy J. It was beginning to look as if Billy J. was going to be a major force in rock 'n' roll on both sides of the Atlantic for quite a while!

The Searchers, who were very big in England, had "Some Day We're

Gonna Love Again" in the U.S. in July, but it was barely Top 40 here in spite of being very strong at home. The Swinging Blue Jeans, who had started off so promisingly with Brit versions of Chan Romero's "Hippy Hippy Shake" and Little Richard's "Good Golly Miss Molly," now abruptly fizzled and made their last chart appearance at #97 with "You're No Good." This was yet another former American song. Betty Everett was the original singer, and it was a hit again for Linda Ronstadt in 1975. The Searchers' version was a big hit in England, but even so marked the end of their string there, as well. Not even a year had passed and the invaders already had begun dying off.

Chad and Jeremy finally made their second U.S. appearance with their follow-up to "Yesterday's Gone," which was their only U.K. hit. Titled "A Summer Song," the mellow strains of this follow-up sounded darn good on the hot August nights of 1964. A Top-10 record, it was the biggest song the duo ever had in the states, yet did nothing in England!

New blood! A new group called the Animals growled their way onto the charts in August, outdoing the Rolling Stones in the rebellion-and-scruffiness department. Their debut disc, "House of the Rising Sun," was based on an old U.S blues number about a prostitute. It was a lengthy song which had to be edited down for the hit 45. And hit is the word. It was not only the Animals' first hit, but also their biggest hit, their only #1 ever, and it became an instant classic. In England, where it was their second record, it was also #1. A final distinction: When "House of the Rising Sun" made the top spot in September of 1964, it was only the second time a British invasion group other than the Beatles made #1.

September—eleven artists. Wow! In the school year of 1963–1964, the British invasion had been an exciting, new phenomenon. The excitement had continued during the summer of '64. In the fall of 1964, kids were going back to school and the British invasion had become an exciting old phenomenon, with a record number of British invasion artists' songs hitting the charts. As the new fall classes started, the Beatles recycled some old classics. Of course, most of the teenybopper girls, the primary buyers of Beatles records, had no idea these songs went back years and years. The Beatles had cut a flip flop, that is, an old Carl Perkins flip side from a flop single from the '50s, called "Matchbox." No doubt to Perkins' delight, this record turned "Matchbox" into a new hit. The Beatles own flip side to Carl Perkins flip side was—get this—an old Lary Williams flip side, "Slow Down." "Matchbox" and "Slow Down" naturally became another two-sided Beatle hit, but as the passion was still in the process of cooling off, neither the A-side nor the flip side made the Top 20! To be fair, it should be made clear that these Beatles songs were just Beatle LP cuts, and were not even on 45s in England. Since the Beatles did not intend them to be on a single, the small slip in popularity can be excused.

The record companies of DC5 and Billy J. decided to sit September out. But a great new group buzzed into earshot. The Honeycombs were named after their novel gimmick—their drummer was female, one Ann "Honey" Lantree. This made the Honeycombs the only invasion combo that included a woman. Percussionist Honey rivaled Dave Clark for sheer percussive excitement and drum pounding, although Dave's hair may have been a bit longer. And in spite of her heavy-handed style, and unlike the rock drummers of later decades, she did not act like her chair was electrically wired. She managed to smile and even hold her hair in place when she played the wildest and hardest of licks and paradiddles. "Have I the Right" was a stinging #1 in England. But Honey and the boys never made it big again at home, with only one more small hit in '64 and two fairly popular songs in 1965. In the United States, "Have I the Right" went Top 5, higher than the new Beatles record.

Gerry and the Pacemakers did it again in September. Each new song by them was more rocking than the one before. "I Like It" was good time rock 'n' roll at its best, and Gerry flashed a winning smile each time he played and sang it. It was Top 20 here, but had been #1 in England the previous year.

Peter and Gordon had their hit this month with one of the longest titles of the invasion, "I Don't Want to See You Again." It had the same ambiance as their first two hits, and it went Top 20 here and did nothing in England. It must have been confusing for these British groups to have songs that were big sellers in one country, but were either small hits, nonhits, LP cuts, or hits in different years in the other.

New invasion group alert! Manfred Mann had changed their name from the Mann–Hugg Blues Brothers some time before—now they took an American record by the Exciters, "Do-Wah-Diddy," and changed its name to "Do Wah Diddy Diddy" and had a #1 record on the U.S. charts with it. This oddly named group descended on the American music scene in early September. "Do Wah Diddy Diddy" was also a #1 in England, but there it was Manfred Mann's third hit, and it came out in early summer, not early fall. Manfred Mann looked British, with the long haircuts combed frontwards. But they tended to appear in more casual dress than other British bands. With "Do Wah Diddy Diddy," they began a career which would soon establish them as the most important British group since the Animals.

The same fall season of '64 ushered in another new group. The Nashville Teens were neither from Nashville, nor were they teens any longer by the time they began having hits. Their "Tobacco Road" was written by John D. Loudermilk, a composer of many U.S. hit records. In England this Nashville Teens record was Top 10, as was the follow-up, "Google Eyes." After a handful of U.K. hits the next year or so, the Nashville Teens faded in England. Their fate was even worse and their fade even faster in the U.S.

"Tobacco Road" was Top 20, then the U.S. follow-up, which had been their third British record, "Find My Way Back Home," was only #98 on the American Top 100! "Google Eyes" and the other U.K. records failed to succeed at all with U.S. teens. Goodbye, Nashville Teens.

Cilla Black tried again in September. With her incredible U.K. success, record after record a hit in England, she was doubtless little concerned about having hits in the United States. Lucky thing she didn't need U.S. hits to make a living, since her new song, "It's for You," a big hit at home, was not even close to Top 40 here.

The Searchers flirted with star status with a Top-20 song, "Don't Throw Your Love Away," their second biggest hit so far. However, "Searchermania" was strictly a British phenomenon.

The Animals followed up "House of the Rising Sun" in September with "Gonna Send You Back to Georgia." What the title suggests seems rather unlikely since they were in England, not the American South. The song wasn't among their nine or ten British hits. Even in the states, where the Animals eventually had twice as many hit records as at home, "Georgia" didn't make the Top 40.

Before rigor mortis could set in, the Animals, who had originally called themselves the Alan Price Combo, released "I'm Crying." This barely made the Top 20, but restored the Animals' reputation as hitmakers—albeit not on the same level as Billy J. Kramer with the Dakotas or Gerry and the Pacemakers.

The British ballad of the month was from the Bachelors. "Wouldn't Trade You for the World" tried to buck the hard rocking odds, but failed to reach the Top 40, even though it made the Top 5 in England.

The excitement of the month was generated by a new hard rock British group, the Kinks. The band, formerly called the Ramrods, began with a few poor showings in England—American Little Richard's "Long Tall Sally," and "Took My Baby Home," "You Still Want Me," and "You Do Something to Me." These songs were issued in the U.S. on Cameo Records, the label that had Chubby Checker, Dee Dee Sharp, and many other hitmakers. The Kinks did not number among the Cameo hitmakers in the states or the U.K.

The Kinks' career took off, however, with a new batch of songs. The first one released, "You Really Got Me," sounded like it was not sung so much as hammered out. Being a new group in England as well as in the United States, which was unusual, they had no backlog of British oldies to follow up within the United States. "You Really Got Me" was #1 in England, Top 10 in the U.S. The Kinks were three times more popular at home than they were in the United States where the competition from all of the big American artists, including those at Cameo Records, was almost overwhelming.

October—five artists. The fall got slow, and so did the DC5. "Everybody Knows" continued their trend to rock ballads. The Dave Clark Five began life together as a soccer team. But they needed to raise money for uniforms, train fare and such. Since Dave was almost as good a drummer as an athlete, they did a few local dances to raise soccer money.

Little did Dave and the team know just how much money they would make and how little soccer they would play! In October of 1964 "Everybody Knows" was the DC5's first (official) release to make "only" the Top 20 in the United States, and it just squeaked onto the British Top 40. But even a Top-20 record is worth a lot of juke box play and television appearances. The Dave Clark Five was not really in trouble.

Neither were the Rolling Stones in dire straits. They had formed as a spinoff of a group called Alex Korner's Blues Incorporated. After three poor showings as the Rolling Stones, they finally made the U.S. Top 10 this late in the British invasion with their last record for the year. Late or not, time was on their side, even if only in the states with "Time Is on My Side." This had originally been sung by American rhythm and blues singer Irma Thomas, who resented the Stones' exact copying of her style so much that she refused to perform the song ever again. By this time, the Stones had already had five hits in England, and their current British hit, "Little Red Rooster," went to #1 in England!

The Searchers, the British giants who had originally scored with a remake of American Jackie DeShannon's "Needles and Pins," did another Jackie DeShannon remake, "When You Walk in the Room," but as usual for them in the U.S., barely made the Top 40. The Searchers had a lot of American releases, quite a few hits, but rarely were their songs big hits, especially in comparison to their Top-5 placings in England.

October brought two new groups over from England, and they were totally different. Herman's Hermits was one of the few invasion artists to sing with a British accent. Their lead singer, Peter Noone, was said to resemble the character Sherman on the Rocky and Bullwinkle cartoon television show, and was misnamed after him. The cartoon name seemed appropriate, since the Hermits were considered one of the more lightweight invasion bands. Influenced heavily by Buddy Holly and stateside girl groups, Herman and the Hermits leaned toward the novelty after a while. For their first U.S. song, on the MGM label, they chose an American girl group tune by Earl-Jean, "I'm Into Somethin' Good." Released as their first song in England only a few weeks earlier, it was #1 there and Top 10 here, a pretty good start for a new group that was something of a novelty.

Also a novelty, but not intentionally, was the Zombies. It was after they won a talent contest in England that they began to record. Musically, the Zombies actually outdid the Kinks in the hammer-rock department.

With more harmony than many others, "She's Not There" went to the top of both countries' charts. The Zombies' sound may have been ahead of its time.

November — six artists. Note that the Beatles hadn't released a new #1 record since July!

Now, in November, the reliable DC5 returned to the sound of their earlier hits, with the very upbeat "Any Way You Want It." By this time they were releasing songs simultaneously in both countries, and "Any Way," though not Top 10 in either country, was quite a bit bigger in this country than in the United Kingdom.

There was slow stuff in November, ably offered by Chad and Jeremy in their third and last song for the year, "Willow Weep for Me." Interesting that they continued to have Top-20 hits in the U.S., when nothing at all was clicking for them at home in England.

The Searchers were still in there, plugging away. They selected yet another U.S. hit oldie, "Love Potion #9" (see page 83) for the invasion treatment. In England, "Potion" was just an LP cut, with their end-of-the-year hit there being "What Have They Done to the Rain." "Rain" would become Top 30 in the United States, but not until the next spring. "Potion" made the U.S. Top 5, even if the Searchers did get the lyrics messed up when they copied the original. One of their errors was singing "Madame Rue" when it should have been "Madame Ruth."

This month Manfred Mann followed up their first United States record, the #1 song "Do Wah Diddy Diddy," with a Top-20 hit, "Sha La La." This new hit was, like "Do Wah Diddy Diddy," another former U.S. song — this one from a Shirelles LP. Manfred Mann's "Sha La La" was a much bigger hit in England. Manfred Mann was a puzzle for U.S. radio listeners. Was Manfred one of the group, or was he a man named Mann, or was it the group name, or both? The answer was, yes and no. The group name was Manfred Mann. They were named after their organ player, called Manfred Mann. But his real name was Michael Liebowitz. Would they have been a success had they called themselves Liebowitz Laddy instead of Manfred Mann?

Dusty Springfield (and Cilla Black and Millie Small) notwithstanding, the British invasion was still almost exclusively a male phenomenon. For that matter, even being male was no help unless you were in a group that looked at least superficially like the Fab Four. The list of big male soloists who were stars of British rock 'n' roll, but invasion no-gos, must have been depressing to many of the British singers. The big U.S. boosters of the British groups and buyers of the British records were the girls. They were the ones who screamed "We love you, Beatles," and cried after the concerts were over. In contrast to the girls, American boys were more likely to picket and protest what many saw as British limey luvver boys, than scream.

Probably 90 percent of all rock 'n' roll records in the United States were purchased by girls in the early '60s, so it was natural that the male invaders would become popular, if they resembled the Beatles and thus attracted the girls.

When any British female singers did arrive, they not only looked nothing like the Beatles—they also tended to sing a totally different kind of rock 'n' roll music. We have already met, and said farewell to Cilla Black. In November, Marianne Faithfull gave it a shot with a haunting record, "As Tears Go By." With her long hair and harpsichord instrumentation, Marianne was patently British. She scored half a dozen hits, all but one in the Top 10, in England. But "As Tears Go By" didn't even crack the Top 20 on our side of the Atlantic.

Another young British woman surfaced in the U.S. in November. Sandie Shaw had just made #1 in England with "(There's) Always Something There to Remind Me"—her very first record. So it made sense to try in the states with the same song. Sandie did not even reach the Top 40, except in the Midwest, where "(There's) Always Something There to Remind Me" was very popular.

December—seven artists. It was the twelfth month of the year, and the twelfth and final month of Phase II of the Beatles British invasion. Although the pace had slowed a bit, and the chart placements tended to be a bit less lofty, the invasion was continuing to be a powerful factor on the American music scene. Another woman gave it the Old British Try, and the word woman is used advisedly. Pet Clark had been a star in England since 1940. When she joined the Invaders, she was a rather mature 30 years old.

Most child stars in the United States have a hard time living down their child-star image, and outliving their kid careers. In other words, none of the other American or British child stars of the '40s and '50s became rock 'n' rollers of the '60s. Petula Clark had been the Shirley Temple of Britain, and she went on to have a dozen U.K. hits pre-1964. Then, in late '64, "Downtown" became her thirteenth hit and her third Top-5 hit.

When "Downtown" was released as Pet Clark's first record in the U.S., it was soon #1 over here. Pet Clark succeeded where no other invading woman had. And as an older singer popular with the kids as well as with many parents, she gave the invasion a kind of respect with the older generation neither it nor rock 'n' roll had enjoyed before.

The record changed Pet Clark's whole life. Even though she had been a star her entire life, having an international #1 hit record caused her to reclassify her entire life into two sections: pre–"Downtown" and post–"Downtown."

The Bachelors hadn't had a new record since June, but in December they released their fourth song, "No Arms Can Ever Hold You." As usual for this duo, it was a much bigger British hit (Top 10) than American (Top 30).

The Animals' next record won the award for the dumbest title of Phase II of the invasion: "Boom Boom." It was in the same rude British blues style the Animals had been using since the beginning with "House of the Rising Sun." As a matter of fact, it was their audiences' reaction to the Animals' stage act which got them the name Animals! Originally, they were tamely called the Alan Price Combo after their keyboard player, but their fans said they acted like animals on stage. It is fun to speculate, as with Herman's Hermits and Manfred Mann, whether or not their success would have been so great had it not been for the name change!

"Boom Boom" was not an Animals hit in England, and it missed the Top 40 in the states. At this point, both Pet Clark and the Bachelors were outselling the Animals on both sides of the ocean.

Also in the harder vein, the Kinks finally came up with a follow-up to September's "You Really Got Me." "All Day and All of the Night" sounded almost the same, and it made the exact same Top-10 position as the first one in the United States, and the same top-of-the-chart success in England.

Gerry and the Pacemakers fired a last 1964 shot across the ocean this month. Their songs so far had been fairly sweet and they stayed that way, which was appropriate for a group which with a different membership lineup had originally called itself Mars Bars. Gerry Marsden and the Pacemakers' fourth U.S. hit, "I'll Be There," was a ballad much like their first hit, "Don't Let the Sun Catch You Crying." "I'll Be There" maintained their Top-20 status in the states and in England.

Remember Honey, the drummer? She and the Honeycombs came up with a solid follow-up for "Have I the Right." As fierce as that debut single had been, "I Can't Stop" was even more dynamic, even to the trick ending done in half-time. Speaking of endings, after the Top 5 "Have I the Right," it was shock all around when "I Can't Stop" did stop, short even of the Top 40. Then their hit career stopped in the United States, and in England as well. In England, "I Can't Stop" wasn't even a single, and the Honeycombs' three other British records became only very small hits over there.

The last month of the invasion, fittingly, included a new Beatles release. "I Feel Fine" was a fine hit, reaching #1. Yet it was the first Beatles record since September, and the first #1 to come out since July. Quite a change from the first few months of the year, when the Beatles dominated some 10 percent of the chart.

"I Feel Fine" ushered in Phase III of the invasion. It signalled the beginning of the end of original, light Beatles material, and the beginning of the experimental and unconventional. The opening note was supposed to be either feedback (probably), or the sound of an electric guitar string vibrating against a metal cigarette lighter (less likely)—or both. If you liked the Bachelors, it sounded like hell. If you liked the Zombies, it was great! If you were a Beatlemaniac, you didn't judge, you just bought. Whether you liked the intro to "I Feel Fine" or not, you bought the record to hear the rest of the song whenever you wanted to, and the record went to #1. The flip side, "She's a Woman," also went Top 5, convincing any doubters that the Fab Four were still #1 in the British invasion!

As December 1964 ended, so ended Phase II of the Beatles British invasion. Marking the end of Phase II with the calendar is not arbitrary. At this point, the newness of the invasion had certainly worn off. To many younger record buyers and radio listeners, the British sound was now a natural element of rock 'n' roll radio. To older kids, the groups were no longer a novelty. To the record companies, it was no longer "sign them fast, no matter what they sound like." From now on to sell even a few copies, a song had to be really good, and so did a group, no matter if they were American or British.

Perhaps the most important legacy of the invasion of 1964 was that, for the first time, the suits at the record companies, television executives, and adults in general finally took rock 'n' roll seriously, if not as a musical force, certainly as a financial industry. Up to this time, rock 'n' roll was considered a fad which would pass, just kids' stuff, never accepted by the establishment, always fighting an uphill battle. From now on, rock 'n' roll would dominate the establishment and ultimately become the musical establishment in the United States and the world.

Phase III: 1965–1969

After 1964, there were just a few new invasion artists. In fact, the ones that came in Phase III were not really a part of the British invasion. They were for the most part just rock 'n' roll artists who happened to be from England, more like occupation forces than invading battalions. Meanwhile, the Phase II artists finished out their careers as the '60s went on. And a few lasted beyond the '60s.

1965-1969

Of course, the Beatles continued their string of hits beyond 1964. John, Paul, George, and Ringo had roughly 30 more hits in the states, many two-sided, with almost half of those making national #1. In England, they had only about half as many chart songs, with 11 making #1. A funny thing about English record companies. They would often reissue old hits, and boom, the songs would make the charts a second time as singles. For the Beatles, such varied songs reissued in the '70s that made the charts a second time included "Penny Lane," "Strawberry Fields Forever," "Help," "Hey Jude," and "Yesterday."

The Beatles had broken up by the end of the '60s. In those days, most big, popular rock 'n' roll artists in the United States had successful careers of about five to six years. These years are marked from the time an artist's hits started, not from the time the group formed. The Beatles began forming back in the mid-'50s. The hits began around 1963. The end came in 1969, six years later. Classic. The Beatles as a group were big, but not bigger than the system which, in one way or another, chewed groups up and spit them out when the flavor (if not the talent) was gone.

The second-string Beatles, the Dave Clark Five, experienced much the same fate, if on a smaller scale. They had 16 more U.S. hits, including one #1, "Over and Over" (originally by American Bobby Day) and four Top 10s. By the end of four years, the DC5 were finished in the United States. It was little better in England, where they lasted for five years. Classic pattern.

Billy J. Kramer with the Dakotas, who had seemed so important in the summer of 1964, never had it so good again. It is hard to believe that they had so many big hits in just a few months, then faded with just two later American "hits," both in 1965, and neither making the Top 40. In England they had started earlier than in the U.S. so their run was for three years there, but only one year here.

Herman's Hermits did better than most of the British invasion groups. With their strong British accents and novelty approach to the music, their appeal was more enduring than the others, especially for the teeny-bopper record buyers. Both of their #1 hits were novelty tunes, sung with thick accents: "Mrs. Brown You've Got a Lovely Daughter" and "I'm Henry VIII, I Am." To illustrate how important the novelty element of their music was to their success in the U.S., neither of these songs were even singles in England, where the accents would mean nothing special. "I'm Henry VIII, I Am" was really just a joke, an LP filler to which Herman didn't even know all the verses — that's why he says, "Second verse, same as the first!" They and their British fans were astounded that it became their best-selling U.S. 45.

The Hermits had 18 U.S. hits and 17 British hits up through 1968, five years in total once again. Their big year was '65, with seven hits, all Top 10, and then two #1's. The last Top-40 U.S. hit was "I Can Take or Leave Your Loving" in 1968. In England they lasted longer, into 1970, and had four more Top 10s. After that, Peter "Herman" Noone had two more Top-20 U.K. hits as a solo artist.

The Honeycombs didn't survive in America past 1964 at all, although they did have two British hits in 1965. The Swinging Blue Jeans had their three U.S. "hits" all in 1964. The story was about the same in England, except for one small hit earlier, in 1963, and another later, in early 1965.

In 1966, a duo à la Peter and Gordon and Chad and Jeremy, but named David and Jonathan, had two small hits in England and a Top-20 version of the Beatles' "Michelle" in the United States. But nothing else, anywhere. Chad and Jeremy had eight more U.S. hits, half in the Top 40. One that didn't make the Top 40 was the old Billy J. number, "From a Window." As brief as Chad and Jeremy's career was stateside, it was a mere flash in the pan in England, where their only hit was "Yesterday's Gone" in 1963, which barely made the British Top 40 at all.

The biggest duo of the invasion, Peter and Gordon, did much better than David and Jonathan or Chad and Jeremy. With 11 U.S. hits post-'64, and half of those Top 40, they stayed around through 1967. In '66 they had two Top-10 novelty tunes, "Lady Godiva" and "Knight in Rusty Armor," and a brief revival in the 1980s. "Knight" was not a hit in England, while "Lady" made the Top 10 as their final British hit in 1966. Peter and Gordon were popular for two years in England and three in the U.S. But their total run lasted only about three years.

The Bachelors had five more U.S. hits in 1967, but each one was less popular than the last, until the final hit didn't even make the Top 80. They did much better in England, with about 10 more hits after 1964, including "Marie" in 1965, "Hello Dolly" in 1966, and an almost-#1, also in 1966, "Sounds of Silence."

The Hollies were one of the few invasion groups that didn't really catch on until after 1964. Their first record was 1964's massive flop remake of American Doris Troy's "Just One Look." Reissued in the U.S. in 1967, it almost made the Top 40. "Bus Stop" and "Stop Stop Stop" made the Top 10 in '66, "Carrie Ann" in '67, and "He Ain't Heavy, He's My Brother" in '69. They kept their name alive with non–Top-40 records off and on through 1975, plus a surprise hit in 1983, for an overall run of 22 songs in 10 years, or 23 songs in 18 years if you include the '83 hit. All of this was in the states. In Great Britain, they had an impressive 21 hits after 1964, with Top 10s and Top 40s clear through the mid-'70s. In terms of longevity they were one of the most popular of all of the invasion groups. They lasted much longer than the five to six year rule, just about double it. Even longer, if you count the freak occurrence of an isolated U.S. hit remake of the Supremes' "Stop in the Name of Love" in 1983, 10 years after their last Top-40 record.

Freddie and the Dreamers have not been mentioned yet. Freddie had a background which included singing skiffle and working as a milk man. As a rock 'n' roll group, Freddie and the Dreamers gained much of their experience working in the Beatles' old stomping grounds, Hamburg, West Germany. Of all the significant British invasion groups, Freddie and the Dreamers were the last to arrive. It wasn't because they were newly formed. In England, they had had their first hit in 1963. "If You Gotta Make a Fool of Somebody" was their first of nine over there, and was very big. Their last was in 1965, the American song "Thou Shalt Not Steal." But in the U.S., their first hit was 1965's "I'm Telling You Now." This had been their second hit in England, but in '63, not '65! And after four more hits, all in 1965, they too faded away. Freddie later became the host of a kids' television show, which seemed about right, as his records were often very teeny-bopper oriented yet pure rock 'n' roll nonetheless.

The Fortunes were a less important invasion artist that did not cross the ocean until 1965. "You've Got Your Troubles, I've Got Mine" was Top 10. Their follow-up, "Here It Comes Again," made the Top 40. "This Golden Ring," 1966, didn't. In England, their first two songs were Top-5 hits, in '65; "This Golden Ring" was Top 20 in '66, and then they had a Top tenner each in '71 and '72. Of all the British groups, their mismatch of American/British hits made perhaps the least sense.

Back to some bigger fish — the Animals endured longer than most. They succeeded 14 times after 1964 up through 1968, with most making the Top 40. After a while the name was changed to Eric Burdon and the Animals. Later still, Eric formed War, and had a hit in 1970 and a flop in 1971. War did not have any hits in England, but as the Animals, Eric had a dozen British hits, mostly Top 40, through the end of the decade. Six years for the overall British run, about like usual (with one odd entry, "The Night," in 1983). But only four years in the United States.

The other scruffy group was the Rolling Stones. They were the slowest invasion group to catch on during Phase II. But their popularity has lasted up into the 1990s and shows no sign of stopping. Obviously, the Stones were the most successful of all of the invasion groups, including the Beatles, as a unified "group."

The hard-rocking Zombies were very short-lived. They had three hits post-1964, with only one in the Top 40. Then they popped up surprisingly with "Time of the Season" as a Top-10 swan song in 1969. That was a lot better than their U.K. success, which ended abruptly after only the two hits, "She's Not There" and "Tell Her No"! The Zombies really lasted just about six months.

The also hard-rocking Kinks fared better. They had nine American hits post-'64, the majority Top 10 if you overlook two poor showings in their last year, 1967. In England they were much more important, having 17 hits lasting up to 1972, with many Top-10 hits year after year. The Kinks' popularity originally lasted just short of three years in the U.S. As their hard rock style became more popular, they staged one comeback in 1970–'71, and another from '78 to '84, totalling another 13 hits.

Remember how Billy J. was paired with the Dakotas? Well, Wayne Fontana and the Mindbenders, who missed the first year of the invasion, started together with Fontana as the organizer, then split up. Their first British hits were in 1963, three remakes of U.S. songs: "My Girl Josephine," "Road Runner," and "Um Um Um Um Um Um." While they didn't have the big chart-toppers many groups had, they did score 10 times between '63 and '67 in England. The Mindbenders had four more hits without Wayne Fontana, ending in 1967. The combined group had a #1 first time out with "The Game of Love" in America, which was also their biggest U.K. record in the same year, 1965. Why it took two years for them to export their music is a mystery, as is the reason Fontana left when the hits were finally coming. In the United States, the Mindbenders without Wayne made a big splash with "A Groovy Kind of Love," then faded after one flop in '66. One Mindbender, Eric Stewart, went on to join 10 cc. But the overall run of hits was three years in England, one in the U.S.

Gerry and the Pacemakers were major invasion stars in their day. Unfortunately, except for the obscure "Girl on a Swing" in 1966, their slide down was a quick one in 1965. With five hits overall, they began on the Top 10 with "Ferry Cross the Mersey," missed the Top 40 with "You'll Never Walk Alone," and disappeared at #90 with "La La La." The story was even more grim in England, with only three in '65 and nothing after that! From international star to oldie in two British years and one U.S. year! Surprisingly poor showing for a major invasion star.

Among the big groups, Manfred Mann were and are considered a group of the first order of importance. This reputation was built on a grand total of just six U.S. hits, however. Of their four post-'64 hits, only two were Top 40. The last, "Fox on the Run" in '69, barely hit the upper 90s on the Top 100. In England there were over a dozen post-'64 hits, mostly Top tenners, up through 1969. Then in 1973, Manfred Mann's Earthband had one hit in England, but failed to place at all in the United States.

That leaves the Searchers as the last of the big groups. They had four records in '65 and two in '66, but only two of these six made the Top 40. Only a two-year run, one song on the Top 40. The run was comparable in England, the main difference being three hits in 1963, making the run of hits last for three years in the U.K.

The Nashville Teens were taken care of in Phase II, where they had both of their U.S. hits. There were three U.K. hits in '65, but they were of minor popularity, making the Teens essentially a one-shot artist in the states with "Tobacco Road."

Phase I artist Cliff Richard had one U.S. hit post-'64, a very, very minor entry to the Top 100 in 1968, "Congratulations." In England, Cliff had over 35 post-'64 hits through the mid-'70s, and most of those were Top 10. No British artist or group has ever outsold him, and the only non–British artist to beat Cliff was Elvis. He is still big today, internationally. Even "Congratulations" was #1 overseas. Cliff, who began in 1958 and was then supposedly outgunned by the beat groups of the invasion year, actually had many British hits during the invasion year, then persevered and outlasted them all.

Phase III artists Freddie and the Dreamers, the Fortunes, and Chad and Jeremy have already been reviewed. These artists seemed to fit the mold of the Phase II 1964 Beatles British invasion acts, even though their first U.S. hits were not on the charts until 1965, 1966, or 1967. Eleven other artists do clearly fall under Phase III of the British post-invasion.

The main thing that seems to define Phase II versus Phase III artists is when they began to have hits in the U.S. In almost every case, all of the British artists from 1955 on were successful in the U.K. before they were exported to the U.S. Sometimes the difference was only a month or two, but often it was a year or two. The sound, look, and ambiance of British groups changed in 1965. The group names were often non sequiturs, the songs more like folk- and acid-rock than traditional rock 'n' roll. So, Freddie and the Dreamers, whose first U.S. hit was in the spring of 1965, qualify as Phase II because their British hits began in 1963 and their songs and name were light. But the Yardbirds, whose first U.S. hit was also in the spring of 1965, qualify as Phase III because their first British hit came early in 1965, not 1963, their name had an obscure meaning, and their song titles and lyrics were strange!

The Yardbirds were five guys with a lot of replacements over the years. They looked more like the Stones than the Beatles, but their music was more serious than the Beatles' at this point. They had nine U.S. hits of steadily decreasing popularity and increasing strangeness from Top-10 "For Your Love" in 1965, Top-20 "Over Under Sideways Down" in 1966, Top-50 "Ha Ha Said the Clown" in 1967, and Top-100 "Ten Little Indians" in early 1968. Group members like Jeff Beck, Eric Clapton, Jimmy Page and others formed other groups such as Led Zeppelin in later years, but the Yardbirds themselves lasted less than 35 months, when they broke up due to lack of popularity. Their U.K. success was even a bit poorer than their American run.

Hedgehoppers Anonymous is a group whose name illustrates the name-style difference between Phase II and Phase III artists. Phase II groups had fairly straightforward names, often including their own names (for example, Billy J. Kramer with the Dakotas, Gerry and the Pacemakers, Freddie and the Dreamers, and Peter and Gordon). The Yardbirds' name had been kind of obscure, referring to bums who hopped freight trains. Hedgehoppers Anonymous, well, who knows what that referred to. Their only U.S. hit was "It's Good News Week," but the title was ironic, with lyrics like "someone's dropped the Bomb somewhere contaminating atmosphere and blackening the skies." The song was Top 5 in the U.K., but was not even Top 40 in the states. Their producer, Jonathan King, later had a hit or two of his own, including "Everyone's Gone to the Moon" in 1965.

A trio of solo artists appeared in Phase III who were unknown in the United States in Phase II. The first to find fame, early in 1965, was Georgie

Fame. Georgie (real name Clive Powell) had just three legitimate U.S. hits, but only the first was even Top 40. "Yeh, Yeh" was a strange, breathless song which placed in the Top 30 in 1965. He did better in England. There, "Yeh, Yeh" was #1 and led to a string of songs that placed anywhere from #30 to #1. In 1968, Fame scored big after a year of no hits of any kind in the U.S. He sang a song based on the popular if historically inaccurate movie *Bonnie and Clyde*. "The Ballad of Bonnie and Clyde" was a hit on both sides of the Atlantic, but was a far cry from "Yeh Yeh." In all, Clive Powell's career consisted of four years of hits in the states, not counting 1968.

Another solo artist in '65 was Donovan (real name Donovan Phillip Leitch), who was heavily inspired by Bob Dylan. He became a major force in England, with Top-10 hits every year from 1965 to 1969. After that, he did television work and other non-rock work. In the U.S., he had only four Top-10 hits, and 10 lesser hits between '65 and '73. His best-known songs included "Sunshine Superman" and "Mellow Yellow" in '66, "Hurdy Gurdy Man" in '68, and "Atlantis" in '69. In all, he lasted about five years stateside.

The most conventional Phase III solo artist, and the last from 1965, was Tom Jones. "It's Not Unusual" got him off to a good start in early '65 in both countries. A pair of movie themes, "What's New Pussycat?" and "Thunderball," furthered his career. Soon he became an international star with his own television show, outgrowing both the invasion and rock 'n' roll.

In 1966, a few new groups straggled over from England. The Troggs' name was frequently mispronounced to rhyme with "rogues," but really rhymed with "dogs," being short for the group's original name, Troglodytes. Troglodyte means cave dweller, and the Troggs were early punk-rockers. In England they had eight or nine major hits between 1966 and 1968, but only three in the U.S., all in 1966: "Wild Thing" at #1, "With a Girl Like You" in the Top 30, and "I Can't Control Myself" which missed the Top 40. "Night of the Long Grass," "Hi Hi Hazel," and their other 1967 British hits never did them any good in the United States. But in 1968, "Love Is All Around" got the Troggs back into the U.S. Top 10 one last time. A two-year run was all she wrote for the Troggs.

The Spencer Davis Group, a hard-rock band, began in England in 1965 with three songs that were never heard in the United States. In early 1966, "Keep On Running" went to #1 over there. Released a few months later in the United States, it placed in the 70s. Then, in the United States, "Gimme Some Lovin'" and "I'm a Man" were Top 10, but the next two records missed the Top 40 altogether. Just one United States year. They did better in England, where Davis had started his adult life as a university instructor.

Dozens down and three to go. Very minor were the Easybeats, who originated in Australia. They had two hits in England, a Top-10 "Friday on My Mind" in '66, and Top-20 "Hello, How Are You" in '68. Their music was somewhat frantic, very distinguishable from Phase II music of the likes of Gerry and Billy J. This was probably the responsibility of their producer, Shel Talmy, who also produced the records of the hard-rocking Kinks, as well as the Who. In the United States, the Easybeats were one-shot artists. Only "Friday on My Mind" was very successful, making the Top 20 in '67.

With two yet to go, we come to Engelbert Humperdinck. Arnold Dorsey's life and name were changed by the manager of Tom Jones, who also became Arnold/Engelbert's manager. After changing Arnold's name, the manager steered Engelbert into a career similar to Tom Jones', including hits on the same record label that Jones was on, Parrott Records; a television series; and leaving rock 'n' roll behind. The first hit was, not surprisingly, a former American hit, "Release Me," and sold well in both countries in 1967.

The most important Beatles British invasion group of Phase III was probably the Who. They had some two dozen hits in their first decade in England, beginning in 1965 with "I Can't Explain," "Anyway, Anyhow, Anywhere," and "My Generation" in the Top 10. These early songs did not make it in America, but "Happy Jack" got them on the U.S. Top 40 for the first time.

The Who is considered a major, successful rock band, but the facts are not that glowing in terms of their British invasion status in the U.S. They were just not that popular as a singles artist in America. While they had many chart songs of medium popularity, they scarcely qualify for the 1964 invasion, since their first big single and only Top-10 hit in the U.S. in 10 years of recordings was "I Can See for Miles" late in 1967.

Which brings us to the women. Priscilla White, a.k.a. Cilla Black, scored in the mid-'60s with "Alfie" in '66, making it her third and last hit. ("Alfie" was better known as Cher's big hit that year, Dionne Warwick's the next year, and Eivets Rednow's the year after that.) She was a much bigger star in England, with over 20 hits, about half in the Top 10, from 1963 through the '70s. America missed a lot of good music when we ignored the female invaders.

Lulu (Marie McDonald McLaughlin) had local popularity in England. This local success got her into a band, the Luvvers. Lulu and the Luvvers had over a dozen British hits from '64 through the '70s. "Shout," an old song by the Isley Brothers and by Joey Dee, was released twice by Lulu, in '64 and '67, but was a major flop both times. No wonder, since it was very hard rock, unlike the style of the hits she had in the U.S. in between the two "Shout" release dates. Like Tom Jones', her career was helped along by a movie theme, hers being "To Sir with Love" in 1967. Her other hits, in '67 and '68, such as "Morning Dew," a Top-30 tune, were not biggies and are largely forgotten, making her essentially a one-shot artist in the United States.

Marianne Faithfull fared somewhat better in here, with one Top 40 in 1964 and three in 1965 along with her last non–Top 40 in '65. "Summer Nights" and "Come and Stay with Me" were delights. "Come and Stay with Me" was written by that American the Searchers liked so well, Jackie DeShannon. It would have been nice to have heard more of Faithfull. But, unlike Cilla, Marianne didn't have any more success at home in Britain than she did here, so we probably didn't miss out on as much in her case. It was all over in the span of a year.

But Sandie Shaw — well, she is another story! In the United States, she had three hits in about a year. Not one of those three was Top 40 nationally, although "(There's) Always Something There to Remind Me" and "Girl Don't Come" were very big in the Midwest. Her failure to catch on here is the biggest shame of the entire invasion, comparable only to the Cliff Richard fiasco, and at least his was corrected later. Sandie Shaw was a huge star in England, where she had 20 hits in England after 1964. "Remind Me" was her first, and it was #1. She was a British star of the first magnitude, but a one-year fizzle here.

Another outstanding woman was Dusty Springfield. Following her three Top-40 U.S. hits in 1964, she continued an impressive string of successes. She had only one release on the Top 100 in 1965, but then in 1966 she made the big time again with the Top-5 hit "You Don't Have to Say You Love Me." From then on she bounced from the Top 10 to the Top 40 to the Top 100 through 1970. In all, she had 17 U.S. hits. Her record of hit records in England was virtually identical, making her not only one of the biggest and most lasting of the invaders, but a major force in rock 'n' roll back home as well.

Petula Clark did the surprising. She won the Best Rock 'n' Roll Song of the Year Grammy Award for "Downtown." In 1989, a remixed/updated "Downtown" was released without her knowledge and scored once again. She was a rock 'n' rolling/pop woman in the male-dominated Beatles British invasion. Plus, her being a former child star and about 10 years older than most of the male groups' members, made it doubly surprising that she was popular at all. "Downtown," her first hit, was in the last month of Phase II. In Phase III, she had four Top-40 hits, including another #1, "My Love." In all she had 18 U.S. hits of one size or another after 1964, making her one of the most successful invaders of the bunch, male or female. In England, she lasted into the '70s. She always had a strong pop tendency, but then, so did much of rock 'n' roll.

The Beatles British Invasion
of the U.S. Charts: An Overview

How well did the British groups do in the invasion? Some were popular for only one year or less, others for considerably longer. Here is the breakdown of the Phase II Beatles British invasion forces. (An asterisk indicates artists who had one very minor hit or small comeback record later, but whose main career ran for a shorter period.)

One Year or Less

Billy J. Kramer with the Dakotas	Freddie and the Dreamers
The Honeycombs	Millie Small
The Swinging Blue Jeans	The Zombies
Marianne Faithfull	The Nashville Teens
Wayne Fontana and the Mindbenders	Cilla Black*
	Sandie Shaw
The Fortunes	Gerry and the Pacemakers

Two Years

Chad and Jeremy	Manfred Mann*
The Bachelors	The Searchers

Three Years

Peter and Gordon*
The Kinks*

Four Years

The Animals
The Dave Clark Five

Over Five Years

The Beatles	Dusty Springfield
The Hollies	Petula Clark

Over 20 Years

The Rolling Stones

So that is the chronological story of the Beatles British invasion. Phase I was a trickle of artists, each having one or two hits in the United States in the 1950s and early '60s. Then, in 1964, Phase II saw around two dozen artists make the international transition. In Phase III, all but a few—the Beatles, the Stones and Pet Clark—faded into rock 'n' roll oblivion within a couple of years. It was fun while it lasted, but for most, it just didn't last.

Over the years, the legend of Phase II has grown in the collective memory. Everyone who was a teenager in 1964, regardless of his or her musical tastes, has fond memories of the era. Other authors have written entire books reviewing the artists who came from England with music for moderns in the '60s. No one is putting down the music or the invasion; it is just being put into perspective. Those years were indeed magic ones for the youth and music of America. The word magic is not used lightly. There seems to have been a magic spell cast over America that year. People tend to remember that time as the day when the British dominated the charts, and the American music and artists were shunted aside.

Was the Beatles British invasion actually a sudden and terribly damaging assault on American rock 'n' roll, or was it one brief attack, which has lived on in rock 'n' roll history more for its emotional impact than for its depth, strength, or breadth? And, of course, it paved the way for the British groups of the 1970s and the '80s. Now that we have surveyed the music and the artists of the Beatles British invasion, we can address those questions, which are the subject of the remaining chapters of *The Beatle Myth*.

Regardless of the answers, the Beatles and British music were right for the times, and the times were wonderful. In the late 1960s, the '70s, and the '80s, there were additional artists from England doing punk rock, new wave, and underground rock. There has been talk of new British invasions. But Phase IV will never equal the magical excitement of Phase II in 1964.

Chapter 2

The American Roots
of the Beatles British Invasion

Rock 'n' roll means excitement. It meant excitement when Elvis gained national popularity in the mid-1950s. Dance-craze songs of the '60s meant excitement. Surf and drag music meant excitement. It meant excitement when a rock 'n' roll tour came to town. It even meant excitement when a local band played at a school dance.

Of all the sources of excitement rock 'n' roll has focused on since 1955, two rate above all of the rest. The first was the excitement stimulated by Elvis Presley, and maintained by countless other singers and groups who followed. Some feel there could not have been rock 'n' roll without Elvis. We will never know for sure if that is so, but there is no denying that a new type of musical excitement was building around the country in the 1950s. It is a certainty that something had to give. The excitement that Elvis generated no doubt served as a catalyst which speeded up the emergence of the music, and to some extent defined its nature and introduced the concept of the white rock 'n' roll singer.

Obviously Elvis alone could not have carried rock 'n' roll. Without Bill Haley and his Comets, the Orioles, Clyde McPhatter, the Drifters, Little Richard, Chuck Berry, Fats Domino, Frankie Lymon and the Teenagers, the Five Satins, and literally dozens of other local and national rock 'n' roll pioneers, neither Elvis nor the new music would have sustained. Elvis was the centerpiece, but the other artists were the place settings, the courses, and the desserts. Elvis drew everyone's attention to a multicourse meal which was just waiting to be devoured. Elvis was the entree, the "biggie." Still, if he had been alone upon a bare table, he could not have maintained the excitement, kept the crowds, and musically nourished all of America's teens by himself.

And American teens were hungry in the mid-'50s! Even without an Elvis centerpiece, the kids would have come to the rock 'n' roll table to devour the musical meal sooner or later.

This oversized excitement was duplicated when the Beatles arrived ten years later. By then the meal was well under way, and there was a full menu of rock 'n' roll for the Beatles to build upon. The teenagers who had lived through the first decade of rock 'n' roll, however, were now in their mid-to-late 20s, and were no longer buying either the 45s played on the radio or the pimple cream the music sold on the airwaves. In the place of these former teens there was a new rock 'n' roll generation which had been in kindergarten when Elvis and the others first broke upon the scene.

The Beatles took the place of Elvis as the centerpiece of the new generation's new rock 'n' roll. The Beatles attracted a much larger group of dinner guests than had ever before dined together because the baby boomers were the biggest crowd yet. The Beatles seemed even more important and influential than Elvis. Looking back, the reason for this is clear. Mixing metaphors, whereas Elvis had been a trailblazer, fighting his way through the dominant pop music scene, the Beatles were easily accepted into the hearts of millions of already established fans as the new centerpiece of an established musical form which already had millions of devotees and hundreds of distribution and radio outlets. The path was already there — the Beatles had only to follow it.

As any good dinner guest should, the Beatles brought their own covered dishes and desserts with them to the American rock 'n' roll dinner table. Like Elvis before them, the Beatles alone created great excitement. But the other groups the Beatles brought on their coattails gave an added spice and variety to the teenager's musical menu by multiplying the excitement manyfold.

For 10 years, British teens had enjoyed British groups as well as the hits of such American artists as Brenda Lee, Elvis, Ricky Nelson, and the Everly Brothers. American kids knew only American music. True, there had always been a few records a year trickling from British artists, but American kids really had no idea that these songs were British. The first year American teens got to enjoy their fill of British rock 'n' roll was 1964. Not only the centerpiece Beatles but also the side dishes, which included Billy J. Kramer with the Dakotas, Herman's Hermits, the Animals, and Manfred Mann, were eagerly devoured.

For pure excitement, the Beatles possibly outshone Elvis. But it was the side orders that made the real difference, creating the feeling of the British invasion. After all, there was no massive "hillbilly invasion" following Elvis' success.

Cover Versions — A Popular Music Tradition

No musical artist or group, including Elvis and the Beatles, ever developed without musical roots. True, many times those roots are obscure to the great mass of fans, so when new artists suddenly spring forth as apparent overnight successes, the public often thinks that the artists originated their music, rather than adopting and adapting the music of other artists.

A common practice in the early days of rock 'n' roll was for a white artist to record a song which had already been released by a black artist. Generally, the original black version was on a small record label and produced on a tight budget in a back room somewhere with maybe only one microphone. These records often were not being well distributed and, more important, were not played on radio stations with large, white audiences. In order to "cover" the white audience not reached by the black record, a white artist would often use the black original record as a demo, record his own version of the song, and perhaps have a hit. The term "cover version" referred to the fact that the white version was recorded to cover another market not covered by the original version.

The various markets for musical cover versions did not pop into existence in 1955. The big band era saw many versions of a given song appealing to fans of country music, blues, male vocalists, female vocalists, vocal groups, instrumental fans, and novelty fans.

The song "Down Yonder," for example, was introduced in 1951 by Del Wood, then quickly covered by Lawrence Cook, Champ Butler, Joe "Fingers" Carr, Freddy Martin, and the Fran Petty Trio; each version made the Top 30.

The cover tradition originated in the prephonograph days when sheet music was the medium, and every local performer covered all popular songs for his audience.

"Cover version" refers not to a rip-off, and not even to a recording. It is an audience which is covered by a different version of a song, an audience that is different than the one covered by a previous version.

It was only in the later '50s that cover versions began to be regarded as unfair white rip-offs of original black hits. The assumption made was that, had the cover version not come out and stolen sales from the original, the original would have been a big hit for the original, black artist on the small record label. This is probably a misconception, however. The original black versions would, in most cases, never have become hits because of their limited audience. People who would never have bought the original because the original performance had no appeal for them bought the cover version. Some original versions, for example "Work with Me Annie," had blue lyrics and primitive instrumentation. The cleaned up version by Georgia Gibbs, "Dance with Me Henry," saved that song from oblivion. The Gladiolas' "Little Darlin'" was too poorly recorded and distributed to have ever become a hit, but the Diamonds' Mercury Records cover version sold in the millions. The composer royalties the original black composers got from the white cover versions made black artists far more money than they would have made from the limited sales of their own versions to their own audience. It was not a question of "which version was better," but rather, "which version was more suitable for which audience." A Cadillac is better than a Chevrolet; yet a Cadillac is not suitable for most people.

Some time in the 1970s, the term "cover version" was expanded to apply to any rerecording of a song, not just to versions popular simultaneously with audiences of different racial, regional, or stylistic categories. So when Tiffany recorded the Beatles' "I Saw Him/Her Standing There" in 1988, radio DJs and television VJs referred to it as a cover version. It was not, in the classic sense, because it had been 25 years since the Beatles' version. On the other hand, it can be argued that the young Tiffany audience in 1988 is different than either the young Beatles audience of 1964 or the old, oldies Beatle fans of 1988. Since there is no way to make everyone quit misusing the term "cover version," perhaps it would be better to add the dimension of time to the list of various audiences to be covered by various artists.

The King of the Cover Versions?

Admit it. The first thing that usually comes to the minds of most '50s fans when the name "Pat Boone" is mentioned is "Pat Boone = cover artist." Pat Boone has been crowned "King of the Cover Versions" to state the matter in complimentary terms, and is certainly viewed as an adopter and adapter, not an originator.

What is the first thing that comes to mind when you hear the names Elvis Presley, Fats Domino, or the Beatles? Creativity? Genius? Originality? Certainly not cover versions!

In their wonderful rock and roll reference book, *Behind the Hits,* authors Bob Shannon and John Javna mention Pat Boone only once. Do they mention how popular Pat Boone was (second only to Elvis)? No. Do they tell how many hits he had? No. Do they reveal how many teenagers were first exposed to rock and roll, and how many adults learned to accept rock and roll, via Pat Boone's records? No. Here is what they say: Pat Boone "had a history of doing 'cover' versions of songs. . ." (page 74).

Pat Boone is consistently characterized as *the* unoriginal artist whose career in the '50s rock 'n' roll scene consisted of rerecordings of other artists' material. "Wop boppa lou bop, ba loom bam boom" (or "words" to that effect) were first uttered by Little Richard, but Pat Boone said 'em, too.

It is true that Little Richard, not Pat Boone, wrote the song "Tutti-Frutti." But, once written, a song can be performed by anybody, as long as they pay royalties on public performances for profit, including records. It can hardly be held against Pat Boone legally that he sang Little Richard's song, and in the process, outsold Richard on the song. If it were illegal to record a song you did not write yourself, then Frank Sinatra, Barbra Streisand, Bill Haley, Chubby Checker, the Shirelles, Ronnie Spector, Peter and Gordon, Diana Ross, the Everly Brothers, Pavarotti, Andres Segovia, and practically every other artist of the 20th century would be behind bars!

In all, Pat Boone charted on Billboard 60 times up to 1978. By the standards of punk, acid rock, MTV, British invasion, and even Motown, Pat's music was pretty tame. Many claim that his songs were pop, not rock 'n' roll. That is a foolish position to take. The MOR radio stations of the 1950s would no more play one of Pat Boone's records like "Tutti-Frutti" or "Don't Forbid Me" than they would play Elvis. Had Pat Boone been making hits a decade or so later, his music, with its less driving beat and gentler delivery, would have been called a kind of soft rock, much like the music of Simon and Garfunkel ("Bridge Over Troubled Water," "Scarborough Fair"), the Carpenters ("Close to You," "Yesterday Once More"), or even the Beatles ("Michelle," "Yesterday"), each of whom did songs which bore little resemblance to Little Richard's music, but were still a legitimate part of rock 'n' roll.

Even so, for Pat Boone to sing "Wop boppa lou bop, ba loom bam boom" (or "words" to that effect) was wrong according to his critics. An artist, they say, should stick to his own material, if he is to be taken seriously as an artist.

Here is a complete list of Pat Boone cover records. Note the relative popularity of each version (Billboard rank)—apparently Pat was doing something right according to the first generation of rock 'n' roll record buyers who often preferred his versions to the originals.

Pat Boone's Singles	*Original Artists*
"Ain't That a Shame" (#1)	Fats Domino (#10)
"At My Front Door" (#7)	El Dorados (#35)
"Tutti-Frutti" (#12)	Little Richard (#17)
"Long Tall Sally" (#8)	Little Richard (#6)
"I Almost Lost My Mind" (#1)	Ivory Joe Hunter
"Good Rockin' Tonight" (#49)	Roy Brown,
	Wynonie Harris, Elvis

Pat had 60 hits, and six of those were covers—just 10 percent of his successful 45s were cover versions. And, his reputation as a rip-off cover artist is built on that? There is one element of truth to Shannon and Javner's statement about Pat's having a "history" of doing covers; almost all of them were hits in the first 13 months of his long career.

For comparison, let's look at some other well known, big artists of the early and semi-early days of rock 'n' roll, and see what cover records they released.

Fats Domino—An "Unsung" Cover Artist

Fats Domino had a lot of hits in his day, a few more even than Pat Boone, about 66. Some people may not have liked Pat Boone's style. I for one never bought one of Pat's singles. But I never bought Little Richard, Fats Domino, or El Dorado records either! Fats Domino's style has seldom if ever been criticized by rock 'n' roll fans, and Fats is still regarded as an important rock 'n' roll figure after all these years. He has never been lambasted for covering other artists' songs, or for not writing his own hits.

Besides singing "Wop boppa lou bop, ba loom bam boom," Pat Boones biggest criticism came from his singing "Ain't That a Shame," a song considered to be Fats Domino's property. It wasn't so much that Pat sang songs he did not write that raised people's hackles. It was because he sang songs that were not his own style, songs like "Ain't That a Shame," Fats Domino's big song.

But how many covers did Fats Domino himself have, compared to Pat Boone? Fats' best-known hit was "Blueberry Hill," which he did in his own inimitable style. Surely, had Pat Boone covered "Blueberry Hill," it would have been considered by many to have been an artistic travesty. But the original hit version of "Blueberry Hill" was done not by Fats or some obscure blues artist, but by Glenn Miller! Yes, for his best-known hit, Fats Domino covered a white song and did it over in his own style, much as Pat would take a black song and make it over into his style.

Here is a list of Fats Domino's cover records (45s only):

Fats Domino's Singles	*Original Artist*
"Blueberry Hill" (#2)	Glenn Miller/Ray Eberle (#2, 1940)
"My Blue Heaven" (#21)	Dick Haymes (#5, 1943)
	Dick Kuhn (#8, 1943)
	Gene Austin (#1, 1927)
	Paul Whitman (#1, 1927)
"Your Cheatin' Heart"	Hank Williams
"One Night"	Elvis, Smiley Lewis
"I Can't Give You Anything But Love"	Pop tune
"Isle of Capri"	Gaylords (#15, 1954)
	Jackie Lee (#17, 1954)
"Margie" (#51)	Eddie Cantor (#1, 1921)
"Put Your Arms Around Me Honey" (#58)	1911 hit
"Jambalaya" (#30)	Hank Williams (#1, 1952)
"You Win Again" (#22)	Hank Williams (#10, 1952)
	Brenda Lee
"You Always Hurt the One You Love"	Mills Brothers (#1, 1944)
	Russ Morgan

Fats Domino's Singles	*Original Artist*
"Red Sails in the Sunset" (#35)	Guy Lombardo (#1)
	Bing Crosby (#1)
	8-60 #36 The Platters
	7-51 #24 Nat King Cole
	'57 #57 Tab Hunter
"Ain't That Just Like a Woman" (#33)	Louis Jordan (#17, 1946)
"My Real Name" (#59)	Pop tune
"Magic Isles"	Pop tune
"For You"	Ricky Nelson (#6, 1963)
	Glen Gray and Casa Loma Orch. (featuring Kenny Sergeant)
"When My Dreamboat Comes Home" (#14)	Guy Lombardo (#3, 1937)
"Coquette" (#92)	Guy Lombardo, 1928 theme song
"As Time Goes By"	Rudy Vallee (#2, 1943)
	Jacques Renard (#3, 1943)
"What Will I Tell My Heart?" (#64)	Eddy Howard, 1951
"I'm in the Mood for Love"	Frances Langford (1935)
"I Left My Heart in San Francisco"	Tony Bennett (#19, 1962)
"What's the Reason I'm Not Pleasin' You?" (#50)	Guy Lombardo (#1, 1935)
"Howdy Podner"	Pop tune
"Did You Ever See a Dream Walking?" (#79)	Eddy Duchin (#1, 1933)
"When the Saints Go Marching In"	written in 1896
"Lady Madonna" (#100)	Beatles 1968 popular LP cut

Fats Domino had over four times as many covers as Pat Boone did! And nearly every one was a white song, if songs can be characterized by race, which is questionable. To be fair, Fats may have released 27 cover 45s, but his cover versions were less successful than Pat's, and only some 15 charted. Of his 66 chart hits, 15 or 23 percent were cover versions. That compares to just 10 percent for Pat Boone. And while Pat almost always outsold the originals he covered, Fats seldom outperformed the originals.

How did Fats Domino feel about having his early records covered by Pat Boone? The teenagers of the time loved Pat's cover versions. Uninformed rock fans, writers, and critics of later decades have regarded Boone's covers as uninspired rip-offs. Yet Fats Domino has always regarded Pat's cover versions as blessings from heaven, giving his music exposure that he alone could never have achieved. Fats considered Pat Boone a rock 'n' roll pioneer largely responsible for its ultimate success as well as Fats' own success. He even invited Pat to sing duets with him live on stage.

The bottom line is, Fats is more deserving than Pat of the title "King of the Cover Versions." Hmmm.

Elvis Presley

Let's examine another big artist: Elvis Presley.

Elvis' Singles	*Original Artists*
(On SUN Records)	
"Blue Moon of Kentucky"	Bill Monroe
"Good Rockin' Tonight"	Roy Brown
	and in 1948, Wynonie Harris
"I Don't Care If the Sun Don't Shine"	Country/Pop standard
"Milkcow Blues Boogie"	Kokomo Arnold
"Baby Let's Play House"	Arthur Gunter
"I'm Left, You're Right, She's Gone"	Bill Taylor
"I Got a Woman"	Ray Charles
"Mystery Train"	Junior Parker
(On RCA)	
"A Fool Such As I"	Jo Stafford (#20, 1953)
	Hank Snow (#4, 1953)
"Are You Lonesome Tonight"	Al Jolsen
	Vaughn Deleath (#4, 1927)
"Big Boss Man"	Jimmy Reed (#78, 1961)
"Blue Christmas"	Browns
	Hugo Winterhalter
"Blue Moon"	Glen Grey & the Casa Loma Orchestra (#1, 1935)
"Blue Suede Shoes"	Carl Perkins
"Crying in the Chapel"	Orioles, (#11, 1953)
	Rex Allen (#10, 1953)
	Darrell Glenn (#9, 1953)
	June Valli (#6, 1953)
"Frankie and Johnnie"	Sam Cooke
	Johnny Cash
	Brook Benton (written circa 1850)
"Girls Girls Girls"	Coasters
"Guitar Man"	Jimmy Reed
"High Heel Sneakers"	Tommy Tucker
"Hound Dog"*	Big Mama Thornton (#1, 1953)
"Hurt"	Timi Yuro (#4, 1961)
"I Don't Care If the Sun Don't Shine"	Patti Page (#8, 1950)
"I Feel So Bad"	Chuck Willis (#8, 1954)
"I Really Don't Want to Know"	Les Paul and Mary Ford (#11, 1954)

Elvis' Singles	*Original Artists*
"I've Got a Thing About You Baby"	Billy Lee Riley (#93, 1972)
"It's Now or Never"	Dean Martin "O Solo Mio" (written 1899)
"Lawdy Miss Clawdy"	Lloyd Price
"Love Letters"	Dick Haynes (#11, 1945)
"Love Me Tender"	1861 tune "Aura Lee"
"Money Honey"	Drifters (#1, 1953)
"My Baby Left Me"	Arthur "Big Boy" Cruddup (1953)
"My Boy"	Richard Harris (#41, 1972)
"Old Shep"	Red Foley (1947)
"One Night (with You)"	Smiley Louis, "One Night (of Sin)" (#11, 1956)
"Peace in the Valley"	Red Foley
"Promised Land"	Chuck Berry (#41, 1965)
"Rags to Riches"	Tony Bennett (#1, 1953)
"Shake, Rattle, and Roll"	Joe Turner
	Bill Haley and His Comets
"She Thinks I Still Care"	George Jones, (#1, 1962)
"Such a Night"	Drifters (#2, 1954)
"Surrender"	Italian song "Come Back to Sorrento"
"Take Good Care of Her"	Adam Wade (#7, 1961)
"Tell Me Why"	Crew Cuts
	Gale Storm (1956)
"The Wonder of You"	Ray Peterson (#25, 1959)
"There Goes My Everything"	Englebert Humperdinck (#20, 1967)
"Tutti-Frutti"	Little Richard
"U.S. Male"	Jimmy Reed
"Until It's Time for You to Go"	Neil Diamond (#53, 1970)
"What'd I Say"	Ray Charles (#6, 1959)
"Witchcraft"	Spiders (#5, 1956)
"You Don't Have to Say You Love Me"	Dusty Springfield (#4, 1966)
"You Don't Know Me"	Jerry Vale (#14, 1956)
"You'll Never Walk Alone"	Gerry and the Pacemakers

Interesting, eh? Elvis had eight times the number of covers that Pat Boone had, including almost all his Sun output. Even his "original" songs were sung on demos by Elvis imitators like P.J. Proby for the King to copy. Out of Elvis' 150 hits, around 33 percent were covers, including the "Wop boppa lou bop" rocker. Looks like Pat has to stand in line behind both Fats *and* Elvis for the title "King of the Cover Versions"!

In 1952 Sam Phillips was sued when he had a Sun artist, Rufus Thomas, Jr., record a Sun 45 answer song to Big Mama Thornton's record of "Hound Dog." Titled "You Ain't Nothin' but a Bearcat," it used the same tune and came four years before Elvis' RCA recording of "Hound Dog."

Teenage Generation Gap

If Elvis, Pat, and Fats had music roots in American music of other artists and styles, what were the roots of the Beatles and the other British invasion acts of 1964?

United States teens, devouring as they were British rock 'n' roll for the first time, thought that this new music really was, well, really new. What the young American record fans did not know was that fish and chips is just another way to say perch and potatoes. "A rose by any other name. . . " The music that the British brought over was not really fundamentally different from American rock 'n' roll, it was just served in a new style. Just as a potato is a potato no matter how you cook it, the British music was really just American rock 'n' roll, reheated.

Why didn't Americans, who had come down on Pat Boone for using nonoriginal material, likewise criticize the Beatles and the other British acts when they in their turn borrowed the music of America, often of black America, for their own?

American kids didn't know that they were not listening to original rock 'n' roll when the music had come around for the first time. Rock 'n' roll in those days was aimed only at the junior and senior high school audience. Younger kids listened to kiddie records, older young adults listened to pop music, jazz, or folk songs. So, when the Dave Clark Five remade an American song from 1962 in 1967, the audience of 1962 wasn't around to hear the DC5's version and therefore could not tell the new kids that the song was really an "oldie." And the audience of 1967 had never heard the 1962 version so it still had no idea that the song had previously been an American hit. Such confusion and lack of historical perspective spawned much fame.

Each generation of American high school kids since 1955 has preferred its own music to that of the previous generation some three years past. The transition of the music had always been slow with no sudden, recognizable changes, so there was little or no hostility expressed about the earlier generations' music. In 1964 when the British groups came, there was a sudden and highly recognizable change in music. From then on, many American teens broke into two camps, those who liked the American rock 'n' roll style of the pre-'64 era, and those who preferred the British and British-influenced music of the post-'64 era.

These two camps were antagonistic towards each other and often fell along age lines, with the younger kids being more accepting of the British sound and the older (16- and 17-year-olds) siding with the music that had gone on before.

Hostility is often based on a lack of understanding and knowledge. Quite often, when people get to know and understand a person, place, or thing which seems unusual or wrong, they learn to like it, or at least to accept it. The pre- and post-'64 rock 'n' rollers should at last learn more about one another, and end the Battle of the British invasion. What is the relationship between the two eras?

The music of the British invasion had many sources of inspiration and influence which linked it to the pre-'64 explosion. Besides the British skiffle precursors to British rock 'n' roll, there were British music hall music, and American pop, rock 'n' roll, folk, gospel, country & western, rhythm and blues, Hollywood and Broadway music.

It would be impossible to try to sort out all of these various influences without in-depth interviews with each of the artists of the British invasion, as well as interviews with their managers, producers and arrangers (and parents!).

A great insight into which music most influenced the British invasion artists, however, may be gained by a relatively simple technique: listen to the music recorded by the British invasion artists recorded. An incredibly large proportion of the songs recorded and released by the invasion artists in England and in the U.S. in the mid-'60s, were songs which had previously been popular in the states by American artists!

The Beatles British Invasion "Covers" America

There can be little doubt that any song an artist sings is also a song that influenced him or her, and is also one the artist liked. Of course, the opposite could conceivably be true. When it comes to the British invasion, there is a strong possibility that the British artists and producers pandered to American teens when selecting material, even to the point of recording songs personally repugnant in the hope of getting American teens to buy the records. That is more or less how Pat Boone is regarded by many rock historians and critics. But why an artist would think American kids would want to buy a new, British version of a U.S. oldie-but-goodie is another question.

The pandering theory is, at best, a weak one. British artists did not record for American teens. They recorded songs at home for the home audience. American releases of the same songs were made anywhere from a few weeks to a few years after the British releases, and were controlled totally by the record company officials. Many U.S. singles were just LP cuts in England. It seems far more likely that the British artists used American material because they loved the original American records, which incidentally happened to make nice demo material.

In the first decade of rock 'n' roll, few artists wrote their own songs. Instead, professional songwriters did most of the composing. When they had a song they felt was good, they often made a demostration recording (demo) of the song, and sent the demo around to artists, producers, and record labels. A good demo could showcase a catchy tune, interesting lyrics, or creative gimmick much better than mere sheet music. Especially if the prospective artists could not read music! Any way you consider it, listening to a stack of demo records is a lot easier than sifting through a lot of handwritten sheet music.

Many demos came from the famous Brill Building in New York City. The Brill Building was full of music publishing companies who attracted songwriters, who in turn located their offices in the same building. Such rock 'n' roll composers as Barry Mann, Cynthia Weil, Jerry Leiber, Mike Stoller, Ellie Greenwich, Jeff Barry, Shadow Morton and Howard Greenfield wrote hit songs and recorded demos of their compositions. The Brill Building Publishers and writers are just one example. There were many other writers, such as Bob Crewe, Frank Slay, Bernie Lowe, Kal Mann, David White, John Madara, and Don Covay, who supplied songs for the Philadelphia artists of Cameo-Parkway Records.

In a few cases, demonstration records were actually released by record companies and became hits. For instance, the classic record "Barbara Ann" by the Regents was a demo record which was released without the composer's consent, reaching the national Top 20 in 1961. But in a way, "Barbara Ann" did serve as a demo. The 1965 version, recorded by the Beach Boys with Dean Torrence of Jan and Dean, was released by Capitol Records, this time without the *artists'* advance knowledge, and became a huge, worldwide hit.

Another demo record which got released and became a hit was "It Might As Well Rain Until September." Carole King wrote this song expressly for Bobby Vee. She likewise composed many of Bobby Vee's hits just for him, including "Take Good Care of My Baby," "Walkin' with My Angel" and "Sharing You." While Bobby did record "It Might As Well Rain Until September," Bobby and his management decided to use "Sharing You" for his next single release. Since Bobby's version was not coming out on a 45, Carole's demo was released. It almost made the Top 20.

Of course, no one knew that "Barbara Ann" and "It Might As Well Rain Until September" would be hits. If the artists had known for sure that these songs would be hit material, then the demos would not have been turned down by the hit-hungry artists they were presented to. But there was no way to know if a song was hit material. For every 100 demos that were made, perhaps 99 were never selected by an artist to record. For every 100 demo songs actually recorded by artists, only one or two turned out to be a hit. Picking hits was not an easy task.

When it came to demonstration records, the British artists had access to a unique system. Since they were in England, thousands of miles from the Brill Building, they never got demo records from people like Carole

King. Likewise, since rock 'n' roll had just recently begun to replace skiffle in England, there was no British Brill Building equivalent to supply new songs and demo records for British artists.

The obvious solution: Use U.S. *hit* records as demos! These American songs were imported by British record dealers and brought to England by seamen who worked the Atlantic crossing. American hit records were not only the highest Brill Building quality, but they were also known quantities. The risk had already been taken by a U.S. artist. The British artist knew when a song was hit material — it already was popular in the United States though possibly unknown in England.

The statement is often made how greatly the British invasion artist influenced American rock 'n' roll. In this context, it is generally stated that British rock 'n' roll was different from and superior to the pop "pap" that supposedly characterized American rock 'n' roll in 1960–1963. Few people realized then or now that the American "pap" was in fact the "demo-hits" which were a major influence on British rock 'n' roll from 1962–1969! In fact, a massive portion of the British invasion was retread American music from the pre-'64 era so disdained by Beatles and invasion fans! The British artists must have liked and valued this music, or else why would so many of them have recorded so many American songs for consumption by their British fans?

The Roots of the Beatles British Invasion

Following is a review of British invasion records which were songs that had already been recorded by American artists. This will show where the British acts got their material, who influenced them, and what kinds of music appealed to them.

MANFRED MANN

"Do Wah Diddy Diddy"
In the summer of 1964, Manfred Mann had their third hit in England, "Do Wah Diddy Diddy." It made the Top 20 there. This was also the band's first release in the states, late in the same summer. It was selected for their first U.S. release not because it was an American record, but because it was Manfred Mann's current hit in England. In the United States, "Do Wah Diddy Diddy" went to #1, establishing Manfred Mann as a major invasion artist.

The song "Do Wah Diddy Diddy," however, was originally titled "Do-Wah-Diddy." It was the fourth hit by the Exciters, an American girl group from New York with one male member. "Do-Wah-Diddy" was a Brill Building composition written in 1963 by the married songwriting team Jeff Barry and Ellie Greenwich ("Chapel of Love," Dixie Cups, 1964; "Leader of the Pack," Shangri-Las, 1964; "Da Do Ron Ron," Crystals, 1963). The Brill Building was a New York headquarters for music publishers and a hangout for songwriters. It was a highly respected Mecca of music prior to the Beatles British invasion, then a subject of put-downs after the invasion when some people decided that artists should write their own hits like the Beatles British invasion artists seemed to do.

Early in 1964, besides making the national Top 100, the Exciters' "Do-Wah-Diddy" was a popular Top-40 hit in several parts of the country. Late that summer Manfred Mann's version, which copied the arrangement of the original closely, sounded very familiar to kids who had bought the Exciters' version just a few months before. However, the Exciters' version had not been extremely popular all over the U.S. and averaged only #79 nationally. So to most kids and DJs, Manfred Mann's version was perhaps seen as the only version.

It is ironic that Manfred Mann's first U.S. hit was a remake of a girl group hit. American girl groups were a musical genre that was supposedly inferior to, and replaced by, the British music. Manfred Mann apparently did not agree. For their U.S. and U.K. follow-up to "Do Wah Diddy Diddy," Manfred Mann chose another American girl group record.

"Sha La La"

The Shirelles were one of the first and perhaps the greatest of the American girl groups. It is no surprise in light of "Do Wah Diddy Diddy" that one of their songs would turn up in the British invasion. "Sha La La" had been one of their less important hits in the spring of 1964, the time when American girl groups' popularity was allegedly suffering from a bad case of "British invasion-itis." In fact, after four years of hits, which was longer than the average British group's popularity would subsequently last, the popularity of Shirelles' singles had started dropping off early in 1963; "Sha La La's" #69 status cannot be attributed to the invasion.

Manfred Mann must have really liked American girl groups and known their LPs as well as their hit singles. "Sha La La" was *not* among the several British hits by the Shirelles. Yet, like the Exciters' "Do-Wah-Diddy" before, Manfred Mann heard it and liked it enough to do it as a single. Manfred Mann's "Sha La La" was Top 5 in England and Top 20 in the states.

Manfred Mann had just four Top-40 hits stateside, as compared to a dozen for the Shirelles. Two were those girl group remakes. In England Manfred Mann had many more hits and continued to keep the old-time rock 'n' roll spirit alive.

"Sweet Pea"

Tommy Roe was an American artist from Atlanta who owed a lot, musically, to Buddy Holly. From his first hit, "Sheila" (1962) to his later hits like "Dizzy" (1969), Tommy Roe's songs went to the top of the charts on both sides of the Atlantic.

Manfred Mann knew good songs when they heard them. In 1967, the group stole (so to speak) Tommy Roe's thunder by releasing his song "Sweet Pea" in England, and it became a hit. Manfred Mann was no longer a force in America, and so Tommy Roe's own version of "Sweet Pea" was Top 10 in the United States with no British competition. Not being a U.S. hit, this song was not really a part of the invasion and unavailable for review, but is included to show the roots of the invasion artists' music.

One interesting note is that Manfred Mann had relied on Brill Building types for half of its American hits, while American teen idol Tommy Roe wrote all of his own hit songs. This is the opposite of the common view of American singers and British groups.

PETER AND GORDON

"I Go to Pieces"

Much like Manfred Mann, Peter and Gordon were not particularly known as songwriters (their biggest hits were written by Lennon-McCartney). Their other musical roots were strongly American.

Del Shannon was an American teen idol white male vocalist who — you guessed it — wrote most of his own hits and LP cuts. One of these was a mournful rocker called "I Go to Pieces." Peter and Gordon practically made a career out of doing mournful rockers, Shannon was very popular (with 14 hits) in England, so "I Go to Pieces" was a natural for Peter and Gordon to record.

"I Go to Pieces" was Peter and Gordon's fourth American hit, and made the Top 10. Virtually no one outside Del Shannon's Fan Club knew it was an American song when they heard it on the radio, because it was just an LP cut by the American. And in England, "I Go to Pieces" wasn't played on the radio by either artist.

"True Love Ways"

Another American teen idol with a following in England — and who wrote his own songs — was Buddy Holly. In fact, Buddy Holly was much more popular in the United Kingdom than he ever was in the states. His records were no longer placing in the Top 40 by the time of his death in 1959. When he died in February of that year, Buddy Holly was something of an "oldie" artist already, without a current hit. Ironically, it was Ritchie Valens, not Holly, who was featured in the headline newspaper articles about the plane crash that killed Valens, Holly, and J.P. "The Big Bopper" Richardson. Of the three, Valens was the only one with current hit songs, "Donna" and "La Bamba," a two-sided hit.

However, Buddy continued to do well in Britain for years after his death, well into the mid-'60s. He had a total of 20 chart songs on the Top 50 in England, about twice the number of hits he had on the U.S. Top 100! One of those British hits was "True Love Ways," a slow song quite unlike "Peggy Sue" and "That'll Be the Day." "True Love Ways" was not a Holly single in the United States, but made the British Top 30 in 1960, over a year after Buddy Holly had died.

Peter and Gordon released their recording of "True Love Ways" in 1965. It was their third of seven hits in England, almost making #1. In the United States, it was their fifth of 14 hits, and made the Top 20.

"To Know You Is to Love You"

Also in 1965, Peter and Gordon revived a real oldie from the United States. Phil Spector was a name well known to people in the music business, if not to all rock 'n' roll fans, that same year. This producer's first musical success had been back in the fall of 1958. At that time he formed a musical group called the Teddy Bears. They had only one solid hit, "To Know Him Is to Love Him," on which Phil sang lines like "Da-da-da-da-da-da." The record was #1 in the states and equally popular in England. But in 1965 few American kids knew the song had already been #1 seven years earlier.

Peter and Gordon did the song from a male point of view, and they had to change the title. They called it, "To Know *You* Is to Love *You*." The change was reasonable. The title originally came from Phil Spector's father's tombstone, on which had been inscribed, "To Know Him *Was* to Love Him."

Peter and Gordon's record was Top 5 in England and Top 30 in the United States. It is interesting that while Peter and Gordon had twice as many hits in the states as in their homeland, their few songs that were hits both places were usually bigger at home than over here.

GERRY AND THE PACEMAKERS

One of the British groups with the least reputation for remakes, Gerry and the Pacemakers actually did about as many covers as anyone. They just picked songs no American teens remembered!

"I'll Be There"

American singer Bobby Darin had quite a career. Saddled with heart trouble from a childhood illness, he died in 1973 on the operating table at age 37 with over 40 hits to his credit. His live recording of "Won't You

Come Home Bill Bailey" was one of these hits, and was also a Top-40 song in England. The flip side of "Bill Bailey" was a haunting ballad Darin wrote, and which was a fair-sized hit in the states only. "I'll Be There" was a middle-sized success as done by Gerry and the Pacemakers in both countries, their last big one in England. They still had a lot of good records to come out yet in the United States.

"You'll Never Walk Alone"

This song is well-known for the version Elvis Presley hit with in both England and the states in 1968. Actually from the musical *Carousel*, the original American rock 'n' roll record was a brisk-seller by Patty LaBelle and the Blue Belles in 1964. A year later, Gerry and the Pacemakers also had a U.S. hit with it. However, just to add to the confusion of "originality," the bottom line was that this was the Pacemakers' best-known U.K. record in 1963, a year before the Blue Belles' recording! While it was not a cover of an American rock 'n' roll hit, it was a British version of an American Broadway musical song.

"You're the Reason" was the title of a song which Bobby Darin hit big with in the United States, in 1963. Two years later, Gerry and the Pacemakers had a small success with a record of the same title. This author was unable to find a copy, so it cannot be said with certainty if it is the same song. Also, one of Gerry and the Pacemakers' biggest hits was Gerry's composition, "Don't Let the Sun Catch You Crying" in 1964, which should not be mistaken for Ray Charles' 1960 song of the same title. Finally, an American Gerry and the Pacemakers "Best of" hit anthology LP ends with "Chills," a song written by Carole King and her husband Gerry, also pronounced Jerry, Goffin for their American friend and popular singer Tony Orlando. Why it was included on a hit-compilation album is a bit mysterious, since "Chills" was not a hit in either country by the Pacemakers, and was only the smallest hit possible for Tony Orlando in 1962.

THE HOLLIES

The American roots of the British invasion were also strong with this British invasion band. Formerly the Deltas, their name by the time of the invasion, the Hollies, was inspired by the last name of the leader of the American band the Crickets—Buddy Holly.

"Just Like Me"

The Hollies' very first British hit, released in the spring of 1963, was an American Brill Building–type song, "Just Like Me." Recorded by the Coasters, it was typical early-'60s rock 'n' roll. The Coasters' recording had not been a single, again illustrating how the British so appreciated

American music that they chose American LP cuts to release as their own singles. The Hollies' recording charted only in the U.K., where it was a Top-30 hit, so it was unavailable for review.

"Searchin'"

The Hollies obviously thought that Top 30 was good enough to get the job done. Their English follow-up to "Just Like Me" was another Coasters song, "Searchin'," another Brill–type song written by Leiber and Stoller. "Searchin'" was recorded by the Coasters in 1957 and made it into the U.S. Top 5. The Coasters had three hits in England, "Yakkity Yak," "Charlie Brown," and "Poison Ivy," compared to a long string of U.S. hits. Still, the Coasters' impact in the U.K. was obviously great, as evidenced by the Hollies' imitations. The Hollies' "Searchin'" was Top 20 in England, but at this point the Hollies were still unknown in the United States.

"Stay"

For their third British hit, the Hollies used what seems to be another American hit (also unavailable), "Stay," as a demo. "Stay" was not a Brill Building–type number. Instead, it was written by the man who had a hit with it in the U.S. and the U.K. late in 1960, Maurice Williams and the Zodiacs. The original "Stay" had been #1 in the states, and Top 20 in England.

The Hollies revived "Stay" in England in the winter of 1963–64, just prior to the British invasion, when it went Top 10 there. Subsequently, "Stay" was also a U.S. hit for the Four Seasons.

"Just One Look"

The Hollies' fourth British song, and their first British invasion release in the U.S. was "Just One Look." This release made it four American songs in a row for the Hollies. "Just One Look" was barely cold in the states when the Hollies recorded it. Doris Troy was the American artist who, in the summer of 1963, made the U.S. Top 10 with "Just One Look" as her only hit. Doris was also a one-hit wonder in England — but her one hit there was a different tune in early 1965. Doris Troy was from New York and sang background on some U.S. hits while writing songs for a few U.S. artists before having her own hit. She later moved to London to live.

"Just One Look" was the Hollies' biggest British hit yet, almost reaching #1. In the states, it was one of the less promising debut singles of the entire invasion, reaching only #98 nationally.

After "Just One Look," which was the Hollies' biggest British single to date, they left American songs behind and had great success in both the United States and in England with original songs like "Stop! Stop! Stop!", "Bus Stop," and "On a Carousel." In 1967, at the peak of the Hollies' U.S. popularity, the Hollies' American record company reissued "Just One Look." It failed once again to make the U.S. Top 40.

THE ROLLING STONES

In the long run, the Stones were the most successful of all of the two dozen or so British invasion artists. They are the only invasion group still having U.S. hits in the 1990s. When the Stones first appeared in the states, they were regarded as very scruffy and unmusical. Later into the invasion, as their popularity grew, they were sometimes referred to as "second-string Beatles!"

"Not Fade Away"

The Stones' first U.S. release in 1964 failed to foreshadow the huge success that would follow. The song was the American composition "Not Fade Away," another Buddy Holly number. As their first U.S. hit, it was only Top 30 in the spring of 1964. In England, the Stones' "Not Fade Away" was Top 5, as one might expect considering Buddy Holly's widespread acceptance and popularity there.

A note of interest: The U.S. flip side of "Not Fade Away" was a Beatles song, "I Wanna Be Your Man," which in turn had been the Stones' second chart success in England, just prior to "Not Fade Away." As will be shown, when artists like Peter and Gordon and the Rolling Stones recorded Beatles material, they were in fact making another connection with the American roots of the British invasion.

"Time Is on My Side"

In 1964, a U.S. blues female rock 'n' roll vocalist named Irma Thomas had four hits. The biggest, her first, was a Top-20 hit, "Wish Someone Would Care." This success prompted a pair of LPs. On her LP titled *Wish Someone Would Care,* she sang a song titled "Time Is on My Side." This LP was released in the U.S. in July 1964. The Rolling Stones evidently bought the LP, since they released a 45 version which made the U.S. charts as their fourth U.S. hit in October. It was the Stones' first Top-10 45, and launched their U.S. hit list, but was not released in Britain as a single.

Irma Thomas, a black singer, was as annoyed at the Stones for stealing her song and arrangement as the black groups might have been when Pat Boone covered their songs. From that time on, she dropped the song from her repertoire unless the audiences literally begged for it.

THE SWINGING BLUE JEANS

"Hippy Hippy Shake"

The Swinging Blue Jeans had five British hits and three in the states. Their first American hit was "Hippy Hippy Shake." To virtually every American fan, the Blue Jeans' version was the "original." This song was a staple of many Mersey Beat bands in England, and even the Beatles did it in their live sets. A rare recording of the Beatles' version, accidentally recorded in Hamburg in 1962 and lost for over 20 years, is available on many labels. The Swinging Blue Jeans' version is one of the very best examples of hard, driving, wild British invasion music this side of the Fab Four's "I'm Down."

Chan Romero was an obscure singer/songwriter from the Southwest. In 1959, he recorded the original version of his composition, the "Hippy Hippy Shake," for entrepreneur Bob Keene's Del-Fi records. Keene had just hit it big with Ritchie Valens' "La Bamba," and then, having lost Valens to the plane crash that also took Buddy Holly and the Big Bopper, continued in the same groove with Romero. The story is that this record, which was not a national hit in America, was played on the sound system of the Cavern Club every night in the early sixties, and all the Mersey/Liverpool bands who played at this British rock 'n' roll club, including the Beatles and the Blue Jeans, learned to play it. In England, "Hippy Hippy Shake" was the Swinging Blue Jeans' second, and biggest hit.

"Good Golly Miss Molly"

"Good Golly Miss Molly" marked the third of the Swinging Blue Jeans' five hits in England and the second of their three hits in the United States in the spring of 1964. It had been composed and recorded by Little Richard and was Top 10 for him on both sides of the Atlantic in 1958. The Swinging Blue Jeans' version just missed making the Top 10 in 1964 in England. In the United States, it was Top 40 in the Midwest, but not nationally.

"You're No Good"

The Swinging Blue Jeans' last U.S. hit of even minor proportions was another American number, Betty Everett's 1963 girl-group record, "You're No Good." Her version was not a hit in England, although she did have two other chart successes there. In the United States, Betty Everett's "You're No Good" was regionally popular, but nationally reached only the Top 50. Even so, this Miss from Mississippi outshone the Swinging Blue Jeans, whose version was #97.

In England, the Blue Jeans made the Top 5 with "You're No Good." Little did they dream how near the end was!

"Don't Make Me Over"

In the musically wonderful winter of 1962–1963, Dionne Warwick began her long career with a Top-30 record, "Don't Make Me Over." She later had eight hits in England, but "Don't Make Me Over" was not among them.

Even so, the song must have impressed the Blue Jeans. Early in 1966, it was their last British Top-40 hit. Their American career had already ended.

THE ANIMALS

"House of the Rising Sun"

The Animals' first American hit was an American song, but not an American hit. A blues standard, "House of the Rising Sun," was totally unknown to teenagers.

"Gonna Send You Back to Walker
(Gonna Send You Back to Georgia)"

The Animals' second U.S. hit showed two titles on the label: "Gonna Send You Back to Walker (Gonna Send You Back to Georgia)." It was not among the group's British hits, and made a poor showing in the fall of 1964 in the U.S., missing the Top 40. The American version from January 1964 skimmed the top U.S. 40 as recorded by Timmy Shaw, and used the "Georgia" title alone.

"Bring It on Home to Me"

Sam Cooke had seven hits in England, some of them after his death in 1964. In the states, he had over 40 successful singles. One of these was "Bring It on Home to Me," a Top-20 record in the summer of 1962. The flip side, "Havin' a Party," was also Top 20.

"Bring It on Home to Me" was not among Sam Cooke's British hits. But the Animals heard it and used it to get their fifth hit in both America and England. It was Top 10 at home and Top 20 abroad.

"See See Rider"

Also known as "C C Rider," this song had a long American heritage. Besides Chuck "King of the Stroll" Willis' Top-20 original in 1957, LaVern Baker made the Top 40 with "C C Rider" in 1963, and Bobby Powell did a final, less popular U.S. version in 1965.

This Chuck Willis original was the only other American hit in the Animals' catalog. Interestingly, it was not one of their British singles. It was Top 10 in the United States in 1966.

THE DAVE CLARK FIVE

The Dave Clark Five were the Beatles' main rivals in the early days of the invasion. A major part of the invasion forces, the DC5 was also a group with some of the strongest American rock 'n' roll roots!

"Do You Love Me"

The DC5 started out in the United States with several original songs, including "Glad All Over," "Bits and Pieces," and "Any Way You Want It." But in the motherland, the DC5's very first hit was "Do You Love Me," originally a U.S. Top-5 hit by the Contours, who had eight U.S. hits but were not hit artists in England. Well, perhaps that is overstating the situation. The DC5 knew and liked the Contours' music, and "Do You Love Me," besides being their British debut, later became their fourth U.S. single on the American Top 20.

"Reelin' and Rockin'"

Chuck Berry is often mentioned when American influences on the British invasion acts are discussed. While his influence was actually fairly minor compared to other influences, the DC5 did use one Berry tune, "Reelin' and Rockin'." Released by the DC5 early in 1965, it was Top 30 in both the states and England. Chuck Berry's version had been a hit single in neither country, although in England it was released in 1970 and made the Top 20.

"I Like It Like That"

Chris Kenner, from New Orleans, wrote two songs which have become minor classics, "The Land of 1,000 Dances" and "I Like It Like That." The former song was a minor 1963 entry by Kenner but made famous by Cannibal and the Headhunters in the mid-'60s. The latter was a Top-10 hit by Kenner in the summer of '61, but made even more famous in 1965 by the DC5.

Funny how many of the big Invasion records were not hits in England. "I Like It Like That" was Top 10 in the U.S. but was not a hit in the U.K.

"Over and Over"

Bobby Day, a composer and singer from Los Angeles, scored tremendously big in 1958 with one of the great records of that year. "Over and Over" was the third of six hits for him, a fairly obscure record, since it just missed making the national Top 40 in the states. However, the flip side was a classic called "Rockin' Robin," which was a Top-5 hit, so the record as a whole was very successful.

Someone in the DC5 organization was really plugged into old U.S. rock 'n' roll. Bobby Day never had a hit in England, yet the DC5 knew and recorded "Over and Over." It carried them into the Top 50 in England in 1965, and clear to the #1 spot in America.

"You've Got What It Takes"

And the American/British hits just kept on comin'! The Dave Clark Five should have gotten some kind of an award for remaking as many American records as they did.

Marv Johnson was an early protégé of Berry (Motown) Gordy. "You've Got What It Takes" was a strange-sounding record, but not so strange that it didn't become Top 10 in 1959 as the third of Marv's nine chartings. In England Marv also had hits, five of them, and "You've Got What It Takes" was the first, going into the British Top 5.

Seven years after Marv Johnson's original, the Dave Clark Five revived "You've Got What It Takes." They gave it the usual DC5 treatment: rough vocal, driving drums, and raucous delivery. In England, it was well received into the Top 30. In the United States, it was lovingly embraced into the Top 10.

"A Little Bit Now"

The Dave Clark Five were not snobs. If they wanted to remake a U.S. oldie, they did it, even if the song hadn't been a huge smash. "A Little Bit Now" was the modest follow-up to "A Wonderful Dream" by the Majors, a U.S. vocal group from Pennsylvania. In 1963, the Majors' version of "A Little Bit Now" was only regionally successful, missing the national Top 40. "A Little Bit Now" was noticed by only a few, and forgotten by most.

But "A Little Bit Now" was neither missed nor forgotten by the good ol' DC5. Four years later in 1967 they dusted off this oldie and gave it the usual DC5 treatment. It wasn't a hit in England. In the United States, it did about as well as it had for the Majors. Too bad, since it was an excellent song in both versions.

"Put a Little Love in Your Heart"

By the end of 1967, the Dave Clark Five were total has-beens in the United States, and would never have another hit single going to their credit. Back home they kept plugging away, continuing to rely often on their American roots for material. An American artist who had written many songs over the years was Jackie DeShannon. For her, songwriting came easily. She turned out songs almost as eaily as she turned out LPs, and she had a lot of LPs for an artist who had a great deal of trouble turning out hit singles.

In 1964, Jackie DeShannon toured the U.S. with the Beatles. In 1969, she finally hit the big time chartwise with her own composition, "Put a Little Love in Your Heart." It was her ninth time on the charts, but this one went clean into the Top 5!

The Dave Clark Five knew a good song when it came along, even if it wasn't an oldie yet. They recorded "Put a Little Love in Your Heart" the same year and made the Top 40 in England.

"Good Old Rock 'n' Roll" and "More Good Old Rock 'n' Roll"

By 1970, the Dave Clark Five was finally running out of steam in England. Two of their last successful records were titled "Good Old Rock 'n' Roll" and "More Good Old Rock 'n' Roll." These records were actually medleys of American rock 'n' roll songs. The first squeezed "Sweet Little Sixteen" (Chuck Berry, 1958), "Long Tall Sally" (Little Richard, 1956), "Chantilly Lace" (The Big Bopper, 1958), "Whole Lotta Shakin' Goin' On" (Jerry Lee Lewis, 1957), and "Blue Suede Shoes" (Carl Perkins, Elvis Presley, both 1956) into three minutes and 25 seconds! But their late 1950s–early 1960s American roots showed one last time in the summer of 1970, when they released "Here Comes Summer."

"Here Comes Summer"

This song was the only hit for America's Jerry Keller. He was one of the very few — if not the only — rock 'n' roll star to come from Arkansas and have his own television show in Tulsa, Oklahoma. In the summer of 1959 his own composition, "Here Comes Summer," made him famous for a while by becoming a Top-20 hit. In England, Keller's "Here Comes Summer" was even more popular, going into the Top 5.

In the summer of '70, the DC5's revival of "Here Comes Summer" missed the Top 40. The end was near for the group, whose British act relied more on U.S. hits written by the U.S. hit artists than on their own original compositions. Their final British records included the American numbers "Sweet City Woman" (the Stampeders, 1971) and "Sha-Na-Na" (a.k.a. "Na Na Hey Hey Kiss Him Goodbye," Steam, 1969).

HERMAN'S HERMITS

Unlike many of the British invasion artists who were known in England for one or two years before they had U.S. records, Herman's Hermits were brand new in England in 1964. This meant that Americans got to hear each new song in the same time and sequence as the British kids did.

"I'm Into Somethin' Good"

The first Hermits record in both countries was another Brill Building product, "I'm Into Somethin' Good." To those few who knew of the original version, which had made a small splash a mere two months earlier by the black American female singer Earl-Jean, it was a bit of a shock to hear a male, thickly accented voice singing "I'm Into Somethin' Good" in the fall of 1964.

Earl-Jean was the name on the American record. She had already had success as a part of the American girl group the Cookies, but "I'm Into Somethin' Good" was her first solo record. Carole King and hubby Gerry Goffin supplied the words and music for Earl-Jean, as they had previously done for the Cookies, but this was her only hit.

Earl-Jean's U.S. Top-40 effort was not a hit in England, but Herman's

Hermits must have gotten a copy of the record someplace. Their remake was #1 in England and Top 20 here.

"Silhouettes"

Of all of the roots of the British invasion songs, the primo classic was "Silhouettes." In 1957, the Rays made rock 'n' roll history taking this one-shot into the U.S. Top 5. Steve Gibson and the Redcaps charted mildly with their cover version, and the Diamonds ("Little Darlin'," 1957), made the U.S. Top 10 in 1957 with their own recording of "Silhouettes."

In England, "Silhouettes" did not chart by *any* artist in 1957—their loss. Herman's Hermits made up the loss in 1965 by making "Silhouettes" their third hit in both the U.S. and England. Their version of the song was considerably faster, and lacked the '50s ambience of the original. But it was a Top-5 smash in both countries.

"Wonderful World"

The influence of Sam Cooke appears once again in the roots of the British invasion. Back in 1960, one of Sam Cooke's memorable ballads was "Wonderful World," Top 30 in England and Top 20 in the states. The late Sam Cooke, killed in 1964, and his version were virtually unknown to the newest crop of American teens of 1965 when the Hermits updated the song in the invasion style—guitars, drums, and heavy emphasis on the beat.

Somewhat surprisingly, the Hermits' version did much better than the original. It made the British Top 10 and the American Top 5.

"A Must to Avoid"

For once, the roots of the British invasion are not hand-me-downs! Instead of remaking a U.S. oldie, Herman's Hermits actually commissioned a song to be written for them—by an American.

The American chosen was a relative unknown: Phil Sloan. Also known as P.F. Sloan and Flip Sloan, Phil was more of a songwriter than a recording artist. With partner Steve Barri he wrote many hit songs and LP cuts for Jan and Dean, including "I Found a Girl" and "(Here They Come) From All Over the World (The TAMI Show Theme)."

Calling themselves the Fantastic Baggies ("Baggies" was California beach slang for surfer swimming trunks), Phil and Steve had some success as surf artists in the U.S. and in Australia. One of their better known compositions was a new theme song for the American syndication of the British television series "Secret Agent Man." The original British theme had been a harpsichord instrumental, but for the American release of the television show it was felt a new theme was called for. Johnny Rivers sang the resulting song, "Secret Agent Man," and soon after the series showed up on American television, requests began coming in for a recording on a 45.

In the wake of the Beatles' film *A Hard Day's Night*, Herman's

Hermits made a deal to do a film of their own titled *A Must to Avoid*. On the strength of his "Secret Agent Man" theme Phil Sloan got the assignment of writing this movie's theme of the same name. The movie wasn't so hot. It didn't have much of a plot. But the song sung by the Hermits, not Johnny Rivers, did quite well—Top 10 in both the U.S. and the U.K.

What? You say you remember the song "A Must to Avoid," but never heard of a movie by that name? Well, the movie was renamed after the song was recorded. The new name was *Hold On*, and Phil was commissioned to write a song for that title, too. It wasn't a single, though.

GEORGIE FAME

"Yeh, Yeh"

Clive Powell scored in 1965 an unusual U.S. hit that out-yeah-yeah-yeah-ed even the Beatles' "She Loves You." "Yeh, Yeh" had a much softer sound than most invasion music. Still, it sounded verrry British. Of course, the tune had been done before, as the follow-up by Cuban-American band leader Mongo Santamaria to his 1963 hit, "Watermelon Man." This U.S. version, a virtually vocal-less instrumental, has a title punctuated differently ("Yeh-Yeh!") and is so different musically from Georgie Fame's later British version as to be hard to recognized as a cover.

THE MOODY BLUES

"Go Now"

For such a well-known group, the original Moody Blues had few hits, only two on the Top 40 during the British invasion. Their first and biggest, "Go Now," was an obscure U.S. record recorded by Bessie Banks and written by Jerry Leiber and Mike Stoller.

THE SEARCHERS

The Searchers were probably the champion invaders when it came to American roots. Practically every time they released a record, some American songwriters started getting royalty checks from a song they thought was long forgotten. Even the Searchers' flip sides sometimes had American roots. And their LPs . . . but that's another story. The Searchers were prolific, with a great many U.S. single releases, but their American hit-song success was limited. They made the charts over a dozen times but in the short span of only about two years. And while their hits usually did very well in England, less than half hit the Top 40 in the U.S.

"Sweets for My Sweet"

Jangling guitars were the sound of the Searchers, plus some mildly harmonious vocals. Other than the Beatles, in fact, the sound of the Searchers perhaps best typifies the characteristic sound of the British invasion. The American Drifters, who had 18 hits in England, provided the "demo" for the Searchers' first British hit, "Sweets for My Sweet." Funny that the Drifters' song chosen by the Searchers was not among those 18 Drifters' hits in Britain! In the summer of 1963, "Sweets for My Sweet," which had been Top 20 by the Drifters in the states, was #1 in England as rendered by the Searchers. It became very popular in 1964 in the Midwest by the Searchers, but never made the national Top 100.

"Sweet Nothin's"

It was pretty rare for a British group to do an American song which had been a slow song by an American female vocalist, but the Searchers did every kind of American song imaginable.

Brenda Lee was just a little girl in 1960 when she had a Top-5 hit in both the U.S. and England with "Sweet Nothin's." Her catalog was big, some 18 hits in England alone, a true American success story for someone so poor as a child that she would often arrange to be playing at a neighbor's house each day at noon, just to be sure she would get something to eat for lunch.

In the fall of 1963 the Searchers paid Brenda Lee tribute, if not money, by choosing her 1960 song for their third British record. It was not Top 40, and the Searchers learned a lesson from that poor showing, staying away from American girl songs — for about a month.

"Needles and Pins"

"Needles and Pins" was one of the records American kids were buying back when the Searchers were doing "Sweets for my Sweet." The composers of "Needles and Pins" were unknowns at the time — Sonny Bono and Jack Nitzsche. Sonny later became a star with Cher; Jack Nitzsche had an instrumental hit in 1963 with "The Lonely Surfer," arranged many Phil Spector hits, and won an Oscar 20 years later for one of his many Hollywood movie scores.

"Needles and Pins" has a very interesting aspect to it. The Searchers' version, which was #1 in England and Top 20 in the United States, was typical of the British sound of the Searchers. It featured jangling guitars, and with their way of pronouncing "needles and pins-ah" became a patented Searchers' trademark. But when you listen to the Jackie DeShannon 1963 preinvasion original, recorded even before the Searchers had their first British hit, you hear the same "pins-ah" lyric and the same jangling guitar sound which supposedly typified the British invasion sound!

Talk about roots of the British invasion! Good old American early '60s rock 'n' roll, even girl group music, was the stuff the invasion records were made of, even if no one recognized it.

"Just Like Me"

Remember the Hollies' first British hit — "Just Like Me"? That old Coasters' LP cut got yet another lease on life when the Searchers cut the song in 1964. In England it was only an LP cut, but in the states it was a non–Top-40 single. Both the Hollies and the Searchers sort of homogenized many songs like "Just Like Me" when they recorded them, turning them into a sort of British-invasion Muzak with a big beat but, at times, little individualism.

"When You Walk in the Room"

Remember Jackie DeShannon and the Dave Clark Five's 1969 British version of her hit, "Put a Little Love in Your Heart"? And of course, there was Jackie's very influential "Needles and Pins." A minor hit of Jackie's from January of 1964 got a great revival by the Searchers in the fall of '64.

Jackie DeShannon wrote many songs, including "When You Walk in the Room." Her own recordings usually sold poorly, so it was lucky for her that American artists like Brenda Lee ("Dum Dum," 1961) and Bobby Vee ("You Won't Forget Me," 1964) and invasion groups like the Searchers often chose her songs to record. Their British version of "When You Walk in the Room" went to #1 in England and slipped into the edge of the U.S. Top 40.

"Love Potion Number 9"

The reliance of the British invasion on American songs was truly amazing in 1964. In England, of course, American songs were probably welcome by teens, and in the U.S. the release decisions were made by record execs who probably favored recognizable titles over unknown quantities.

The Clovers were known for years as the group who did "Love Potion Number 9" in 1959 — and not much else, although they had many U.S. rhythm 'n' blues hits. That record hadn't been a hit in England, and was only Top 30 in the U.S. But the Searchers really lived up to their name when it came to searching out good American oldies to record.

"Love Potion Number 9" was one of the Searchers' biggest successes in the U.S., making the Top 5. In England it was not a hit.

"Bumble Bee"

LaVern Baker was an American rhythm and blues singer with a considerable following among rock 'n' rollers. Another of her songs, "C C Rider," was recorded by the Animals. LaVern's records never did extremely well on the pop charts, with her 1960 hit "Bumble Bee" not even making the Top 40. This poor showing in the U.S. and no showing at all in England did not deter the Searchers from once again using an American oldie for their newest release. The Searchers' "Bumble Bee" followed the original fairly closely, although with a less soulful delivery. As so often happened, "Bumble Bee" by the Searchers was a hit only in the U.S. where it was Top 5 in the winter of 1964–65.

"Hi-Heel Sneakers"

During February 1964, month two of the British invasion, Tommy Tucker, a one-shot artist in America, had a bluesy Top-30 hit called "Hi-Heel Sneakers." The Searchers must have had someone in the states sending them the latest American hit records, since "Sneakers" was not a hit in England.

The Searchers' version was on the flip side of "Bumble Bee," and while it did not gain national popularity, was a hit in the Midwest. As was so often the case, the Searchers sort of homogenized the song, taking away all rhythm and soul from the music on this recording. Homogenized and removing soul sound too sanitary. A better characterization might be to say they tightened up the songs compared to the looser bluesy style of the originals.

"Take Me for What I'm Worth"

The last Searchers' American oldie remake was perhaps their oddest. "Take Me for What I'm Worth" was written by ol' Phil "P.F." Sloan and had been featured on his Dunhill LP, *Songs of Our Times*. Phil was writing and singing in a Dylanesque, folk-protest style at this time (1965). His best-known work from this time, and from the same side of his LP, was "Eve of Destruction," a hit as recorded by Barry McGuire. Phil played the guitar parts on Barry McGuire's hit version. Phil's other British invasion involvement was with Herman's Hermits, but his Hermits songs were written expressly for the Hermits. This contrasted with his relationship with the Searchers, which was nonexistent. Phil had no contact with the Searchers, and had never presented demos of his songs to them, so he was both thrilled and surprised when they chose to do one of his songs.

"Take Me for What I'm Worth" was the Searchers' second-to-last chart song in the U.S., and it didn't even graze the Top 40. In England, it was Top 20. This was, as stated, all a big surprise to Phil Sloan.

The LP Covers

So far, the review of the roots of the British invasion has been limited to songs released as British 45s or as British invasion U.S. 45s. But the British artists' American rock 'n' roll roots go a lot deeper than that. For every hit song the British had, there were a flip side and ten or so LP cuts, and a large proportion of these were also American songs. In fact, in many cases, the songs chosen for U.S. singles were mere LP cuts in England.

An example of the British LP cut that became an American hit single is "Just Like Me" (also known as "Ain't That Just Like Me"). The Searchers never expected that song to leap from their British LP onto the American singles charts.

A full listing of the LP roots of the British invasion would become a seemingly endless review. To give an idea of the extent to which the American influence on British artists was hidden away on LPs, a few representative examples of non-45 rpm, American LP, British invasion artist cuts are given:

Searchers LP Cuts	*Original American Version*
"Hi-Heel Sneakers"	Tommy Tucker, 1964
"It's in Her Kiss"	Betty Everett, 1964
"Sea of Heartbreak"	Don Gibson, 1961
"What'd I Say"	Ray Charles, 1959
"Hully Gully"	Olympics, 1960
(a.k.a. "Monkey"	Freddy Cannon, 1963
and "Peanut Butter")	Marathons, 1961
"Mashed Potatoes"	Joey Dee, 1963
(a.k.a. "Hot Pastrami")	Dartells, 1963

Hollies LP Cuts

"You Must Believe Me"	Impressions, 1964
"That's My Desire"	Sensations, 1962
"Lawdy, Miss Clawdy"	Lloyd Price, 1954
"Candy Man"	Roy Orbison, 1961
"Sweet Little Sixteen"	Chuck Berry, 1958
"Mickey's Monkey"	Miracles, 1963

Herman's Hermits LP Cuts

"The End of the World"	Skeeter Davis, 1963
"Heartbeat"	Buddy Holly, 1958
"Sea Cruise"	Frankie Ford, 1959
"Walkin' with My Angel"	
(written by Carole King)	Bobby Vee, 1961
"I Understand (Just How You	
Feel)"	G-Clefs, 1961
"Mother-in-Law"	Ernie K-Doe, 1961

Kinks LP Cuts

"Louie Louie"	Kingsmen, 1963

Billy J. Kramer with the Dakotas LP Cuts

"Da Do Ron Ron"	Crystals, 1963
"Dance with Me"	Drifters, 1959

Billy J. Kramer with the Dakotas LP Cuts	*Original American Version*
"Pride" (composed by Madera and White of Danny and the Juniors)	
"I Know"	Barbara George, 1961
"Great Balls of Fire"	Jerry Lee Lewis, 1957
"It's Up to You"	Rick Nelson, 1962
"The 12th of Never"	Johnny Mathis, 1957
"Twilight Time"	Platters, 1958
"Under the Boardwalk"	Drifters, 1963
"When You Walk in the Room"	Jackie DeShannon, 1963
"Tennessee Waltz"	Sam Cooke, 1964
"Irresistible You"	Bobby Darin, 1961

Georgie Fame LP Cuts	
"The Monkey Time"	Major Lance, 1963
"Pride and Joy"	Marvin Gaye, 1963

Rolling Stones LP Cuts	
"Mercy, Mercy"	Don Covay, 1964
"Hitch Hike"	Marvin Gaye, 1964
"Good Times"	Sam Cooke, 1964

Skiffle, music hall, jazz, traditional and Broadway music influences notwithstanding, apparently the largest single influence on British artists who took part in the mid-'60s invasion of the United States was American artists' rock 'n' roll songs.

The LPs chosen for the sampling of roots of the British invasion were selected totally at random, with one exception. The Beatles are being saved until last because they had such very extensive American roots.

THE BEATLES

When it comes to the roots of the British invasion the Beatles are unique. They recorded a great many U.S. songs, four of which were Beatle hits in America, but not one was even released as a single in England. This last bit of information is very unusual, since the other invasion artists almost invariably released their own versions of American songs on 45s in England.

With all the other invasion artists, only American songs that were chart singles in the U.S. or England were reviewed, except in the special LP-cut section. In reviewing the Beatles, their U.S. LP versions of American songs are also included in addition to their American singles. This was done because Beatles LPs sold so widely and were played so liberally that most cuts were as familiar to American teenagers as 45s were for other artists.

"Act Naturally"

Ringo got to sing lead on country star Buck Owens and His Buckaroos' song "Act Naturally." Very, very few Beatles fans had ever heard of this song before it was on the Beatles LP *Yesterday and Today*, although it was well known to country music fans. This marked almost the sole instance of country music entering the roots of the British invasion.

"Anna (Go to Him)"

"Anna" was one of three chart records Arthur Alexander had in 1962. Alexander didn't write his biggest record, "The Fool," but he did compose "Anna," which he sang in a blues style that apparently appealed to John Lennon. "Anna" appeared on an extremely rare 1964 VJ 45.

"Baby It's You"

Manfred Mann scored a U.S. and U.K. hit with one Shirelles song, "Sha La La." The Beatles were also Shirelles fans, as evidenced by their recording of an old Shirelles 1962 Top-10 hit, "Baby It's You." The Beatles' version has now eclipsed the rather delicate and haunting Shirelles original in most people's memories. The Beatles' version was very heavy-handed and rough, lacking most of the sensitivity that marked much of the Beatles' later work.

"Bad Boy"

Larry Williams' "Bad Boy" was much better suited to the Beatles' style than was "Baby It's You." Larry Williams was a wilder rocker than even John Lennon, and his work may be familiar from his non–Top-40 U.S. hit from 1957, "Short Fat Fanny." The song was also played in England, as was his better-known "Bony Moronie." The Beatles, like most British kids, were obviously into flip sides. "Bad Boy" had been the flip side of "Short Fat Fanny." Talk about roots! The flip of an American flop being recorded by the Beatles.

"Boys"

The Shirelles appear for a third time, making them one of the most frequently emulated American artists of the male-dominated Beatles British invasion. It may be noted that none of the female British invasion artists figured in the *roots* of the Beatles British invasion at all, not relying on American influence to gain either the British or American charts.

"Boys" was a Shirelles LP cut, and was included by the Beatles on their first LP. Since it was an uptempo rocker at least by Shirelles' standards, the Beatles' version was faithful to the original.

"Chains"

The Cookies were one of the best, if more short-lived, of the American girl groups. They were the brain-children of Carole King and her husband. In fact, on the 1963 Top-20 version of "Chains" by the Cookies, Carole's voice can be very clearly heard. Chalk up another victory for the Brill Building enclave!

One of the Cookies was Earl-Jean, whose "I'm Into Somethin' Good" provided demo-inspiration for Herman's Hermits. The Cookies themselves could rock when they were called upon to do so. One of their other hits, "Don't Say Nothin' Bad (About My Baby)," actually featured a line, "so girl you better shut your mouth!" The Beatles therefore did "Chains" justice when it appeared on their first LP, even if their harmonies were a bit off the mark. The Cookies' original version was charted in England the same year the Beatles cut it, 1963.

"Devil in Her (His) Heart"

The Donays were an obscure girl group who never gained fame. But their recording of "Devil in His Heart" must have served as a convincing demo for the Beatles, since no other versions are known. This is a very pure early-'60s girl group song, something that the Beatles specialized in back then.

"Dizzy Miss Lizzy"

Larry Williams' music was the Beatles' inspiration once again. "Dizzy Miss Lizzy" was a minor U.S.-only hit in 1959. The Beatles' early LP version was a rocking success for them, as would be expected.

"Everybody's Trying to Be My Baby"

Carl Perkins was idolized by the Beatles far out of proportion to the former's popularity in the states. "Blue Suede Shoes" was the only one of his five appearances on the U.S. Top 100 to enter the ranks of the Top 40. In the decades since the Beatles released their version of Perkins' material, he has enjoyed enhanced status and considerable touring success. "Everybody's Trying to Be My Baby" never became a hit.

"Honey Don't"

It was unusual for Ringo to sing lead, but sing it he did on "Honey Don't," an early Beatles' LP cut. The song had been a Carl Perkins LP cut in the '50s. The Beatles did a good job locating it since Carl had darn few U.S. hits, and only one in England, "Blue Suede Shoes"! Perkins was not half the rocker Larry Williams was, so had John sung "Honey Don't," it may or may not have worked, but by Ringo, it was perfect.

"Kansas City"

Jerry Leiber and Mike Stoller wrote the song about the second biggest city in the state of Missouri, "Kansas City." "Kansas City" was a big #1 hit in America back in 1959, one of two hits by Wilbert Harrison. Why a Liverpool band would sing the song was a mystery, except that Harrison (Wilbert, not George) could rock his guitar when called for, and so the song was right up the Beatles' early rock alley. The Beatles' version, with Paul on lead vocal, was excellent.

"Hey Hey Hey Hey"

The Beatles stuck this obscure Little Richard Penniman song onto "Kansas City" without any label credit going to Richard for either the title or the composing. This song was about as wild as Paul could hope to get.

"Long Tall Sally"

Now we're talkin'! American kids liked Little Richard enough in 1956 to send his "Long Tall Sally" to the Top 20. British kids liked Little Richard's original version even better, making it Top 5 over there. The Kinks had a version, but the Beatles' satisfyingly rocking rendition has pretty well overpowered all other versions since it appeared as an early cut on a Beatles LP and subsequently on compilation reissues.

"Match Box"

The Beatles did have their favorites. Carl Perkins showed up again in the Beatle repertoire. "Match Box" was about as obscure as the roots of the Beatles invasion could have been. Very few U.S. Beatle fans had any idea the song was American. That was because it was a Carl Perkins 1957 flip side, and the hit side, "Your True Love," missed the Top 40 by about 25 points.

The Beatles liked the song, and many say they improved greatly on the original. Today, Carl Perkins performs the song live — the Beatles version, not his own.

"Misery"

Obscure! In 1963, a group called the Dynamics popped up with "Misery," a song that enjoyed limited success only in the states, where its standing did not warrant its inclusion in the national Top 40. The Beatles' LP version raised the song to new heights, and made a bundle in royalties for the American composers, who no doubt had been disappointed by the Dynamics' un-dynamic record sales record. The Beatles performed the song in a subdued manner, and probably not one Beatlemaniac in 10,000 knew that their version was not the original.

"Mr. Moonlight"

Dr. Feelgood and the Interns is pretty obviously a fake name: the group never existed. Their two chart singles were performed by Piano Red, a.k.a. Willie Perryman. Neither was a Top-40 hit, and one has to wonder just how the Beatles came by these things. "Mr. Moonlight" was just a flip side of a flop 45, but made a mighty nice Beatle LP cut.

"Money"

Barrett Strong was an early Berry Gordy (founder of Motown) pro-tégé. Strong's recording of "Money" propelled him to stardom in 1960. As familiar as the song is today, however, it may be the Beatles' LP version which accounts for much of "Money's" familiarity. Barrett Strong's version barely made the U.S. Top 20, and he could have become better known had he not turned down a song Berry Gordy offered him as a follow-up to "Money." As a second choice, Gordy gave the song to another, new group, the Miracles. The song, "Shop Around," was a top-of-the-chart success for the Miracles in 1960.

The Beatles did a fine rave-up of "Money" and the song remains one of their more popular nonhit oldies.

"Rock and Roll Music"

Chuck Berry is much like Little Richard, an early rocker who still has a following. Along with the far more popular Elvis Presley, Berry is considered largely responsible for the music we have since called rock 'n' roll.

"Rock and Roll Music" was an obviously contrived song. Even the title was chosen to be as commercial as possible. But then, that has always been the goal of rock 'n' roll—appeal to kids and get them to spend their allowance and odd-job money on your records!

In 1958, Chuck Berry had a U.S. only, Top-10 hit with "Rock and Roll Music." The song proved perfect for the Beatles and especially John, and is another one of their best known early LP cuts.

"Roll Over Beethoven"

Capitol Records of Canada released the Beatles' rendition of Chuck Berry's "Roll Over Beethoven." The sales overflow across the U.S. border registered enough sales to slip this tune, which had been Chuck Berry's second hit way back in 1956, into the Top 100 in 1964. No one in England ever intended this to be a Beatles single.

"Slow Down"

Larry Williams was a major fave of the Fab Four. "Slow Down" added to "Dizzy Miss Lizzie" makes two Williams songs they recorded. "Slow Down" was an obscure LP cut before the Beatles released it on an LP. Virtually no one was the wiser and felt it was an original Beatle song. This was understandable, as it sounded very natural, one of the Beatles' most wonderful remakes.

"'Til There Was You"

Now things get a little strange. John was a rocker. Ringo and George went with the flow. But Paul McCartney was much more pop-oriented than John. The Beatles' producer, George Martin, had a background in pop and show music. This unusual combination of interests and background resulted in "'Til There Was You."

"'Til There Was You" was a Beatle LP cut. The song gained prominence when the Beatles performed it live on the Ed Sullivan show in 1964, the only ballad they included in their sets. The song was written for the Meredith Wilson musical *The Music Man*, where it was sung by Marian, the female librarian! An original U.S. hit version was sung by, of all people, Anita Bryant, who made it a Top-30 hit in 1959.

Anita Bryant had two British hits ("Paper Roses" and "My Little Corner of the World," both 1960). "'Til There Was You" was not one of them, so it is not clear if Paul's inspiration was from her or from the musical. Either way, the roots of the British invasion were undeniably strongly American in Beatles music, as well as convoluted, as the Beatles tapped many sources to find inspiration and material.

"Twist and Shout"

Of all of the Beatles' American roots, the best received was without a doubt "Twist and Shout." John Lennon delivered the song in a hoarse, bluesy style emulated later by Janis Joplin and much later by half of the singers on MTV. The song was recorded at the tail end of the recording session since John's way of belting out "Twist and Shout" always totaled his voice for the rest of the day!

The Isley Brothers did the first hit version of "Twist and Shout," which included yells and vocal pileups. Surprisingly, it now sounds mild in light of the Beatles' wild version, although the arrangement so associated with the Beatles was copied note for note and harmony by harmony from the Isley Brothers.

The Beatles' version hit #1 on the U.S. charts in the summer of—1986! Use of the track in two popular movies introduced the song to a new generation.

"Words of Love"

As every loyal Beatlemaniac knows, the inspiration for the name "Beatles" came at least in part from the insect-name of Buddy Holly's American group, the "Crickets." When the Beatles put the Buddy Holly 1957 45 cut "Words of Love" on one of their mid-'60s LPs, they paid Buddy Holly an equally great tribute. The Beatles' version of "Words of Love" is the most faithful remake of any of the American songs the Beatles ever recorded. This is especially notable since the song is a rock 'n' roll ballad.

Overview

The roots of the Beatles British invasion included 31 songs which were American hit singles later released as invasion 45s in the U.S. Besides those 31, another 20 or so were American songs that became invasion artists' *British* hits. Too numerous to count were other American hits which became LP cuts by invasion artists, and American songs which were British hits recorded by noninvasion British artists.

Confusing, these various categories of songs. Let's limit ourselves to the 42 invasion singles and Beatle LP cuts which were originally American recordings by American artists. Whenever fans of the early Beatles and of the British invasion speak of the relative merits of the invasion music versus preinvasion American rock 'n' roll, the American is considered a poor, distant second. In fact, words like "watered down," "pop," "pabulum," "uninspired," and "commercially motivated" are constantly repeated to describe U.S. music between the death of Buddy Holly in early 1959 and the arrival of the Beatles in early 1964. Those five years are seen as the nadir of American rock 'n' roll by U.S. fans of the invasion. Very strongly made is the claim that the beauty of the Beatles British invasion music was that it had its roots in the original, 1955–1957, untamed, American rock 'n' roll.

But how did the invasion artists themselves view the American artists, and more significantly, how did they view American rock 'n' roll music of the period 1959 through 1964? A table of the number of invasion hits and Beatle recordings drawn from each year up to the invasion tells the story.

Year of American Version	Number of Invasion Songs with American Roots	Number of Beatle Songs with American Roots
1955	0	0
1956	0	5
1957	2	2
1958	5	3

Year of American Version	Number of Invasion Songs with American Roots	Number of Beatle Songs with American Roots
1959	4	3
1960	3	2
1961	1	1
1962	2	5
1963	5	2
1964	7	0

Many rock historians assert that American rock 'n' roll had become a barren wasteland following the death of Buddy Holly, the shame of Jerry Lee Lewis after marrying his 13-year-old cousin, the jailing of Chuck Berry, and the drafting of Elvis. According to this belief, American music between 1959 and the invasion of 1964 is worthless. It was the Beatles and the British who, by reviving early American rock 'n' roll traditions of Chuck Berry and his contemporaries, saved rock 'n' roll from dying out completely.

The Truth About the In-Between Years

The facts as revealed in this study of the roots of the Beatles British invasion tell a different story.

1. Only five Beatle songs and no other British invasion records had visible roots in 1955–56 American music — just under 10 percent of the 52 recordings of American songs that were invasion hits, British hits by invasion artists, or Beatles LP cuts.

2. Even including the transitional years of 1957 and 1958, only 24 songs are found — accounting for less than half (46 percent) of the roots of the Beatles invasion.

3. The other 54 percent, or 28 songs, comes from the period of supposedly weak American music, the early '60s.

The myth that American music of the early 1960s was a vast wasteland, from which America was saved by the Beatles British invasion, is false. Obviously, the British artists did not feel the American music of the post 1958 period was weak, because they loved it enough to emulate it and rerecord the songs.

Thus, the hard facts reveal that the largest single musical influence on British artists, whom we grew to know as British invasion artists and who are often credited with revitalizing rock 'n' roll, was American rock 'n' roll hits of the period 1959–1964. It is a terrible irony that so many American rock 'n' roll fans and critics labor under the misconception, spread by many opinionated authors, that the American preinvasion music was different from the invasion hits and relatively worthless. To a large measure, in fact, the invasion songs were precisely the same maligned American music coming right back at us. The myth of post–Holly, pre–Beatle American rock 'n' roll's being a musical wasteland is seen to be false when viewed in the light of these facts.

There is a precedent for this illogical antipathy toward early '60s American rock 'n' roll by the invasion generation. This process is perfectly illustrated in the epic rock 'n' roll movie *American Graffiti*. John Milner (played by Paul LeMat) is driving around in his hot rod. John is a hood, a Fonzie-type character who is several years out of high school, yet still very youthful and interested in rock 'n' roll music. This night, he is cruisin' in his car and groovin' to the sounds of the late 1950s and the early '60s. Suddenly, he hears a new group, the Beach Boys, singing their first hit record. He reaches for his car radio and turns the song off, referring to it as "surfin' shit."

John did not realize that the Beach Boys' two main musical influences on their early records like "Surfin'" and "Surfin' U.S.A." were Jan and Dean's 1959 hit "Baby Talk," and Chuck Berry's 1958 record "Sweet Little 16." Both of these were songs and artists John probably liked. But he didn't hear the roots, all he heard was a new group on the radio.

So, what should John Milner have said when he heard "Surfin'"? "Wow! That sounds just like the music from my high school days! Good old rock 'n' roll!"

But John, an older guy, put down the new music because superficially it seemed different. It wasn't what he considered "real" rock 'n' roll, so he rejected it. In the mid-'60s and since, Beatles and invasion fans have turned the tables, and put down the older music because, superficially, it seemed different. In retrospect however, we can see it was not really different.

The point is that music is music. Everyone's taste is a bit different from anyone else's. People who are into the Beatles British invasion are no more justified in putting down preinvasion music than fans of opera are justified in putting down country music. Instead, everyone should revel in the reality that we live in a free country which allows everyone to engage in the pursuit of personal happiness. Music isn't intrinsically good or bad, it is simply preferred or not. If we like it, we should be glad we can listen to it. If we don't like it, we should just not listen to it. Criticizing it is unbecoming, illogical, and unnecessary.

One fan of the invasion has already seen the light. Linda Ronstadt, in a 1985 NBC "Today" show interview, was asked why she was redoing old songs instead of current rock. Her reply was enlightening—she was, as the interviewer put it, rejecting a '60s state of mind. "It really was staggering, what happened in the '60s. There was just wholesale rejection of everything that had come before. Which is sort of an ungrateful thing to do [by] the most ungrateful bunch of monsters ever! I am a part of that generation, so I can criticize it myself!"

The Beatles British invasion music was wonderful, exciting, and dynamic. But to say preinvasion music was any less so is not only inconsiderate and opinionated, but reveals a profound lack of knowledge of the roots of the invasion.

Chapter 3

144 "Yeah Yeah Yeah's" Can't Be Wrong!

Among the Beatles' mop-top haircuts, Beatle boots, and the Beatles' collarless suit coats, the most notable Beatle trademark during the Beatles invasion was the phrase "Yeah! Yeah! Yeah!" In fact, those three words became so closely associated with the Beatles that people began to think they'd invented the words for use in rock and roll music. It was certainly justifiable that the Beatles were well known for using the word "yeah" in their early songs. In 1964 they were especially known for the phrase "Yeah! Yeah! Yeah!" which was featured prominently in one of the greatest rock 'n' roll songs of all time, "She Loves You."

The Beatles were seen on American television for the first time on January 3, 1964. It was a BBC film that Jack Paar had made of them performing "She Loves You" on stage in England. Unknown in the states at the time, the Beatles' "She Loves You" was a hit in England, where it reached #1 a few weeks after entering the charts on August 31, 1963. Seeing this performance on Jack Paar, I was entranced by the Beatles' use of the familiar phrase, "Yeah, Yeah, Yeah!"

"She Loves You" was not the only song on which the Beatles used "Yeah Yeah Yeah." On their first American Capitol LP *Meet the Beatles,* the song "It Won't Be Long" featured the phrase. In the aftermath of the #1 popularity in the states of the "She Loves You" single and the huge popularity of the *Meet the Beatles* LP, the "Yeah Yeah Yeah" phrase became synonymous with Beatles music itself.

And to think Paul McCartney's father, feeling "Yeah Yeah Yeah" lacked dignity, tried to convince Paul to change it to "Yes Yes Yes!"

The Beatles had quite a predilection for the word "Yeah." On their first American LP, cut one, side one, and hit #1, was "I Want to Hold Your Hand," which began with "Oh Yeah ...." Also on side one, "All I've Got to Do" used "Yeah" at the end of several lines. On side two, "Little Child" repeated the "Oh Yeah" phrase some more, while the final cut, "Not a Second Time," gave us "Oh Yeah" at the end of several lines again.

No wonder the Beatles were the "Yeah Yeah" group in 1964!

More "Yeah-ing" was in evidence. The Beatles' first Brtitish chart topper, and also a U.S. hit, was "Please Please Me." A variation of the "Oh Yeah" was sung on "Please Please Me," namely "Woe, Yeah." And on the flip side of "She Loves You" was a nice little ditty called "I'll Get You." It began with the now familiar "Oh Yeah, Oh Yeah."

In later years, the Beatles sang "Day Tripper, Yeah." Yeah, the phrase "Yeah Yeah Yeah" was certainly melded, deservedly, with the name the Beatles in the 1960s.

The "Yeah" phrase is so solidly connected with the Beatles that it has become part of the collective cultural pop consciousness. To illustrate this fact, let's jump from the mid-1960s to a time 22 years later, and the movie *Peggy Sue Got Married*, a time travel science fiction/fantasy starring Kathleen Turner. As Peggy Sue, she went back in time, from her 1986 25-year high school reunion to her actual 1961 high school days.

The important fact was that she was in 1961 but had all of her 1986 knowledge intact. Did she use her knowledge to prevent the assassination of President Kennedy? Did she use her knowledge to make money playing the stock market? Did she try to nip the Viet Nam War in the bud? No, she used her advanced knowledge to pass on to her boyfriend (played by Nicholas Cage), an aspiring rock 'n' roll singer and songwriter, the lyrics to "She Loves You," a song which at this point in time in the movie hadn't been written yet. She figured these lyrics would allow him to scoop the Beatles' sound, not due for two or three years, and allow him to become successful and famous.

At the end of the movie, however, Cage sang "She Loves You" to Turner with one teeny-weenie revision of his own: He changed the line she provided, the Beatles' classic "Yeah Yeah Yeah," to the more traditional rock 'n' roll phrase, "Woe Woe Woe!" When Turner heard how he had changed the classic lyrics, she cringed — Cage had missed the whole point and, not taking her "Yeah Yeah Yeah" suggestion, would not become famous after all.

The primary idea of the scene was that "Yeah Yeah Yeah" was the hook that made the Beatles famous. Unlikely. But the scene's secondary idea was that Cage's character, existing as he did in the pre-Beatles, pre-1964 rock 'n' roll dark ages, rejected "Yeah Yeah Yeah" as musically unfamiliar and odd, especially when compared to "Woe Woe Woe!"

It is true that the Beatles made "Yeah Yeah Yeah" a household word — with adults. Remember, in rock 'n' roll's first decade, only *kids* were into the music. There were no television shows like "Entertainment Tonight" to expose adults to rock lyrics, and certainly no MTV to bring rock 'n' roll into the living room. Except for the afterschool "Bandstand," rock 'n' roll was more of a bedroom music, something kids listened to on transistor radios while doing homework. And to kids, deeply into rock 'n' roll, not only the word "yeah," but also the phrase "Yeah Yeah Yeah," was already a household word.

To adults including parents and reporters of the 1960s, and to kids of the '80s, '70s, and the late '60s, it appeared then and now that the "Yeah" phrase sprang spontaneously from the brilliant joint consciousness of the Lennon-McCartney composing team.

To the kids of the '50s and early '60s, the phrase was as familiar as Popsicles and Cherry Cokes.

The Roots of "Yeah Yeah Yeah"

A review of pre–Beatles rock 'n' roll supports the notion that "Yeah Yeah Yeah" was a standard rock 'n' roll refrain well before "She Loves You" raised people's awareness of it. The following review includes 45s and LPs, and identified 144 recordings which used some form of the phrase "Yeah Yeah Yeah" before "She Loves You." Sometimes the "Yeah Yeah Yeah" in these older songs sounds quite different from the way the Beatles used it. Different rhythms, musical styles, cultural backgrounds, and accents make "Yeah Yeah Yeah" come out in many forms. Sometimes it came out as "Yeah Yeah Yeah Yeah." Still, between 1951 and 1964, "Yeah Yeah Yeah" was used in a minimum of 144 records before the Beatles had a U.S. hit with "She Loves You." All 144 recordings are listed chronologically in the Appendices.

This list of "Yeah Yeah Yeah" songs shows a clear trend up to 1963, as shown in the "Yeah Graph." In the whole of the 1950s up through 1958, only 14 songs were found that had the "Yeah" phrase. For the next three years the occurrence of "Yeah" songs was much greater each year, with 14 found in 1959, 14 in 1960, and 24 in 1961. Then, suddenly, "Yeah Yeah Yeah" took off in popularity, with 31 songs in 1962 and a whopping 48 in 1963.

One point is clear: Peggy Sue's boyfriend would not have found "Yeah Yeah Yeah" unusual or unacceptable in the pre–Beatles '60s. When the Beatles used the phrase, they were riding a wave of the lyric's popularity, not innovating a rock 'n' roll refrain. Moreover, while "Yeah Yeah Yeah" was a great hook for "She Loves You," it was probably not the magical touch that pushed the Beatles over the top and in the movie it would not necessarily have pushed Cage's character's musical career over the top. The Beatles' use of the phrase is not notable. What would have been notable in 1963 would have been if the Beatles had not used a lot of "Yeah Yeah Yeahs!"

"Yeah Yeah Yeah" Recordings

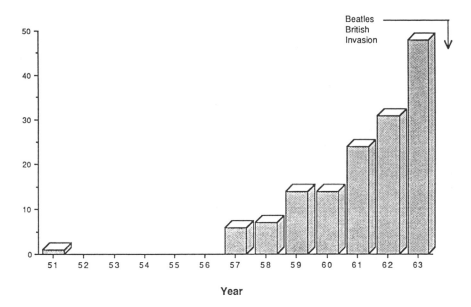

The number of "Yeah Yeah Yeah" occurrences before the Beatles' "She Loves You."

A second point is perfectly clear: Great as the Beatles, Lennon-McCartney, and "She Loves You" were, they did not invent "Yeah Yeah Yeah." Nor did they introduce "Yeah Yeah Yeah" into rock 'n' roll. They didn't even popularize the phrase. Instead, what they did do was to expose adults, the press, and perhaps subsequent generations of rock 'n' rollers to "Yeah Yeah Yeah." And in the process, it was turned into the Beatles' own refrain. But they were just the most famous in a long line of artists, 99 percent of whom were American, who used the phrase routinely.

Which raises the question: If "Yeah Yeah Yeah" was not original with the Beatles, then what songs are likely candidates to have exposed the Beatles to the phrase and thereby inspired them to sing it? It is impossible to know for sure. It could have been a British (or French or German) song, an LP cut, a flip side, or a live performance. But we can look at the known American artists who sang "Yeah Yeah Yeah" before the Beatles, see what year these pre–Beatles "Yeah Yeah Yeah" songs were recorded, and examine how popular they all were in the U.S. and England. This can give some clues as to which records were likely to have been heard by the Beatles. However, it cannot be conclusive.

Category 1. Each of these 23 "Yeah Yeah Yeah" songs made the U.S. Top 10 before "She Loves You" was popular in the states (January 25, 1964):

Song	Artist	Rank	Date
"All Shook Up"	Elvis Presley	#1	3/57
"Boys"	Shirelles (flip side of "Will You Love Me Tomorrow")	#1	11/60
"Quarter to Three"	U.S. Bonds	#1	5/61
"The Duke of Earl"	Gene Chandler	#1	1/62
"Good Luck Charm"	Elvis Presley	#1	3/62
"Locomotion"	Little Eva	#1	6/62
"Fingertips"	Little Stevie Wonder	#1	6/63
"My Boyfriend's Back"	Angels	#1	6/63
"Sugar Shack"	Jimmy Gilmer and the Fireballs	#1	9/63
"You Can't Sit Down"	Dovells	#3	4/63
"Da Do Ron Ron"	Crystals	#3	6/63
"If I Had a Hammer"	Trini Lopez	#3	7/63
"Volare"	Bobby Rydell	#4	7/60
"Loop-De-Loop"	Johnny Thunder	#4	12/62
"Party Lights"	Claudine Clark	#5	6/62
"Her Royal Majesty"	James Darren	#6	2/62
"Mocking Bird"	Inez Foxx	#7	6/63
"Don't Say Nothin' Bad About My Baby"	Cookies	#7	3/63
"Let's Get Together"	Hayley Mills	#8	9/61
"The One Who Really Loves You"	Mary Wells	#8	3/62
"Little Diane"	Dion	#8	7/62
"You Got What It Takes"	Marve Johnson	#10	11/59
"Love Came to Me"	Dion	#10	11/62

Category 2. Each of these 33 "Yeah Yeah Yeah" songs made the U.S. Top 40 before "She Loves You" appeared.

Song	Artist	Rank	Date
"Alone"	Shepherd Sisters	#20	9/57
"Crazy Love"	Paul Anka	#15	4/58
"I'm a Man"	Fabian	#31	1/59
"First Name Initial"	Annette	#32	11/59
"If I Can't Have You"	Etta and Harvey	#12	9/60
"Twistin' USA"	Danny and the Juniors	#27	9/60
"Hucklebuck"	Chubby Checker	#14	10/60
"Story of My Love"	Paul Anka	#16	1/61
"Little Devil"	Neil Sedaka	#11	6/61
"The Mountain's High"	Dick and Dee Dee	#2	8/61
"Big John"	Shirelles	#21	10/61
"School Is In"	U.S. Bonds	#28	10/61
"Everlovin'"	Ricky Nelson	#16	11/61
"Multiplication"	Bobby Darin	#30	12/61
"Do the New Continental"	Dovells	#37	1/62
"Twistin' Matilda (and the channel)"	Jimmy Soul	#22	3/62

Song	Artist	Rank	Date
"The Alvin Twist"	Chipmunks	#40	3/62
"Uptown"	Crystals	#13	5/62
"Dancin' Party"	Chubby Checker	#12	6/62
"That Stranger Used to Be My Girl"	Trade Martin	#26	10/62
"Hotel Happiness"	Brook Benton	#13	11/62
"Comin' Home Baby"	Mel Torme	#36	11/62
"He's Sure the Boy I Love"	Crystals	#11	1/63
"Call on Me"	Bobby "Blue" Bland	#22	1/63
"Let's Turkey Trot"	Little Eva	#20	2/63
"Hot Pastrami"	Dartells	#11	4/63
"Come and Get These Memories"	Martha and the Vandellas	#29	4/63
"Killer Joe"	Rocky Fellers	#16	5/63
"If My Pillow Could Talk"	Connie Francis	#23	5/63
"The Kind of Boy You Can't Forget"	Raindrops	#17	8/63
"A Love So Fine"	Chiffons	#40	9/63
"Can I Get a Witness"	Marvin Gaye	#22	10/63
"Kansas City"	Trini Lopez	#23	11/63

Category 3. Each of these 26 "Yeah Yeah Yeah" songs made the U.S. Top 100 before "She Loves You."

Song	Artist	Rank	Date
"Yea Yea"	Kendall Sisters	#73	3/58
"Jeannie Jeannie Jeannie"	Eddie Cochran	#94	3/58
"True True Happiness"	Johnny Tillotson	#54	8/59
"A Year Ago Tonight"	Crests	#42	12/59
"Shortnin' Bread"	Paul Chaplain and His Emeralds	#82	8/60
"Whole Lotta Shakin' Goin' On"	Chubby Checker	#42	10/60
"Twistin' and Kissin'"	Fabian	#91	11/60
"The Continental Walk"	The Rollers	#80	4/61
"Temptation"	Everly Brothers	#27	6/61
"Mr. Happiness"	Johnny Maestro	#57	7/61
"Twisting U.S.A."	Chubby Checker	#68	12/61
"Duchess of Earl"	Pearlettes	#96	3/62
"Walk on with the Duke"	Duke of Earl	#91	4/62
"Thou Shalt Not Steal"	John D. Loudermilk	#73	4/62
"Hit Record"	Brook Benton	#45	5/62
"Lolita Ya-Ya"	Ventures	#61	8/62
"Stubborn Kind of Fellow"	Marvin Gaye (1st Hit)	#46	10/62
"Locking Up My Heart"	Marvelettes	#44	3/63
"He's Got the Power"	Exciters	#57	3/63
"I Got a Woman"	Ricky Nelson	#49	3/63
"What a Guy"	Raindrops	#41	4/63

Song	Artist	Rank	Date
"Come Go with Me"	Dion	#48	6/63
"Yeh-Yeh!"	Mongo Santamaria	#92	6/63
"A Breath Taking Guy"	Supremes	#75	7/63
"That Boy John"	Raindrops	#64	11/63
"Do-Wah-Diddy"	Exciters	#78	1/64

Category 4. Each of these 28 "Yeah Yeah Yeah" songs was a nonhit single released before "She Loves You."

Song	Artist	Date
"Alone"	Brother Sisters	1957
"Whenever You're Ready"	Bob Luman	1957
"My Baby's Gone"	Johnnie and Joe	1957
"Steady"	Steve Lawrence	1957
"Sweet Baby Doll"	Johnny Burnette	1958
"A Boy and a Girl"	Shepherd Sisters	1958
"Boogie Woogie Feelin'"	Tony Cassanova	1959
"Heartaches of Sweet 16"	Kathy Linden	1959
"The Switch"	Bobby Please and the Pleasers	1959
"These Lonely Tears"	Little Joe Cook	1959
"Cutie Pie"	Johnny Tillotson	1960
"Robot Man"	Jamie Horton	1960
"Suzie Jane"	Ron Holden	1960
"Big John"	Carol and Anthony	1960
"Baggy Pants"	Jan and Dean	1961
"Tell Me Mama"	Janie Grant	1961
"Vacation Time"	Johnny Maestro	1961
"Pin the Tail on the Donkey"	Paul Peek	1961
"Olds-Mo-Williams"	Paul Peek	1961
"Locomotion Twist"	Oliver and the Twisters	1961
"I Want a Love I Can See"	Temptations	1962
"Daddy"	Debbie and the Darnels	1962
"I Dig This Station"	Gary U.S. Bonds	1962
"He's Braggin'"	The Tip Tops	1963
"What I Gotta Do to Make You Jealous?"	Little Eva	1963
"The Trouble With Boys"	Little Eva	9/63
"The Ghoul in School"	Fortunes	1963
"Over Yonder"	Appalachians	1963

Category 5. Each of these 15 "Yeah Yeah Yeah" songs was an LP cut released before "She Loves You."

Song	Artist	Date
"Some Kind of Nut"	Danny and the Juniors	1958
"Do the Mashed Potatoes"	Danny and the Juniors	1958

Song	Artist	Date
"Fever"	Ray Peterson	1959
"I Sympathize with You"	Conway Twitty	1959
"Poetry in Motion"	Bobby Vee	1960
"Stewball"	Coasters	1961
"Patricia"	Ray Peterson	1961
"Counting Teardrops"	Barry Mann	1962
"Rabian, Teenage Idol"	Bobby "Boris" Pickett	1962
"Even Though You Can't Dance"	Raindrops	1963
"When the Boy's Happy"	Raindrops	1963
"One Last Kiss"	Bobby Rydell	1963
"What a Party"	Freddy Cannon	1963
"What's Happening"	Major Lance	1963
"He's Braggin'"	The Orlons	1963

Category 6. These 5 songs were "Yeah Yeah Yeah" flip sides released before "She Loves You."

Song	Artist	Rank	Date
"School Days" (Flip side of "The Class")	Chubby Checker	#38	5/59
"Twist and Shout" (Flip side of "Always Late [Why Lead Me On]")	Top Notes	–	7/61
"The Conservative" (Flip side of "Don't Hang Up")	The Orlons	#4	10/62
"Lover Boy" (Flip side of "Do the Bird")	Dee Dee Sharp	#10	3/63
"I Want a Boy for My Birthday" (Flip side of "Will Power")	Cookies	#72	7/63

Category 7. These 2 recordings were "Yeah Yeah Yeah" songs in England by British artists before "She Loves You" was recorded (July 1, 1963):

Song	Artist		Rank	Date
"Tall Paul"	Barry Sisters		–	1/59
"Walkin' Back to Happiness"	Helen Shapiro	UK	#1	9/61

Category 8. Each of these 34 songs featured "Yeah Yeah Yeah" and was recorded in the U.S. approximately 18 months before "She Loves You" was popular in the U.S.

Song	Artist	Rank	Date
"Counting Teardrops"	Barry Mann	—	1962
"Rabian, Teenage Idol"	Bobby "Boris" Pickett	—	1962
"The Conservative"	Orlons	#4	10/62
(Flip side of "Don't Hang Up")			
"I Want a Love I Can See"	Temptations	—	1962
"Her Royal Majesty"	James Darren	#6	2/62
"The Alvin Twist"	Chipmunks	#40	3/62
"Twistin' Matilda"	Jimmy Soul	#22	3/62
(and the channel)			
"Thou Shalt Not Steal"	John D. Loudermilk	#73	4/62
"Uptown"	Crystals	#13	5/62
"Hit Record"	Brook Benton	#45	5/62
"Locomotion"	Little Eva	#1	6/62
"Party Lights"	Claudine Clark	#5	6/62
"Little Diane"	Dion	#8	7/62
"Stubborn Kind of Fellow"	Marvin Gaye (1st Hit)	#46	10/62
"Hotel Happiness"	Brook Benton	#13	11/62
"Comin' Home Baby"	Mel Torme	#36	11/62
"Loop-De-Loop"	Johnny Thunder	#4	12/62
"The Sweetest Boy"	Kittens	—	1963
"He's Sure the Boy I Love"	Crystals	#11	1/63
"Call on Me"	Bobby "Blue" Bland	#22	1/63
"Let's Turkey Trot"	Little Eva	#20	2/63
"He's Braggin'"	The Tip Tops	—	3/63
"He's Got the Power"	Exciters	#57	3/63
"Lover Boy"	Dee Dee Sharp	#10	3/63
(Flip side of "Do the Bird")			
"Killer Joe"	Rocky Fellers	#16	5/63
"If My Pillow Could Talk"	Connie Francis	#23	5/63
"He's Braggin'"	The Orlons	—	6/63
"Fingertips"	Little Stevie Wonder	#1	6/63
"Da Do Ron Ron"	Crystals	#3	6/63
"Yeh-Yeh!"	Mongo Santamaria	#92	6/63
"My Boyfriend's Back"	Angels	#1	6/63
"If I Had a Hammer"	Trini Lopez	#3	7/63
"Kansas City"	Trini Lopez	#23	11/63
"Do-Wah-Diddy"	The Exciters	#78	1/64

Category 9. These 18 songs were U.S. "Yeah Yeah Yeah" records which were hits in England before "She Loves You" was recorded. For each song, the date and level of its British popularity is given.

Song	Artist	Rank	Date
"You Got What It Takes"	Marve Johnson	#4	2/60
"Volare"	Bobby Rydell	#22	8/60
"Quarter to Three"	U.S. Bonds	#7	7/61
"Little Devil"	Neil Sedaka	#12	5/61
"Temptation"	Everly Brothers	#27	6/61

Song	Artist	Rank	Date
"Let's Get Together"	Hayley Mills	#11	10/61
"The Mountain's High"	Dick and Dee Dee	#37	10/61
"Jeannie Jeannie Jeannie"	Eddie Cochran	#31	11/61
"Everlovin'"	Ricky Nelson	#20	12/61
"Multiplication"	Bobby Darin	#5	1/62
"Dancin' Party"	Chubby Checker	#19	8/62
"Locomotion"	Little Eva	#2	9/62
"Comin' Home Baby"	Mel Torme	#13	1/63
"The Conservative"	The Orlons	#39	12/62
(Flip of "Don't Hang Up")			
"Her Royal Majesty"	James Darren	#26	3/62
"Let's Turkey Trot"	Little Eva	#13	3/63
"Da Do Ron Ron"	Crystals	#5	3/63
"Mocking Bird"	Inez Foxx	#36	2/63

Category 9 is highly interesting. Out of these 18 songs over one-third are considered "girl group" records. The Beatles were evidently quite taken with girl groups like the Ronnettes, and many early Beatles recordings were American girl group records. For instance, the Beatles recorded "Chains" by the Cookies, who had "Yeah Yeah Yeah" records in 1963; "Boys" by the Shirelles, who had a 1961 "Yeah Yeah Yeah" record, as well as the Marvelettes' "Please Mr. Postman"; and the Donays' "Devil in His (Her) Heart." Moreover, all of these Category 9 songs were being played in England while the Beatles were preparing to record "She Loves You."

The Beatles idolized Elvis Presley. Elvis' "Yeah Yeah Yeah" songs which were #1 records in the U.S. and the U.K. included "All Shook Up" and "Good Luck Charm." Clearly, Elvis could have inspired the Beatles right there. Chubby Checker was very big in England as he was in the states. Of all the artists contributing songs to the "Yeah Yeah Yeah" Hall of Fame, Chubby Checker had the most—five songs. His claim to the phrase is at least as good as the Beatles' and his five include only his pre–"She Loves You" recordings!

Just because all those were hits does not rule out other songs. We know the Beatles listened to many obscure American records and songs, because of some oddities that they recorded including songs which barely cracked the American charts, like Larry Williams' "Dizzy Miss Lizzie" and Little Richard's "Kansas City/Hey Hey Hey"; American LP cuts (The Shirelles' "Boys," Carl Perkins' "Honey Don't," and Buddy Holly's "Crying, Waiting, Hoping"); flip sides of hits, like Carl Perkins' "Slow Down," and Larry Williams' "Bad Boy"; flip sides of nonhits like Carl Perkins' "Match Box" and Dr. Feelgood's "Mr. Moonlight"; non–rock 'n' roll songs like Buck Owens' "Act Naturally" and Anita Bryant's "'Til There Was You"; and total obscurities like Chan Romero's "Hippy Hippy Shake" and Arthur Alexander's "Anna."

Any one of many songs or records, even ones not in the lists given here, might have exposed the Beatles to "Yeah Yeah Yeah." But there are some likely candidates in categories 1 through 9. Rather than copying any one song, the phrase was probably picked up by the Beatles as part of the customary rock 'n' roll form, along with basic guitar chords, instrumental breaks, and fade-out endings. It is doubtful that any of the Beatles now know or ever did know just where they may have picked up the phrase.

Besides the triplet, there is that heavy use the Beatles made of "Yeah," "Oh Yeah," and "Woe Yeah" on songs like "I Want to Hold Your Hand" and "Day Tripper." So many U.S. rock 'n' roll songs from the pre–Beatles era used these phrases that a list would be impractical to gather. A few examples:

"Love Came to Me" by Dion in 1962
"Oh Yeah, Maybe Baby" by the Crystals in 1962
"Tell Him" by the Exciters in 1962
"Don't Say Nothin' Bad About My Baby" by the Cookies in 1963
"Walk Like a Man" by the Four Seasons in 1963
"I'm Gonna Change Everything" by Jim Reeves (a 1962 U.S. hit and a bigger hit that year in England)

Even after all of the review and discussion about "Yeah" and "Yeah Yeah Yeah," many additional possibilities for the source of Beatles inspiration no doubt remain.

Consider Sheila, the "Ye Ye" girl (pronounced "yeah yeah") from France. Sheila used this phrase when she sang, and with it became the #1 teenage singer in France in the early '60s. She sold 2.5 million records in that small country between 1962 and 1964, and even had a U.S. hit 20 years later in 1981. Sheila (real name Annie Chancel) and her version of the "Ye Ye Ye" phrase even spawned a line of "Ye Ye Clothing." On one Sheila LP released in America ("Sheila, the Ye Ye Girl," Phillips 144) she actually performed three familiar tunes from among the 144 songs on the "Yeah Yeah Yeah" list: Brook Benton's 1962 "Hotel Happiness," the Rocky Fellers' 1963 "Killer Joe," and the Orlons' 1963 "Yeah Yeah Yeah" flip side, "Don't Hang Up." Either Sheila was directly inspired by these songs, or else "Yeah Yeah Yeah" was so common overseas in the early days of rock 'n' roll that you simply could not do an LP without running into a few "Yeah Yeah Yeah" songs.

Perhaps the most interesting of all of the pre–Beatle "Yeah Yeah Yeah" records is the original, American version of "Twist and Shout." The first hit version of "Twist and Shout" was by the Isley Brothers in 1962. When the Beatles' version became a U.S. hit the second time it was released in America, in 1964, the Isleys' original hit was ignored by radio DJs and critics alike.

As time passed, and the oldie revival of the late '60s continued to grow in the 1970s, '80s, and '90s, the Isley Brothers' version was uncovered and played again. And it was invariably billed as "the original 1962 American version of the Beatles' 1964 hit, 'Twist and Shout'."

In reality, the original American version of this classic rock 'n' roll composition was done a year before the Isleys' record. The Top Notes released a 45 on Atlantic records (Atlantic #2115) in the summer of 1961, "Always Late (Why Lead Me On)." This was a slow ballad that failed to catch on. Unnoticed on the flip side was a little up-tempo number called "Twist and Shout."

Funny thing about The Top Notes' "Twist and Shout." It has a long fade out that consists chiefly of 31 seconds of "Yeah Yeah Yeah!"

And to think that "Twist and Shout" was one of their early records that the Beatles did not sing "Yeahs" on. In any event, the Beatles certainly continued the tradition, becoming the greatest in a long line of "Yeah Yeah Yeah" singers.

"Yeah Yeah Yeah!"

The Truth Behind the Beatle Myths

Myth: The Beatles were responsible for the popularity, if not the creation, of the musical lyric "Yeah Yeah Yeah."

Reality: No doubt the Beatles during the British invasion made the phrase "Yeah Yeah Yeah" their own. But far from inventing or even popularizing the phrase, their use of it was certainly an outgrowth of the music from the late 1950s and early '60s that they had used as a model for all their recordings up to that time. It is charming to attribute this phrase to the Beatles but incorrect and unseemly to credit them with the phrase and keep perpetuating another aspect of The Beatle Myth.

As John Lennon said in an interview featured on the "Lost Lennon Tapes" radio show early in 1989, "They say we changed the music. But we used the music that was already there." The same attitude was expressed by John about the other Beatle icons.

The Beatles' long hair has been characterized as a trait original with them, explained once as the result of an accident when George Harrison rushed from a session in the pool to a show without stopping to comb his hair. Since the 1960s the popular press if not the revisionist writers have offered as fact the idea that the "Beatle haircut" was immediately accepted in 1964 and emulated by teen America.

The Beatles had long hair early on, but it was combed back, much like the hair of Elvis and other American and British teen idols. Apparently the late Stu Sutcliffe was the first Beatle to comb his hair forward, or rather his

Hamburg prostitute girlfriend wore her hair that way, and styled Stu's to match. Soon the other Beatles imitated Stu. But the haircut was already being seen in the U.S., notably on the head of young John John Kennedy, son of the late president.

American teens were not quite ready for long hair, however. For years, U.S. male rock 'n' roll stars had worn duck tail/hoody haircuts, the greaser look. But few high school boys imitated it, mostly hoods, greasers, and juvenile delinquents. For Bruce Pollock's *When Rock Was Young,* Phil of the Everly Brothers told a 1950s story about long hair on rock 'n' rollers. Phil told of the caption under a photo published in 1958 of the Everly *Brothers* and the Shepherd ("Alone") *Sisters:* "The only way to tell the difference between rock 'n' roll girls and rock 'n' roll boys is that the boys' hair is longer."

For average boys to imitate the rock 'n' rollers' styles would have been the equal of high school girls adopting Marilyn Monroe's décolletage and make-up. Even if the boys or girls had wanted to adopt the styles of the top celebrities of the day, they probably would not have had the courage to do so. Besides, their parents would never have given permission, nor would the schools' dress codes allow them to do so. At most high schools, boys' hair was not allowed to touch their eyebrows or their ears, even as late as 1970.

In that context, for teenage boys to wear Beatle haircuts in 1964 would be equal to kids wearing MTV punk orange Mohawks today—perhaps one kid in a thousand. Even college yearbooks show the same short hair in 1969 as in 1964, except on the hippies.

Myth: The Beatles created the mop-top haircut, and teen America embraced long hair immediately.

Reality: The Beatles were given the mop-top look in Hamburg, and not by a teenage fan. American kids were already on their way to wearing their hair long, but it would take another 10 years before the look was accepted and became widely worn.

Perhaps the most famous Beatle picture sleeve is for the single "I Want to Hold Your Hand" (also used for the "I'll Cry Instead" and "Can't Buy Me Love" singles). Besides the mop-top hair and Paul's lit cigarette, the Beatles' collarless suit jackets immediately caught the eye. Soon, these were called "Beatle jackets," as if the boys invented the style. In fact, since few if any kids had ever seen anyone wearing one in person, the prevailing notion was the Beatles created these jackets. And as with the haircut, in later years the idea developed that the style became popular with young men in America.

In reality the Beatles visited Paris in 1963, and their manager, Brian Epstein, got them fixed up in the latest French fashions. After all, Epstein was upper middle class and always well dressed, while the Fab Four were working class and tended to leather and denim. Much as Berry Gordy and other U.S. managers spiffed up the girl groups and teen idols in America, Epstein created a new, clean, modern image for his boys. On the "Lost Lennon Tapes" program in 1989, John said that the Beatles were not fashion originators. He said that they were emulating what was being worn by other people who they thought were cool.

One act that apparently was cool was the American rock 'n' roll duo Jan and Dean. These West Coast surfers sported the collarless look in 1963, before the Beatles. They can be seen in a press photo dated 1963 wearing what appears to be the same basic suits worn by the Beatles on their famous picture sleeve. They have the same outfits on in photos taken over Labor Day weekend in 1963, on stage in Brooklyn. One of these Jan and Dean collarless-jacket photos can be seen on the back of disk jockey Murray the K's live LP from this show, KFM Records #1001.

Myth: The Beatles originated the collarless suit jacket, and American teens adopted it.

Reality: As with the "Beatle haircut" and the refrain "Yeah Yeah Yeah," the Beatles were not originators or even popularizers, but emulators, and very few American teens in turn emulated their extreme styles.

Another famous Beatles photo was on the back of their premier U.S. Capitol Records LP, *Meet the Beatles*. This photo was taken at the same session as the "I Want to Hold Your Hand" sleeve photo; they are wearing the same collarless suit jackets. However, this photo is full length, and the Beatles are standing. Since their pre–bell bottom slacks are very tight and short, their footgear is clearly visible. They are wearing black leather, high-heeled, ankle-height boots, also purchased in Paris. These immediately became known as "Beatle boots," again with the implication that the Beatles were fashion originators.

Returning to Jan and Dean, on their 1962 Liberty Records *Golden Hits* LP cover photo, their footgear can be clearly seen, and are the same black leather high-heeled, ankle-height boots worn some two years later by the Beatles. Long before the Beatles were photographed wearing these boots, they were commonly worn by celebrities, and could be (but seldom were) purchased in stores across the United States. Perhaps one high school boy in 300 actually wore them.

Myth: The Beatles originated the style that became known as "Beatle boots," which became instantly popular with American teens.

Reality: The Beatles bought footgear which had been available for some time and worn for quite a while by U.S. entertainers, in order to be cool. The style never caught on in the states.

Another part of the Beatle myth is that they were responsible for a repopularization of the self-contained combo as the main unit of American teen music. As a four-member combo, they were heralded for returning rock 'n' roll to its original, "pure" form, disdaining the extra frills like the strings employed by, for example, the teen idols. As legend had it, in the early days Buddy Holly's Crickets, Bill Haley and his Comets, and other self-contained artists, who each did all their own singing and instrumental accompaniment, predominated. Then, in the early '60s, there developed a reliance on studio musicians and background singers, and singers who did not play instruments. Finally, the Beatles and the British invasion groups rescued American teens from the untalented singers and their nameless supporting players and restored the self-contained group to prominence, in fact making it almost mandatory for a group to be self-contained if they were to be respected and to have hits.

This part of the myth is perhaps the shakiest of all. In the first place, most of the early artists the Beatles idolized and emulated, such as Elvis, Chuck Berry, Little Richard, and Larry Williams, were not "self-contained groups." Even the Crickets never sang on any Buddy Holly records. Nameless, or at least unnamed groups like the Picks and the Roses did the background singing on Holly records, which on later hits featured violins.

In the second place, many of the invasion artists themselves were not self-contained. For example, the Beatles used violins on "Yesterday" and "Michelle"; Peter and Gordon, Chad and Jeremy, David and Jonathon, and the Bachelors played only a fraction of the instruments heard on their recordings. Many invasion group singers did not play instruments in their groups, including Billy J., Peter Noone, Mick Jagger, Freddie Garrity (...and the Dreamers), and Denis D'Ell, vocalist for the Honeycombs.

It turns out that there were already many self-contained groups having big hits in the states just prior to the Beatles British invasion. A list of the self-contained American groups with Top-10 hits in the early 1960s shows many such artists, with the number growing as the invasion neared:

1961

Highwaymen	Rosie and the Originals
String-a-Longs	Troy Shondell
Mar-Keys	

1962

Four Seasons	Dave "Baby" Cortez
Joey Dee & Starlighters	Billy Joe and the Checkmates
Booker T. and the M.G.s	Peter, Paul & Mary

1963

Kingsmen	Surfaris
Jimmy Gilmer and the Fireballs	Beach Boys
Four Seasons	Chautay's (sic)

Rockin' Rebels
Kingston Trio
Village Stompers

Peter, Paul & Mary
Rooftop Singers

Fourth, after the Beatles invasion, the number of American self-contained groups did not exactly skyrocket, but followed the upward trend that had been building for the entire decade.

1964

Beach Boys
Four Seasons
Marketts
Rip Chords

Trashmen
Ronny & Daytonas
Rivieras
Ventures

1965

Byrds
Beach Boys
McCoys
Sam the Sham and the Pharaohs
Four Seasons
Junior Walker and the All Stars

Kingsmen
Gentrys
Ramsey Lewis Trio
Turtles
Beau Brummels
Lovin' Spoonful

1966

Lovin' Spoonful
Tommy James & Shondells
? and the Mysterians
Beach Boys
Young Rascals
Royal Guardsmen
Sam the Sham and the Pharaohs
Cyrcle
Mitch Ryder and the Detroit Wheels

Los Bravos
Paul Revere and the Raiders
The Outsiders
Count Five
Syndicate of Sound
Bobby Fuller Four
Four Seasons
Shadows of Knight

Fifth, the Motown explosion of the 1960s was fully of highly respected groups that were not self-contained either vocally or instrumentally, and almost none of whom played instruments.

Myth: The early 1960s saw non–instrument playing singers with studio backup replacing the 1950s self-contained groups, but the Beatles and the invasion groups not only were all self-contained instrument playing artists, but made the form de rigueur in the United States.

Reality: Many respected '50s artists did not play much and were not self-contained units; the same applied to many British groups. But in the early '60s, prior to the Beatles invasion, the self-contained combo was already a trend on the rise.

There are two other "Beatle firsts" which are a part of the Beatle myth. One was started inexplicably in the fall of 1965, the other even less explicably in the mid-1980s when MTV presented their first annual music video awards.

The 1965 myth popped up when the Beatles released the single "Yesterday" at the end of the summer. This was the first time that the Beatles had used string instruments that were not electric guitars. Producer George Martin had suggested using classical instruments such as the viola. When this new sound—new for the Beatles at any rate—was heard, it was hailed as a breakthrough in the rock 'n' roll field.

Ironic! In 1964, the Beatles were heralded for returning rock 'n' roll to its combo roots, sans frills like strings, which it had in reality never left. A year later, the same Beatles were hailed as innovators for introducing a string section to rock 'n' roll!

Documenting the many rock 'n' roll hits using strings which predate the Beatles would be impossible. To name a few—Ray Peterson's 1960 "Corinna, Corinna," the Drifters' 1960 "Save the Last Dance for Me," the Skyliners' 1959 "Since I Don't Have You," Little Willie John's 1960 "Sleep," Buddy Holly's 1959 "It Doesn't Matter Any More," and the Crystals' 1962 "He's a Rebel" all used violins. In their early days, the Beatles even copied, sans strings, an early U.S. recording which used them, "Anna (Go to Him)" from 1962.

Carl Belz, in his otherwise fine book *The Story of Rock,* admitted that many other rock 'n' rollers had previously employed strings, but stated that the Beatles' use of strings in an almost "classical" way *was* new. Belz was wrong. A year before "Yesterday," a song called "When It's Over" was released by Jan and Dean. The flip side of their 1964 hit "Sidewalk Surfin'," "When It's Over" did chart in the Midwest. The LP it came off was full of strings, oboes, a harp, French horns, and other "classical" instruments. To cement the point, the same month that the Beatles' "Yesterday" single was released in America, an LP titled *Jan and Dean's Pop Symphony No. 1* also came out. For this unique LP, college-trained musician Jan Berry arranged and conducted 12 instrumental versions of Jan and Dean hits and LP cuts dating back to the '50s. These were so effective that when a classmate of this writer played an excerpt for his high school chorus teacher, the teacher actually thought it was Beethoven. Besides, the LP was featured numerous times on KXTR-FM, the classical music station in Kansas City.

Myth: The Beatles introduced strings to rock 'n' roll in 1965 with their beautiful hit, "Yesterday."

Reality: Apparently the U.S. adult population and press, who had never heard or anyway listened to rock 'n' roll before 1964, heard the beautiful single "Yesterday" and were impressed at what they thought was a Beatles innovation—string instruments. In fact, countless rock 'n' roll records had already used violins, including "classical" string sections. The Beatles' use of strings was not an innovation in music, but evidently it was a revelation to adults.

The mid-1980s MTV myth was a real boner. At their first annual awards ceremony, a special award was given to the Beatles for their film *A Hard Day's Night* for being the first music video.

What a gaff! There were many, many music videos filmed before *A Hard Day's Night*. A review of four that are easily viewable now on television reruns or obtainable on tape will illustrate this point.

Ozzie Nelson produced a 1961 music video for his son Ricky's song "Travelin' Man," using stock footage superimposition of girls from around the world. When Paul Peterson sang "She Can't Find Her Keys" on "The Donna Reed Show" in 1962, his girlfriend was seen to pull everything from a fire hydrant, an ash can, a television set, and an electric fan from her normal-sized purse. Jan and Dean filmed a color "Surf City" music video for a summer replacement television series in 1963, available on Media Home Entertainment's videotape *Surfin' Beach Party*. The "Surf City" video was shot on location and includes such now standard music video techniques as smoke, scantily clad girls, sight gags, speeded up film, freeze frame, film run backwards, people turning into surfboards, and other special film effects and gags.

And in the Big Band era, music films, one brand of which was named "Soundies," were produced which were music videos utilizing fantasy, rapid cutting, superimposition, and other modern-looking special effects. These were played in theaters, and in special film/audio juke boxes. One of the best from this era is "Deep Purple" by Helen Forrest and Artie Shaw, circa 1940, available on *Best of the Big Bands* from Video Yesteryear in Connecticut. The video begins with the Shaw band with vocalist Forrest performing the song, but quickly fades to a scene of an elderly lady sitting alone in a garden. Sensing a presence, she looks up just in time to see her lost beau from her youth materialize, still youthful in top hat and tails after all these years. He smiles lovingly at her. Following a few moments of astonishment, she somehow herself transforms to a youthful girl, and runs to embrace him. As they talk and kiss, the old woman suddenly reappears and watches the young couple consisting of her youthful self and her lost love of yesteryear. Finally, the beau looks at his pocket watch, says it's time to go, and after a long last kiss, walks away through the solid garden wall as he dematerializes. The young girl watches him depart, herself in turn being watched by the old woman version of herself. Finally, the young girl dissolves, the lonely old woman hangs her head in sad regret over lost opportunities of youth, and the video returns to the bandstand.

Myth: The Beatles invented the music video with *A Hard Day's Night*.

Reality: The Beatles were, in 1964, the latest in a line of hundreds, possibly thousands of musical entertainers who filmed sketches illustrating their hit songs.

The Beatles were the biggest act since Elvis. They were important and influential. But neither boots, long hair, collarless jackets, strings on records, music videos, nor the phrase "Yeah Yeah Yeah" were originated or popularized by the Fab Four.

Chapter 4
The Beatles vs. the Teen Idols

Elvis and Those Who Came After

By far the most successful solo hitmaker in the history of rock 'n' roll was Elvis Presley. So it was natural that comparisons between the boy from Memphis and the boys from Liverpool were made back in 1964. The controversy began as soon as the Beatles began their ascent to superstardom in the United States, when kids who loved Elvis began to resent the fact that the attention which had up to then been reserved for Elvis began to be heaped on the Beatles.

When people began to call the Beatles "the Greatest," Elvis fans who had never heard that phrase used about anyone except the King felt threatened. Soon, many magazines and radio stations began having reader and listener polls to see which artist was bigger.

What was even more interesting to rock 'n' roll fans who liked Elvis and the Beatles was the coattail effects each had on rock 'n' roll. In the wake of Elvis' huge popularity in the 1950s, the rock 'n' roll teen idol was born. All of a sudden, there were lots of good looking, young, slightly hoody male singers who appealed to teenaged, usually female, record buyers.

The classic example of the Elvis-inspired teen idol was the late Ricky Nelson. The story has been told many times about the evening when a girl Ricky was dating swooned over an Elvis record on the radio, and Ricky boasted that he was making a record, too. He had already impersonated Elvis on an episode of his family's television sitcom, "The Adventures of Ozzie and Harriet." Within a week he made his boast come true with a hit record million-seller cover version of Fats Domino's "I'm Walkin'."

Many other teen idols came from slightly different roots. For example, Bobby Vee grew up on country music and liked Elvis. When Bobby Vee recorded his first big hit, "Devil or Angel," his roots would have seemed to be rhythm and blues. Except for one thing—he had never even heard of the Clovers' original R & B version of "Devil or Angel." Bobby Vee got his break filling in for Buddy Holly in concert the day Holly died, and for years sang in a Holly style. In turn, Buddy Holly had been strongly influenced by

Elvis, even imitating some of the King's vocal stylings and singing Elvis songs like "Baby, I Don't Care." Much of the Elvis influence on Holly was disguised by the vastly different voices they possessed, but Holly was still a "junior Elvis."

For Holly, Vee and the other teen idols, the situation wasn't so much one of being outright Elvis imitators as it was following a trail Elvis has blazed, and being accepted by the public, either consciously or unconsciously, because of their resemblance to Elvis.

The Beatles and Those Who Came After

When the Beatles took America by storm early in 1964, the Elvis/teen idol phenomenon was repeated, this time in the form of the Beatles/British invasion. The Beatles, like Elvis before, blazed a trail for similar artists to follow. Very soon, junior Beatles began to appear, from the Dave Clark Five to Peter and Gordon. Many people thought that it was British music per se that was taking the states by storm. But that was not the case. Solo male British rock 'n' roll superstars like Marty Wilde and Cliff Richard didn't catch on. Hugely popular British female solo singing stars like Cilla Black and Helen Shapiro failed to sell records in the United States. No, it was the junior Beatles, or at least groups perceived as junior Beatles, who were accepted by U.S. teens, much as the junior Elvises had been during the previous decade.

In a spirit of fairness, and to give the artists the dignity that is their due, junior Elvis/teen idols will be referred to as "male mainstays," and junior Beatles will be called British invasion groups.

Male Mainstays

The male mainstays could be depended upon. At any given time, they would each have a record (or two, or even a two-sided hit record) on the charts. You could count on it. In the late 1950s and early '60s you could listen to the radio for a couple of hours, and you would invariably hear a song by each of them before long. The male mainstays were so integral to radio programming that the kids almost took them for granted. There was always the "new" Bobby Rydell record coming out, or the "latest" record by Neil Sedaka. They turned out hit after hit after hit after hit. To the kids of the era, these singers *were* rock 'n' roll.

While rock 'n' roll, with its male mainstays, was taking hold with teenagers, the adults still listened to the pop artists, many of whom had been with the big bands of their youth. Two very different musical styles existed side by side, with the older pop form being more accepted. When the new music, rock 'n' roll, came into being in 1955, no serious critic cast aspersions on Frank Sinatra's worth just because Bill Haley and His Comets began having hits. No one criticized the Dorseys for not adopting the new musical style when the Platters and the Penguins made the charts. And no one discounted Bing Crosby's talent when Elvis Presley came into his own. Kids may not have cared for the older artists' music, and their parents may have felt rock 'n' roll was a passing fad, but that was a matter of taste, not of absolute worth.

In turn, when Bobby Vee, Paul Anka, Bobby Darin, and Ricky Nelson came along, no one used the success of these artists to belittle the musical careers of those earlier rockers such as Bill Haley, the Platters, the Penguins, or Elvis.

Yet, for reasons never completely made clear, amid the mid-1960s popularity of the Beatles and the other British bands, the music of the male mainstays was denigrated, and their hit records, success, and importance were all but erased from rock 'n' roll history. In fact, many rock 'n' roll histories skip from the death of Buddy Holly in 1959 to the emergence in America of the Beatles in 1964, as if millions and millions of rock 'n' roll records were not bought by kids in the period of 1959 through 1963.

The Beatles and British invasion artists are the topic of this book, and their success has been thoroughly reviewed in the preceding chapters. Before a discussion contrasting the male mainstays with the British invasion artists can proceed, some information on the American singers is in order. To that end, a list of male mainstay/teen idols was compiled. The criteria used to compile the list were: young, 1960s, rock 'n' roll singer, solo artist, a hoody, greaser haircut, and not primarily a pop, country, opera, rockabilly, rhythm 'n' blues, or soul singer. The criterion for "hit" was a song to make Billboard's Top 100 between 1955 and 1978. The following 17 artists had a total of 490 hits, averaging 29 apiece. An asterisk denotes those who were also primarily songwriters.

Name	First Hit	Last Hit	# of Hits
Ricky Nelson	1957	1973	53
Paul Anka	1957	1977	51*
Bobby Vinton	1962	1977	43
Bobby Darin	1959	1973	41*
Bobby Vee	1959	1970	38
Dion Di Muci	1958	1968	32*
Bobby Rydell	1959	1965	29
Neil Sedaka	1960	1977	29*
Jimmie Rodgers	1957	1967	25
Johnny Tillotson	1960	1965	25
Gene Pitney	1961	1969	24*

Name	*First Hit*	*Last Hit*	*# of Hits*
Frankie Avalon	1959	1962	24
Brian Hyland	1960	1971	22
Tommy Roe	1962	1973	22*
Jimmy Clanton	1958	1969	12*
James Darren	1971	1977	10
Fabian	1959	1960	10

Seventeen male mainstays are listed. Many more stars could have been included in this definition. A few examples: Vic Dana (15 hits), Roy Orbison (30 hits), Frank Gari (3 hits), Buddy Holly (11 hits), Johnny Burnette (5 hits) or Paul Peterson (6 hits). Some discographers might have included Chubby Checker (31 hits) and Del Shannon (16 hits). Instead, here only the 17 *classic* teen idols were listed, with no blacks, country-oriented artists, and rock 'n' roll pop singers included.

In the wake of the subsequent immense popularity of the Beatles and the British invasion groups, the male mainstays have been alternately maligned and forgotten by the music business and by rock historians, if not by their fans. However, Ricky Nelson and his peers — Tommy Roe, Bobby Vee, Bobby Rydell, Buddy Holly, Paul Anka, Bobby Vinton, Frankie Avalon, Neil Sedaka, Dion, and others — were the superstars of their day, the male mainstays of the golden decade of rock 'n' roll. Some, like Bobby Vinton, sang only rock 'n' roll ballads. Others sang many rockers, like Frankie Avalon's "Ginger Bread" and "DeDe Dinah" (1958), Gene Pitney's "It Hurts to Be in Love" (1964) and "(I Wanna) Love My Life Away" (1961), Dion's "The Wanderer" and "Runaround Sue" (both 1961), and Neil Sedaka's "Little Devil" (1961) and "Calendar Girl" (1960).

The myth that teen idol/male mainstay careers were ended by the Beatles British invasion is exploded. Not one of their careers ended in the year of the Beatles British invasion, 1964, and only one had his career end the next year, in 1965.

Now that we have seen the extent of the careers of the male mainstays, the easiest way to evaluate their impact on the music business is to compare their recording successes with those of the invasion groups.

The Invasion "Mainstays"

A list was compiled of all of the male British invasion artists of two or more members, and the number of Billboard Top-100 hits each had between 1964 and 1978, the outside limits of the original British invasion. None of the classic invasion artists was left out. Only the female singers like Cilla Black, Pet Clark, and Sandie Shaw, and the "British teen idols" like

Matt Monroe, Frank Ifield, and Billy Fury, were excluded. The following 22 artists had a total of 314 hits for an average of 14. Again, asterisks denote those who were also songwriters.

Name	First Hit	Last Hit	# of Hits
Beatles	1964	1970	65*
Rolling Stones	1964	1978	39*
Dave Clark Five	1964	1967	24*
Hollies	1966	1975	21*
Herman's Hermits	1965	1968	19
Animals	1964	1978	18*
Kinks	1964	1978	16*
Searchers	1964	1971	14
Moody Blues	1965	1978	13
Peter and Gordon	1964	1967	12
Chad and Jeremy	1964	1965	11*
Gerry and the Pacemakers	1964	1966	11*
Manfred Mann	1964	1977	9
Bachelors	1964	1977	9
Fortunes	1965	1971	6
Billy J. Kramer with the Dakotas	1964	1965	6
Freddie and the Dreamers	1965	1965	5
Zombies	1964	1965	5*
Wayne Fontana and the Mindbenders	1965	1966	4
Swinging Blue Jeans	1964	1964	3
Nashville Teens	1964	1965	2
Honeycombs	1964	1965	2

There are 22 artists in the British invasion list, five more than the male mainstays. Including the Beatles and the Stones, their total number of hits was 314, 170 less than the male mainstays had. More dramatically, the average British artist had just 14 hits, compared to twice as many, 28, for the male mainstays of rock 'n' roll. The teen idols averaged twice as many top 100 records as the Beatles British invasion artists did, debunking the myth that invasion artists had more successful careers.

If the Beatles and the Stones are excluded from list two, the invasion total number of hits would be just 210, or about 10 per artist, compared to 28 for the average male mainstay. Obviously, including the Beatles and the Stones adds to the invasion list.

American Mainstays — The Complete List

So, to the male mainstay list, let's add two more major male mainstays, the original teen idols, Elvis Presley and his friendly competitor, Pat Boone.

Name	First Hit	Last Hit	# of Hits
Elvis Presley	1956	1978	145
Pat Boone	1955	1969	60

When Elvis and Pat are added to the list, there are 695 teen idol hits for an average of 37 chart songs for each. With three fewer artists, the male mainstays had 324 more hits than the 314 the British invasion acts had. The relatively small cadre of male mainstays had twice as many hits as all of the British invasion artists, including the Beatles, combined.

Put another way, the fifth most popular teen idol, Bobby Vee, all by himself, had *more* hit songs than Billy J. Kramer with the Dakotas *and* the Swinging Blue Jeans *and* Wayne Fontana and the Mindbenders *and* Freddie and the Dreamers *and* the Zombies *and* the Nashville Teens *and* Manfred Mann *and* the Manfred Mann Earth Band, combined. You can add to that invasion hit list the longer list of hits of Gerry and the Pacemakers or of the Dave Clark Five or of Chad and Jeremy or of Peter and Gordon or even of the Animals or the Hermits or the entire hit list of the Kinks and you still won't have a combined list of hits equal to the hit list of the Number One most popular of the 17 male mainstays: Ricky Nelson! Not to mention Elvis.

The Comparison of LP Success

The rock revisionists might on occasion concede that some artists who preceded the Beatles British invasion, even the teen idol/male mainstays, could have out-performed the British groups when it came to 45 rpm singles. When they do, however, they are quick to add that the invasion artists placed more emphasis on LPs than 45s. The common position is that before the Beatles, LPs were unimportant and not really a part of rock 'n' roll, which until then consisted of 45s.

To examine that position another survey was completed, of LP charts, comparing the invasion groups against the male mainstays. The comparison could have been made against surf groups or some other genre, but since the male mainstays are the most commonly maligned category, and since we already looked at their 45 track records, it seemed logical to look at their LP chart track record.

Male Mainstays' LPs

Name	# of Charted LPs, 1957–72
Ricky Nelson	14
Paul Anka	10

Name	# of Charted LPs, 1957–72
Bobby Vinton	18
Bobby Darin	14
Bobby Vee	12
Dion Di Muci	8
Bobby Rydell	6
Neil Sedaka	1
Jimmie Rodgers	3
Johnny Tillotson	4
Gene Pitney	11
Frankie Avalon	2
Brian Hyland	2
Tommy Roe	6
Jimmy Clanton	0
James Darren	2

The 16 male mainstays charted a total of 115 LPs, for an average per artist of about seven. Compare this to the invasion artists' LP chartings:

Name	# of Charted LPs, 1957–72
Beatles	26
Rolling Stones	19
Dave Clark Five	13
Hollies	8
Herman's Hermits	10
Animals	13
Kinks	14
Searchers	5
Moody Blues	7
Peter and Gordon	7
Chad and Jeremy	8
Gerry and the Pacemakers	5
Manfred Mann	4
Bachelors	4
Fortunes	1
Billy J. Kramer with the Dakotas	1
Freddie and the Dreamers	1
Zombies	2
Wayne Fontana and the Mindbenders	2
Swinging Blue Jeans	1
Nashville Teens	0
Honeycombs	1

The 22 invasion artists charted a total of 152 LPs, for an average per artist of about seven LPs, matching *exactly* the number of LPs per male mainstay!

The British list includes the Beatles and the Rolling Stones, the two standout superstars of the invasion. Even with that advantage, the invasion groups' performance did not exceed the male mainstays'. Which raises the question, how would the male mainstays stack up if we included the albums of the ultimate teen idols, Elvis Presley and Pat Boone?

Name	*# of Charted LPs, 1957–72*
Elvis Presley	59
Pat Boone	14

When Elvis and Pat are added to the male mainstay listing, the total number of LPs rises to 188, with an average of about 10 per singer, compared to seven per invasion group.

It is actually pretty amazing that the male mainstays compare so favorably with the British invasion artists in terms of numbers of charted LPs. Over the decades, more and more albums have been listed on the Billboard charts. Only five positions were listed in the mid-1940s ten to 25 in the '50s, and 25 to 200 in the '60s.

The Billboard top LP chart had a 200-slot ranking in the late '60s. That meant that an LP by a British band, for instance, could be relatively unpopular in 1967 and still make the charts, say at position number 145.

By contrast, in early 1961, the LP chart had only 25 slots. That meant that an early LP from a male mainstay could be popular enough to qualify for position number 30 or 40 or 50, but never get listed because only the top 25 LPs were listed on the charts.

LPs did not suddenly get popular in 1964 when the Beatles arrived in the U.S. The size of the album charts had been increasing steadily from five positions in 1945, to 25 early in 1961, to 150 in preinvasion 1963, and to 175 and finally 200 in 1967.

Therefore, to make the comparison between all the mainstay and British artists fair, a comparison was made between the number of charted LPs each had, but only including LPs which made the top 25 rankings. In all, the 19 male mainstays had 74 top 25 LPs, for an average of 4 per artist. The 22 British invasion acts totalled 72 top 25 LPs, for a mean of only 3 per artist.

Myth: Before the Beatles British invasion, American rock 'n' roll was totally oriented to 45s, but the British artists shifted much of that orientation to the LP format for the first time.

Reality: The fact is LPs were equally important to rock 'n' roll fans before the British invasion, if not more so.

Why the Chart Comparisons

Why compare the chart success of the male mainstays and the British invasion groups? Why not simply evaluate the music?

Comparing their music really cannot be done, because music is a matter of taste. Ask a star of the Kansas City Lyric Opera who was the better singer, Bobby Vee or Gerry Marsden, or even Elvis Presley or Paul McCartney, and he'll tell you none was any good at all. Then if you ask a fan of the New York Metropolitan Opera to evaluate the Kansas City opera star, the disdain for his voice would probably be just as great. And a jazz vocalist in turn might place little value on the voice of the Met star. Comparing disparate musical styles is just too much of an apples and oranges situation.

An alternative is to compare the careers of various artists. The more popular an artist is, and the longer he or she is popular, the "better" that person is in one sense.

Besides sales during the heyday of an artist's popularity, another angle to consider is the career an artist has after the hits stop coming. The tragic New Year's Eve death of Ricky Nelson in 1985 brought Ricky's name into the fore once again. In death the images of many celebrities are elevated in the eyes of the public, and as a direct result of Rick's tragic airplane accident, Ricky (he changed his name to Rick in 1962) alone among male mainstays was inducted into the Rock and Roll Hall of Fame a month later. At the time of his death, Rick Nelson was performing over 200 shows per year, to full houses. Fabian, Bobby Rydell, Chubby Checker, Johnny Tillotson, Bobby Vee, and Frankie Avalon are also still actively touring.

Who Composes?

A final comparison can be made between the mainstays and the invasion groups: songwriting. Of the 22 British goups, nine, or 40 percent, had a substantial hand in writing their hits. Of the 17 primary male mainstays, seven had a substantial hand in writing their hits, or 41 percent.

The notion that the Beatles wrote all of their own material probably stemmed from their first successful American LP release, Capitol Records' *Meet the Beatles.* Except for the aberrational track "'Til There Was You" from Meredith Wilson's "The Music Man," all of the songs on this "debut" U.S. LP were, in fact, composed by the Beatles.

In England, however, the same LP was released with the same cover, but with a different title, *With the Beatles,* and with a different lineup of tunes. On the British LP, six of the songs were not Beatle compositions, but rather remakes of American oldies. Additionally, *With the Beatles* was the group's second British LP, not their first as in the states. Their first British LP was *Please Please Me*, and this record also included six non–Beatle compositions that were remakes of American hits.

Why Capitol choose to skip over all but one non–Beatle composition on their first U.S. LP is anyone's guess. An album of the six American songs from the first two British LPs would have been interesting. The deletion of the cover versions from *Meet the Beatles* could have been to enhance the Beatles' image, or to increase their royalty payments. If performers write the songs on their records as well as perform them, the royalties they earn will be much greater. Perhaps the Capitol executives felt that American kids would not be receptive to remakes of recent American hits, or maybe they even felt that the Beatles' versions were inferior to the American originals and would make for a weak LP. At any rate, had the original British LP been released in the U.S. unmodified, the image of the Beatles as songwriters and the impression that they "wrote all their own songs" would have certainly been less likely to have emerged. Ultimately, all of the deleted tracks were released in the U.S., but it was too late, the die was cast. Fortunately, the Beatles, especially Lennon and McCartney, did compose many beautiful songs as the years went on—and, of course, did record many more cover versions, as well.

Myth: The Beatles and British invasion acts initiated the trend of artists to write their own hits, something teen idols could not or did not do.

Reality: On a percentage basis, just as many teen idols wrote their hits as did Beatles British invasion groups.

The more popular if perhaps questionable definition of teen idol is an artist who would never have been popular, or as popular, had it not been for promoters, managers, arrangers, publicists. The incorrect, negative connotation of this is that teen idols were not talented, but were merely manufactured stars. In most cases, certainly, those support people were important in the careers of talented celebrities like Jimmy Stewart, Marilyn Monroe, and Humphrey Bogart. But if the teen idols had not had personal worth, then it would be unlikely that they would have had so many hits over three decades to become male mainstays!

A classic example often given of the manufactured teen idol is, ironically the case of Ricky Nelson. It has often been stated that his huge success was entirely due to his exposure on television's "The Adventures of Ozzie and Harriet." This caused millions of teenagers who heard his songs broadcast on the program every week to, zombielike, buy his records much as they would buy Coca-Cola instead of the store brand of cola or some other flavor of soft drink entirely. The assumption is that the massive exposure alone convinced millions of gullible teens that Ricky Nelson must be good if he was on television and that they really didn't exert any judgment before plopping down their money. This argument has three fallacies. One, most of his hits were popular before they were featured on television, and thus gained little from the television exposure. Second, many songs featured on television did not become hits, so obviously there were other factors at work. Third, other young television stars who had exposure of their records on television had miniscule musical careers . . . namely Patty Duke ("Funny Little Butterflies"), Paul Peterson ("My Dad"), and Shelley Fabares ("Johnny Angel"), to name a few.

Male Mainstays Liverpool Style

If you think about it, the biggest teen idols of all of rock 'n' roll were not Paul Anka or Ricky Nelson, but John, Paul, George, and Ringo. First of all, like all teen idols, they were inspired directly by Elvis Presley. They also had hoody haircuts. Not greaser style, but hoody nonetheless.

If ever management promoted a band into popularity, it was Brian Epstein promoting the Beatles. He moved them from bars and strip joints, and forced them literally to clean up their act. He specifically had them cut and wash their hair. He also insisted that they watch their language and smile a lot. Teen idols were always impeccably dressed. Epstein bought for the Beatles matching collarless suits, boots, and other items of dress which were all the rage in Paris at the time.

After he had the Beatles groomed to his specifications, he literally manufactured their popularity, starting when their first British single failed to make the charts in 1962. Brian bought 10,000 copies himself with his own money, simply to get them on the charts!

When the Beatles' first appearance at the London Palladium flopped, Brian had a photographer take a tight shot of a small group of girls he had asked to scream. Then he sent copies of the photo to all of the papers with a press release claiming that 5,000 screaming girls had swamped the theater.

Musically, Epstein teamed the Beatles with arranger George Martin, who put violins on the Beatles' records and, with songs like "Yesterday" and "Michelle," made them respectable enough to be accepted by parents.

The Beatles' early British hits failed when they were first released in the states in 1963. To give the Beatles a push, Capitol Records' publicists spent an unprecedented sum of $50,000 to promote Beatles music into popularity it could not attain without such promotion. The Beatles got onto the Ed Sullivan show because Epstein agreed to just one-half the fee normally paid by Sullivan to performers. In short, manager Brian Epstein, arranger George Martin, and promoters at Capitol manufactured a teen idol career for the Beatles, collectively turning them from young misfits into teen idols!

Had not Epstein ordered John Lennon to never again sing nude on stage (as he did in Hamburg in the early '60s), wearing nothing but a toilet seat hung around his neck, Ed Sullivan (the Beatles' version of Dick Clark) would never have booked them on his "reely big shew!"

None of this discussion is intended as a put-down of the Beatles or the British. Rather, it is to show that rock 'n' rollers are rock 'n' rollers, and that haircuts, clothes, publicity, and swooning girls notwithstanding, teen idol status does not mean that an artist is either untalented or unworthy. It's just part of the package. It's the music "business," after all.

Some younger music fans born after 1955 may have wondered why the media made such a fuss over Ricky Nelson's death. After all, from reading rock 'n' roll histories, one gets the impression that Rick was nothing more than a has-been, a child actor seen on an old black and white rerun sitcom. Instead of a talented male mainstay, reading about Rick would lead them to believe he had been a minor "teen idol" who had one or two hits like "Hello Mary Lou" and "Teenage Idol," before he was booed off the stage ten years later. Or they might see Ricky as someone who attempted a short-lived comeback with "Garden Party" in the early 1970s, then disappeared into nostalgic oblivion.

For those people, it is important to recognize the long-ignored fact that Rick Nelson was not only a male mainstay, he was the third most popular rock 'n' roll singer of the first 25 years of rock 'n' roll (his popularity was outstripped only by the popularity of Elvis Presley and Pat Boone). Sure he was a "teen idol," but that merely means that he was in that elite group that included both the American male mainstays and the Fab Four.

The Beatles no doubt had and still have real talent. But with the promotion, the packaging, the merchandising, the teen music magazines, the posters, and the screaming girls, the Beatles were four male mainstays. Not only that, they often attributed their own early interest in rock 'n' roll to the same guy who inspired all the teen idols — Elvis Presley.

Chapter 5

Who Won the Battle of the Beatles British Invasion?

Ask any popular music fan, and they will tell you with confidence that the British invasion was a big success. And, of course, it was. Suddenly, in 1964, there were many more British rock 'n' roll and rock acts on radio, television and records in the U.S. than there had ever been before.

The Beatles led the way. Their popularity was of unmatched proportions. They were so popular that, as everyone knows, they were the only artists in history to have ten songs on the charts at once, five of them in positions one through five on Billboard's National Top-100 chart!

Soon there were more Britishers' hits in the states than there were U.S. hits! The Dave Clark Five, Manfred Mann, the Hollies, Peter and Gordon, Chad and Jeremy, David and Jonathan, Herman's Hermits, the Rolling Stones, the Who, the Zombies, the Kinks, Billy J. Kramer with the Dakotas, even Marianne Faithfull, Sandie Shaw, and Cilla Black had some hit action in the United States in the mid-'60s.

Yes, American rock 'n' roll was blown off the radio and squeezed off the charts as the British invasion ended the career of one American act after another.

Besides taking over the U.S. rock 'n' roll scene, the British invasion ushered in the birth of a new era of rock 'n' roll, or, in the case of critics of early '60s music, perhaps as the end of the original "rock 'n' roll" era and the dawn of the modern "rock" era.

The fact of the new, young, British artists killing off the older, established U.S. teen idols and other American artists is a view very widely held, and not just by average fans of rock 'n' roll and rock. Most rock 'n' roll writers, rock critics, and even artists themselves have reported how the British invasion did a real number on the hit careers of many, if not most, of the established, traditional American artists. In their book *The Top Ten* (Simon and Schuster, 1982), Bob Gilbert and Gary Theroux discuss at length every record to make the U.S. Billboard Top 10 from 1956 to 1980. For instance, one song they highlight is Dion's "The Wanderer." They quote Dion as saying that "in 1964 the Beatles changed the pop music scene," and the authors attributed Dion's career slide in the mid-'60s to the British invasion.

Behind the Hits is an impressive tome devoted to revealing the stories "behind the hits" of popular records from 1955 on. One assumes writers Shannon and Javna's fascinating stories are true. In telling of the Strangeloves, an American group which pretended to be Australian, they gave this explanation for the group's deception: "The Brill Building, home of songwriters like Ellie Greenwich and Jeff Barry, Carole King and Gerry Goffin, Neil Sedaka and Howie Greenfield, had been the source of hundreds of hit songs in the early sixties. But in 1965, no one wanted to hear American Groups."

Another pair of writers, Bruce McColm and Doug Payne, collaborated on a book, *Where Have They Gone — Rock and Roll Stars,* updating the lives of music stars of the past. They also expound on the effect of the British invasion on traditional American rock 'n' roll artists. For example, in their discussion of Johnny Tillotson's ("Poetry in Motion") fading career in 1964, they argue for what they strongly characterize as the "devastation of the American music scene when the Beatles arrived in February of 1964." They quote Johnny Tillotson: "It was the most difficult period for the American artist to survive." He cites Bobby Vinton and Neil Diamond as the only American artists to pull through.

Similarly, McColm and Payne explain the fade of hits of the great Bobby Vee ("Take Good Care of My Baby"): "The impact and effect [of the British invasion] was immense."

Another duo, Michael Uslan and Bruce Solomon, co-authored *Dick Clark's First 25 Years of Rock & Roll* (Greenwich House, 1981). They are confident that the British invasion wiped out nearly every important established U.S. rock 'n' roll star of the 1950s and early '60s. On the Drifters ("Up on the Roof"): "After 1964, the Drifters took a back seat to the British invasion...." On Dion: "With the coming of the British rockers, most of the old-line American rock 'n' roll stars fell behind." Roy Orbison ("Oh! Pretty Woman"): "But by 1965 ... only Motown artists were effectively combating the British invasion." The superstar Shirelles ("Will You Love Me Tomorrow"): "During the British invasion, the Shirelles cut a few more albums and went back on the road, appearing at colleges, hotels, and clubs all over the country. Doris, however, had had enough ... and retired back to New Jersey." And on Bobby Vee, one of the ten most consistent chartmakers in Billboard's history: "But Bobby Vee, like countless other American rock 'n' roll stars, was displaced by the British invasion."

One of the first rock 'n' roll reference books was the extremely opinionated and questionable one written by the late Lillian Roxon. The *Rock Encyclopedia* (Grosset and Dunlap, 1969) spends pages and pages on unknowns such as the Vagrants and Kenny Ranken, but has no entry for the likes of Tommy Roe and Neil Sedaka, who between them had over 35 hits! She admitted that the Everly Brothers ("Bye Bye Love") were not squelched by the British invasion. But she stated that little else of American music survived it. "They are one of the few original rock 'n' roll acts to live through the English invasion . . . without disappearing entirely from the pop scene."

Lillian Roxon had less kind words for Lesley Gore ("It's My Party"): "It took the Beatles to put a finish to shrill female nastiness."

Peter E. Berry, in his book . . . *And the Hits Just Keep on Comin'*, decided that for surf artists his book's title was a lie thanks to the Beatles British invasion. His opinion, stated as fact on page 51: "The 'Beatlemania' of 1964 would slow this musical race with the times, as the English monopolized the charts and devastated the Beach Boys' tuneful monument to lust and ambrosia. A foreboding of impending disaster was admonished as 'Daddy took her (sic) T-Bird away' in Brian Wilson's classic, 'Fun Fun Fun,' and Jan and Dean found it cumbersome and hair-raising on 'Dead Man's Curve'."

Even the King's peers were not safe. Paul Lichter's book *The Boy Who Dared to Rock* explains that "The Liverpool explosion would send the careers of most of Elvis' contemporaries into a decline that many would never fully recover from."

Then there is the headline on the January 1985 issue of *Record Collector:* "Enchanters on Ritz: Streetcorner Sound Sandbagged Overnight by British Invasion." According to the writer, Joseph T. Slourella, the doo-wop East-Urban street corner a cappella sound of the fifties was wiped out by the 1964 British invasion.

Finally, the "Bobbys" are lumped together by Mark Rowland. In the fall of 1989, he wrote "Rock and Roll's Show of Shows" about "American Bandstand" in the magazine *oldies*. This magazine is published by a satellite national oldies radio network, and Mark Rowland is Pacific editor of *Musician*. Setting up Frankie Avalon, Fabian, and the "Bobbys" — Vee, Vinton, and Rydell — for the big fall at the guitars of the British, Rowland explained away their original success by explaining that "Their ascension filled a void that occurred after Elvis joined the Army, Chuck Berry went to prison, Buddy Holly died and Jerry Lee Lewis was blackballed. . . ." Later in the same paragraph he relates how, "when the Beatles and the Rolling Stones surfaced . . . the Frankies and Bobbys disappeared."

So, the Gospel according to these writers is that established U.S. artists not only didn't have hits after the Beatles and the rest of the British acts arrived, but also that the arrival of the British acts and especially the Beatles was the cause of their demise. However, these writers did not present facts to back up their statements. They just gave general opinions, presumably based on their personal recollections and impressions of what American rock 'n' roll music was like in the mid-1960s. None of these writers made a close or careful examination of the impact of the British invasion on the United States music charts.

The Reality of the Invasion

As a first step in checking the musical facts of 1964 and the impact of the British invasion on U.S. music, let's take the facts surrounding some of the specific assertions made by the just-mentioned authors.

Taking up the last claim first, we examine the "Frankies and the Bobbys" and the "void" that was purportedly created when they supposedly disappeared afer the onslaught of the Stones and the Beatles.

The "void." Elvis entered the Army in May 1958, a year before Buddy Holly died, and four years before Chuck Berry went to prison in 1962 (a long time in rock 'n' roll). Jerry Lee continued to get airplay; the blackballing has been exaggerated. So there was no sudden "void." Plus, during his two year hitch, Elvis had eight very big hits, all but two in the top 10, so again, no void. Jerry Lee was also still there, charting well into the mid-1960s, including every year except '60 and '63. When Buddy Holly died, he hadn't been in the Top 10 for a year, and his latest single had been languishing for weeks, only to begin charting some two weeks afer he died. So Holly's death, tragic as it was, left no chart void. And Chuck Berry was still running around recording until 1962. So the "void" of the late '50s is a pre–Beatle myth.

But, what about the claim that the surfacing of the Beatles and Stones in 1964 caused or even coincided with the disappearance of the "Frankies and Bobbys?" Let's take a look how the "Frankies and Bobbys" fared on record.

Artist	First Hits	Last Hits (and Chart)	
Frankie Avalon	1/58	3/62	(top 40)
		7/62	(top 100)
Fabian	1/59	2/60	(top 40)
		10/60	(top 100)
Bobby Vee	8/59	4/68	(top 40)
		11/70	(top 100)
Bobby Rydell	6/59	1/64	(top 40)
		2/65	(top 100)
Bobby Vinton	6/62	9/74	(top 40)
		1/80	(top 100)

Frankie Avalon was already gone by some two years when the Stones and Beatles arrived. Fabian had already been gone for four years by the time of the Beatles British invasion. Bobby Vee thrived after the invasion. His biggest seller in fact was "Come Back When You Grow Up," in 1967. Bobby Rydell not only lasted past the 1964 invasion; his second biggest hit, "Forget Him," actually peaked in 1964. The Vinton version of Bobby continued to hit for a comfortable 16 years after the invasion, having two of his four #1 hits post–Beatles British invasion.

In short, the "Frankies" disappeared well before the British arrived, while the "Bobbys" lasted on average seven and a half years after the British invasion.

Another claim was that Neil Diamond was one of the few Americans to survive the invasion. Interesting. Neil did not "survive" the invasion. His hits didn't even begin until 1966, over two years after the invasion. Also, his hits were penned and produced by Jeff Barry and Ellie Greenwich, who were the powers behind such pre–British invasion songs and acts as "Tell Laura I Love Her" by Ray Peterson, "Da Do Ron Ron" by the Crystals, and "I've Had It" by the Bellnotes. Although Ellie did not get label credit for "I've Had It." She and husband Jeff even had hits of their own, calling themselves the Raindrops and singing their compositions "What a Guy," "The Kind of Boy You Can't Forget," and "That Boy John." The British invasion, besides coming well before Neil Diamond's career began, did not hurt Jeff and Ellie's writing/producing career at all. The point is, Jeff and Ellie, the composers behind many girl groups (such as the Dixie Cups, with their 1964 #1, "Chapel of Love") and pre–Beatle American solo male singers, survived the invasion. Neil himself, far from being a "survivor" of the invasion, actually surfaced and thrived after the Beatles emerged as the biggest and best act in the history of rock 'n' roll and popular music.

Speaking of Jeff and Ellie, theirs were the kinds of Brill Building songs "no one wanted to hear" in 1965, according to one pair of authorities, driving the American Strangeloves to pretend to be Australian. Looks like Jeff and Ellie's songs survived the invasion after all. Not only that, the Strangeloves served as producer on an American group's #1 single in 1965, the McCoys' "Hang on Sloopy."

There were multiple claims that Bobby Vee was wiped off the U.S. charts by the British. Bobby's biggest hit of all time was the aforementioned "Come Back When You Grow Up." It sold two million copies. But that was in 1967, three years after the Beatles! Although Bobby's most popular records were pre-1964, he had over a dozen chart records after the British invasion.

Roy Orbison, supposedly stopped by the British, had his biggest hit, "Oh, Pretty Woman," in very late 1964 (the peak of the invasion), and had ten other chart songs after that. And Dion, who admitedly had his biggest hits pre-1964, did have solid success post-1964 with "Abraham, Martin, and John."

And was Lesley Gore's "shrill nastiness" ended by the British invasion? Well, Lesley had only three hits before the British invasion, but 16 after. Lillian Roxon was way off base on that one.

The Beach Boys, far from being devastated, produced postinvasion classics like "Good Vibrations" and "Kokomo" and have survived through to the '90s, when Brian Wilson began doing what some say is his finest work. As for Brian's friends Jan and Dean, when Jan Berry had a near-fatal car accident in 1966, Jan and Dean were still producing hits, had a television series in production on NBC's fall schedule, were filming their own movie, and had begun their own record label. And following their 1978 CBS-TV biopic, they resumed touring, with 1987 being the biggest year of their career. That was also the year they became the first U.S. rock group to tour China.

Remember the phrases the revisionist writers used: "devastation of the American music scene"; "most difficult period for the American artist to survive"; "effect was immense"; "a back seat to the British invasion"; "with the coming of the British rockers, American stars fell behind"; "countless displaced"; "disappearing entirely"; "Beatles put a finish"; monopolized the charts."

As the cases just cited illustrate, the effect of British invasion has been distorted by many writers, including this one in the first paragraphs of this chapter. When the facts are checked, we see their propaganda for what it is — opinions. Artists who were said to have survived the invasion actually came after it. Other artists who were supposed to have had their careers ended by the invasion in fact did quite well after the English acts arrived. And artists who were reportedly destroyed by the Beatles British invasion hadn't been on the charts for years prior to the invasion anyway.

Other Rock 'n' Roll Invasions

No doubt about it, the Beatles were without peer, and they had a massive influence on the American charts. Their talent was seemingly limitless, and the British invasion artists who followed them across the Atlantic were wonderful. American music was never the same afterwards. With that said, it must in all honesty be added that the impact of the British invasion, great as it may have been, just was not nearly as massive as people claim. A careful look at the hit songs of the period shows that it neither marked the end of individual American artists' careers nor took over the charts in general, as so often claimed. Yet it is a sure bet that listing a few post-1964 hits by Bobby Vee will not convince everyone that the Beatles and the other British did not overpower the U.S. and win the battle of the British invasion.

It is true that the music of the British invasion was special. That music was a wonderful movement, a sound and feel which have seldom been matched. But, does seldom mean never?

The year 1964 was special. But was it unique? Was it different from other rock 'n' roll years? Was 1964 truly the time of a major revolution in U.S. rock 'n' roll? Was the coming of the British really a new phenomenon, a capital-I "invasion," or merely another page in the evolution of popular music in America — just another musical influence, like many before and after?

The British invasion, in fact, was not the first "invasion." Musical "invasions" mean the incoming or spread of a new music on the public's consciousness, music usually harmful to the popularity of other established music. New music, by new artists, spreading across the country and onto the charts, is what constitutes a musical "invasion." Applying that definition to rock 'n' roll music over the years shows that by 1964 there had already been several other "invasions" in its short history. One important invasion was the "twist invasion," with artists like Chubby Checker, Hank Ballard, Sam Cooke, Joey Dee, Jimmy Clanton, Billy Joe and the Checkmates, Gary U.S. Bonds, Rod McKuen, and Danny and the Juniors. Each of these artists, along with many others, had one or more "twist" records in the early 1960s. At this time, even records which did not mention the twist were given a twist beat for dancing. Even adults who had consistently shunned rock 'n' roll got on the twist bandwagon! "The Twist" ushered in the era of the dance song invasion, like "The Fly," "Mashed Potatoes," "Gravy," "Pony Time," "The Bristol Stomp," and many, many others.

Soon after the twist invasion, there was the girl group invasion of the early 1960s. The Crystals, the Angels, the Shangri-Las, the Ronnettes, the Pixies Three, Dee Dee Sharp, the Jaynettes, Marcie Blane, the Sensations, the Paris Sisters, the Cookies, the Ad Libs, Little Eva, the Exciters, the Secrets, the Chiffons, the Orlons, the Shirelles, the Chantels, the Dixie Cups, the Dixiebelles, and many more girl groups produced hit after hit in a style that was new and exciting. The girl groups' popularity was definitely hurtful to other music, squeezing it off the charts for a time.

Next came the surf and drag invasion. The Beach Boys, the Hondells, the Rip Chords, the Astronauts, Dick Dale and the Del Tones, Jan and Dean, Bruce and Terry, the Surfaris, the Shangri-Las, the Ventures, the Chantey's, the Routers, the Marketts, Bruce Johnston, the Four Seasons, Paul and Paula, Johnny Cymbal, the Newbeats, the Trashmen, the Detergents, the Trade Winds, Jack Nitzsche and many others had hit songs, flip sides, and LP cuts about the beach and the drag strip in the mid-1960s. And skipping the lyric content of music of the surf and drag invasion, there was the vocal harmony. The falsetto-topped harmony of the surf and drag invasion, typified by the Beach Boys, had a major effect on later non–surf and drag music by artists big and small, such as the Mamas and Papas, the Byrds, the Turtles, the Raspberries, Randy and the Rainbows, and many others.

The early 1960s instrumental invasion was another major force in rock 'n' roll. Mr. Acker Bilk, Floyd Cramer, Horst Jankowski, Chris Barber's Jazz Band, Kenny Ball, the Ventures, Louis Prima, Lawrence Welk, Perez Prado, Santo and Johnny, David Rose, Billy Vaughn, Joregen Ingmann, Duane Eddy, the Mar-Keys, the Marketts, Ferrante and Teicher, Sandy Nelson, Kokomo, Dave "Baby" Cortez, Ace Cannon, Boots Randolph, Bill Black, B. Bumble and the Stingers, the String-a-Longs, Billy Joe and the Checkmates, the Chanteys, the Surfaris, Percy Faith and Bert Kampfert, among others of course, had major instrumental hits all in the pre–Beatle early '60s. Together, they invaded the charts displacing other artists' music.

And so it goes. Twist songs, dance songs, girl groups, surf and drag songs, instrumental songs — they each had their spurt of popularity.

What Made the Beatles British Invasion Different

What sets the British movement apart? If it was just another movement, then why do people write articles and books about it and not write articles and books about the other "invasions"? Well, the other movements in music were perceived as a part of the fabric of rock 'n' roll, woven into the Top 40 without disruption. For instance, the surf acts came in all shapes and sizes and from all parts of the country, from Los Angeles, Denver, Nashville, and New York. Some groups featured vocals, some did only instrumentals, there were all kinds of styles. With all of the different kinds of surf groups, and all of the different regions they came from, there just was no way to get a fix on the music and call it more than a trend or movement. It was just rock 'n' roll.

In the same way, the girl groups were made up of from one to six members per group. They came from many different cities, some were white, others were black, they could be young or relatively old. Some included a male member or two.

As for the instrumentalists, they were anonymous. The songs were enjoyed on their own merits and the merits of their music. No one went after instrumental records as a category, but as good records by individual artists. Likewise, the "twisters" had just one thing in common — a dance.

In short, these other invasions were not distinctive in any way that would set them apart, except their music. And since they came from all over the United States, they did not physically invade at all. They just happened. As a result, the fans, the DJs, and perhaps most importantly the music companies and the press, by and large classified it all as rock 'n' roll, and did not make a big deal out of the subtypes of music.

But the British acts were distinctive. Love them or loathe them, they stood out. Anyone could see they were different. Never mind if they were good, or better than the American artists. They talked differently—cute, with their British accents. Almost all of them looked funny—they copied the Beatles' haircuts and wore suits that were tailored by European tailors. Nearly all of them emulated the combo image of the Beatles, playing their own guitars and drums, something done by darn few twisters and girl groups! And, they came from another country. How easy for the publicists and writers to hang a tag on this music, without necessarily evaluating, understanding, liking, or even hearing the music! Voilà, the British invasion. How simple for DJs and kids alike to connect the music as a coherent whole, even though it was not. The Beatles, Bachelors, and Rolling Stones were really much more diverse musically than were the Beach Boys, Jan and Dean, and the Rip Chords. All three of those surf and drag groups had members in common who wrote songs with one another and who even sang on one another's discs.

As an illustration of this point, take two of the Beatles' (and other British acts') trademarks, the so-called Beatle haircut and the so-called Beatle boots. For years, West Coast kids had been wearing Beatle haircuts, only they were called surfer haircuts. California kids may have started out the day with slicked-back hair. But after a day on the beach, the salt water and the sun took the Brylcream right out of their hair, and the sun or Clairol bleached it blonde. But did we hear about a surfer haircut? No, it wasn't until this recognizable invasion from England appeared that the same haircut was tagged with a name.

Why was the Beatle haircut so famous? Besides being rather outrageous to adults, Capitol Records helped the hair issue along. Capitol sent, free and unsolicited, cases of free Beatle wigs to record stores and radio stations across the country as a part of their promotional campaign for the Beatles.

If the haircut was not original with the Beatles, then did the Beatles really start the Beatle boots? Well, next time you are in a rare record store, take a look at the cover of the Liberty LP *Jan and Dean Golden Hits*, released in 1961. As you will see, Jan and Dean were wearing "Beatle boots" years before the boots got the name from the press.

Reappraising the Common Wisdom

Of course, most 1960s music historians and writers spend little time discussing clothes and hair styles. Instead, they write about the music, and what really set the British invasion apart from other musical movements, the sheer dimension of the invasion. The prevailing opinion: The British artists literally took over the U.S. charts, and their popularity killed the careers of many U.S. artists of long standing, as well as stopping cold the various U.S. musical movements such as surf and girl groups which were underway as of 1963.

Right? Isn't that what music historians and critics write? Once the American kids heard the British music, they just lost interest in wimpy American music such as that of Bobby Rydell, the Everly Brothers, the surfers, the girl groups, Roy Orbison, and the rest. Who wanted to hear the U.S. wimps when you could enjoy the pounding Dave Clark Five. Right? Right?

Let's look at the facts.

SURF AND DRAG

Did the British wipe out the surfers?

A popular notion is that surf and drag music was shut down by the British. But the fact is that the biggest car song ever in the states, the only drag record to ever make #1, was the Beach Boys' "I Get Around," and it was the #1 U.S. hit in the summer of 1964, months after the invasion was supposedly dominating the charts. Jan and Dean had classic top-tenners such as "Dead Man's Curve" and "The Little Old Lady (from Pasadena)" in 1964. Jan and Dean and the Beach Boys together (although only the Beach Boys were credited on the label) had a worldwide #1 with "Barbara Ann" in 1965. Clearly, beach music was not destroyed by the British.

Another way to look at the mortality of surf and drag after the Beatles is to look at the overall hit song data. Considering all of the S & D hits ever to make Billboard's Top 100, 56 songs in all, how many were hits before the British invasion, and how many were hits after? If the invasion killed the surfers, then there should have been virtually no surf and drag songs after January 1964.

Check this out: Three S & D songs made #1 in the states. One was preinvasion, "Surf City," by Jan and Dean. Two were postinvasion, the Beach Boys' "I Get Around" and "Leader of the Pack" by the Shangri-Las. So much for the British invasion's killing the surf and drag #1 hitmakers. There could conceivably have been more #1 surf and drag songs had the British not come across the ocean. But we don't know that. All we know is there were more #1's after the invasion which was supposed to have creamed the surf movement than there had been before.

How about the national Top 10? Fourteen surf and drag songs made the positions two through ten. But only five preceded the Beatles, while nine became hits after the Beatles led the British invasion against the S & D invasion! There were actually more surf and drag hits after the invasion than before. It begins to look like the British did not really "wipe out" the surf sound after all.

Continuing the survey of surf and drag songs, 21 records of this genre hit the Top-40 spots from #11 to #40 in the golden era of rock 'n' roll. Here the balance was preinvasion, with 13 songs being hits before 1964, and eight being hits in 1964 or after. Even so, those eight mean that about 40 percent of the medium-sized surf hits were popular after the Beatles supposedly spun them all off the face of the turntable!

The last category of S & D songs to be examined is songs that didn't make the Top 40. The national charts have 100 places, whereas most radio stations have a local chart of only 40 hit songs. The reason for the bigger national chart is to list mild-sized hits, and songs which were not national hits but which did have regional Top-40 success and made positions 41 through 100 on a national basis. (Some examples of such records are found in the Beatles' songs "Roll Over Beethoven" #68, "All My Loving" #45; the Hollies' "Just One Look" #98; Buddy Holly's "Heartbeat" #82; the Rolling Stones' "Not Fade Away" #48; Jan and Dean's "From All Over the World" #56; and the Beach Boys' "Blue Birds Over the Mountain" #62.) There were 18 surf and drag songs with this degree of national success, with the pre- and postinvasion division being equal, with nine on either side of January 1964.

Total it up and what do you get? From Numbers 1 to 100, 56 surf and drag hits made Billboard. Twenty-eight preceded the British acts' arrival, and an equal number, 28 competed successfully with the British acts for chart space after January 1964. Evidently, the British invasion did not wipe out the surf and drag invasion. Rather than stopping it, the British invasion came right in the middle of it, seemingly having no effect on it at all.

GIRL GROUPS

So much for the theory that the British killed the surf sound. How about the girl groups? Did they curtsey and then bow out after the British boys arrived in 1963?

The biggest groups, the Supremes, the Ronnettes, and the Shangri-Las, had their biggest hits *after* the British invasion took place. The Dixie Cups' "Chapel of Love" was #1 simultaneously with "I Get Around" in 1964. Again popular opinion is wrong—the girl groups got along fine sharing the charts with the British.

Major U.S. Artists

"Okay," the argument could be made, "some U.S. music slipped through the advancing British ranks. But overall, the British music not only dominated the U.S. charts, the British records also ended the careers of many long-time U.S. hitmakers, such as Roy Orbison, the Everly Brothers, Bobby Rydell, and Fabian."

Two big questions remain: One, did the British invasion of 1964 take over the U.S. charts? And two, did the British invasion end the careers of many long-time U.S. acts? These are the claims made by the rock critics quoted previously. Are they false claims?

The hits of the 1950s and the '60s are still the only place to look for the answers to these questions. To discover the truth, a survey was made of the hit artists of the pre- and postinvasion eras. The success and failure rates of both U.S. and British artists from 1955 to the end of the '60s were then examined. The purpose of this analysis is two-fold. One, to discover which American artists' careers, if any, were ended by the British invasion, and two, to determine the extent to which the U.S. charts were taken over by the Beatles and the rest of the British invasion.

Every major artist of the 1950s and '60s was included in this analysis. A major artist was defined as an artist who had at least five chart records over a span of three or more calendar years.

Lesser and one-shot artists were not included, because no writers have ever made claims that their careers were devastated by the Beatles. A list of the major artists and the years they had hits follows:

Artist	Years	Artist	Years
Steve Alimo	1962–66	Teresa Brewer	1955–61
Davie Allen	1965–67	Brothers Four	1960–65
Herb Alpert	1962–	James Brown	1958–
Animals **(British)**	1964–68	Maxine Brown	1961–69
Paul Anka	1957–	Ruth Brown	1957–62
Annette	1959–61	Browns	1959–61
Association	1966–	Anita Bryant	1959–64
Frankie Avalon	1958–62	Solomon Burke	1961–
Bachelors **(British)**	1964–67	Jerry Butler	1958–
LaVern Baker	1956–65	Byrds	1965–
Hank Ballard	1959–62	Glen Campbell	1961–
Beach Boys	1962–	Ace Cannon	1961–64
Beatles **(British)**	1964–	Freddy Cannon	1959–66
Bee Gees	1967–	Clarence Carter	1967–
Belmonts	1961–63	Mel Carter	1963–66
Brook Benton	1958–	Cascades	1963–
Chuck Berry	1955–65	Alvin Cash and the	1965–68
Bill Black's Combo	1959–68	Crawlers	
Bobby Bland	1957–	Johnny Cash	1956–
U.S. Bonds	1960–62	Champs	1958–62
Booker T. and the MGs	1962–	Gene Chandler	1962–68
Pat Boone	1955–	Chantels	1957–63
Box Tops	1967–	Ray Charles	1957–

Artist	Years	Artist	Years
Ray Charles Singers	1955–65	Dick and Dee Dee	1961–65
Chubby Checker	1959–	Bo Diddley	1959–67
Chiffons	1960–66	Dino, Desi, and Billy	1965–68
Chipmunks	1958–62	Dion	1960–
Chordettes	1955–61	Bill Doggett	1956–61
Lou Christie	1963–	Fats Domino	1955–68
Jimmy Clanton	1958–	Donovan **(British)**	1965–
Dave Clark Five **(British)**	1964–	Doors	1967–
Dee Clark	1958–63	Lee Dorsey	1961–
Pet Clark **(British)**	1964–	Ronnie Dove	1964–
Classics IV	1967–69	Dovells	1961–63
Cleftones	1956–62	Rusty Draper	1955–63
Patsy Cline	1957–63	Drifters	1955–66
Coasters	1956–64	Duprees	1962–65
Eddie Cochran	1957–59	Bob Dylan	1965–
Nat King Cole	1955–65	Duane Eddy	1958–64
Perry Como	1955–	Tommy Edwards	1959–62
Arthur Connely	1967–	Shirley Ellis	1963–67
Contours	1962–67	Betty Everett	1963–
Sam Cooke	1957–66	Everly Brothers	1957–67
Jill Corey	1956–58	Exciters	1962–66
Don Cornel	1955–57	Percy Faith	1956–60
Dave "Baby" Cortez	1959–66	Ferrante and Teicher	1960–
Don Covay	1961–65	5th Dimension	1967–
Cowsills	1967–	Fireballs	1959–
Floyd Cramer	1958–62	Eddie Fisher	1955–67
Johnny Crawford	1961–64	Five Americans	1966–68
Crests	1957–60	Five Stairsteps and Cubie	1966–69
Crew Cuts	1955–57	Flamingos	1959–66
Bing Crosby	1955–60	Fleetwoods	1959–63
Cryan' Shames	1966–68	Eddie Floyd	1966–69
Crystals	1961–64	Fontaine Sisters	1955–58
Vic Damone	1955–65	Frankie Ford	1963–68
Vic Dana	1961–66	Connie Francis	1958–
Danny and the Juniors	1957–63	Aretha Franklin	1961–69
Bobby Darin	1958–	Stan Freeberg	1955–60
James Darren	1959–67	Bobby Freeman	1958–64
Sammy Davis, Jr.	1956–62	Ernie Freeman	1957–62
Skeeter Davis	1960–64	Marvin Gaye	1962–
Bobby Day	1957–59	and Tammy Terrell	1967–
Doris Day	1955–62	Gerry and the Pace-	1964–66
Jimmy Dean	1957–65	makers **(British)**	
DeCastro Sisters	1955–59	Georgia Gibbs	1955–58
Joey Dee and the	1961–63	Don Gibson	1958–61
Starlighters		Bobby Goldsboro	1962–
Dells	1962–	Dickie Goodman	1961–
Jackie DeShannon	1963–	Lesley Gore	1963–67
Neil Diamond	1966–	Edie Gorme	1956–
Diamonds	1956–61	Gogi Grant	1955–61

Artist	Years	Artist	Years
Grass Roots	1966–	Gladys Knight and the Pips	1966–
Bill Haley and His Comets	1955–60	Buddy Knox	1957–61
Roy Hamilton	1956–63	Patty LaBelle	1963–66
Happenings	1966–	Major Lance	1963–65
Clarence "Frog Man" Henry	1956–62	Frankie Lane	1955–
		Julius LaRosa	1955–57
Herman's Hermits **(British)**	1964–68	Steve Lawrence	1957–64
		Brenda Lee	1957–
Al Hibbler	1955–57	Dickie Lee	1961–65
Hilltoppers	1955–57	Peggy Lee	1956–
Al Hirt	1964–68	Lettermen	1961–
Brenda Hollaway	1964–67	Barbara Lewis	1963–67
Hollies **(British)**	1964–	Gary Lewis	1965–
Buddy Holly	1957–59	Jerry Lee Lewis	1957–68
Johnny Horton	1959–62	Ramsey Lewis Trio	1964–
Englebert Humperdinck **(British)**	1967–	Little Anthony and the Imperials	1958–
Tab Hunter	1957–59	Little Milton	1965–
Brian Hyland	1960–	Little Richard	1955–65
Impressions	1961–	Little Willie John	1956–61
Intruders	1959–	Trini Lopez	1963–68
Isley Brothers	1959–	Lovin' Spoonful	1965–
Burl Ives	1957–64	Lulu **(British)**	1967–
Chuck Jackson and Maxine Brown	1961–68 1965–67	Frankie Lymon	1956–60
		Barbara Lynn	1962–68
Walter Jackson	1964–67	McCoys	1965–68
Wanda Jackson	1960–62	Gene McDaniels	1961–63
Etta James	1960–	Jimmy McGriff	1962–68
Joni James	1955–60	McGuire Sisters	1955–61
Sonny James	1956–	Clyde McPhatter	1956–64
Tommy James and the Shondells	1966–	Mamas and Papas	1966–68
		Henry Mancini	1960–
Jan and Dean	1959–66	Herbie Mann	1966–
Jay and the Americans	1962–	Manfred Mann **(British)**	1964–
Johnny and the Hurricanes	1959–61	Marketts	1962–66
		Martha and the Vandellas	1963–
Betty Johnson	1956–59	Dean Martin	1955–
Marv Johnson	1959–61	Al Martino	1959–68
Jack Jones	1962–68	Marvelettes	1961–
Tom Jones **(British)**	1965–	Barbara Mason	1965–68
Kitty Kallen	1955–62	Johnny Mathis	1957–65
Bert Kampfert	1960–66	Sergio Mendez	1966–
B.B. King	1957–	Mickey and Sylvia	1956–61
Ben E. King	1961–76	Mitch Miller	1955–61
King Curtis	1962–68	Roger Miller	1964–66
Kingsmen	1963–66	Mills Brothers	1955–68
Kingston Trio	1958–63	Garnet Mimms	1963–66
Kinks **(British)**	1964–67	Miracles	1959–

Artist	Years	Artist	Years
Guy Mitchell	1956–60	Cliff Richard **(British)**	1959–68
Willie Mitchell	1964–	Righteous Brothers	1963–67
Monkees	1966–	Johnny Rivers	1964–
Chris Montez	1962–67	Marty Robbins	1956–68
Moody Blues **(British)**	1965–	Eileen Rodgers	1956–58
Jane Morgan	1956–59	Jimmie Rodgers	1957–67
Jaye P. Morgan	1955–60	Tommy Roe	1962–
Ricky Nelson	1957–	Rolling Stones **(British)**	1964–
Sandy Nelson	1959–64	Ronnettes	1963–66
New Christie Minstrels	1962–65	Ronny and the Daytonas	1964–66
New Colony 6	1966–	David Rose	1956–62
Newbeats	1964–	Billy Joe Royal	1965–
Wayne Newton	1963–68	Royal Guardsmen	1966–68
Ohio Express	1967–	Ruby and the Romantics	1963–65
O'Jays	1963–	Jimmy Ruffin	1966–68
Olympics	1958–66	Bobby Rydell	1959–65
Roy Orbison	1956–67	Mitch Ryder and the	1965–68
Orlons	1962–64	Detroit Wheels	
Buck Owens	1964–	Sam and Dave	1966–
Patti Page	1955–68	Sam the Sham and the	1965–67
Little Junior Parker	1957–64	Pharaohs	
Les Paul and Mary Ford	1955–61	Tommy Sands	1957–60
Peaches and Herb	1966–	Mongo Santamaria	1963–69
Carl Perkins	1956–59	Santo and Johnny	1959–64
Peter and Gordon	1964–67	Freddie Scott	1958–61
(British)		Jack Scott	1958–61
Peter, Paul and Mary	1962–	Linda Scott	1961–64
Ray Peterson	1959–63	Searchers **(British)**	1964–66
Esther Phillips	1962–67	Neil Sedaka	1958–66
Wilson Pickett	1962–67	David Seville	1956–59
Webb Pierce	1957–60	Shadows of Knight	1966–68
Gene Pitney	1961–	Shangri-Las	1964–66
Platters	1955–67	Del Shannon	1961–66
Playmates	1958–62	Dee Dee Sharp	1962–65
Elvis Presley	1956–	Shirelles	1958–67
Johnny Preston	1959–61	Shirley and Lee	1956–61
Lloyd Price	1957–64	Dinah Shore	1955–57
Ray Price	1957–67	Simon and Garfunkel	1966–
Gary Puckett and the	1967–	Joe Simon	1959–
Union Gap		Nina Simone	1965–
James and Bobby Purify	1966–68	Frank Sinatra	1955–
Lou Rawls	1965–	Nancy Sinatra	1965–
Johnny Ray	1955–69	Percy Sledge	1966–
Otis Redding	1963–	Jimmy Smith	1962–68
Jimmy Reed	1957–63	Sonny and Cher	1965–67
Della Reese	1957–66	Joe South	1958–
Jim Reeves	1957–66	Spanky and Our Gang	1967–
Paul Revere and the	1961–	Dusty Springfield	1964–
Raiders		Jo Stafford	1955–57

Artist	Years	Artist	Years
Edwin Starr	1965–	Sarah Vaughan	1955–66
Connie Stevens	1960–65	Bobby Vee	1959–
Dodie Stevens	1959–61	Ventures	1960–
Ray Stevens	1961–	Bobby Vinton	1962–
Billy Stewart	1962–67	Vogues	1965–
Gale Storm	1955–57	Adam Wade	1960–65
Strawberry Alarm Clock	1967–	Junior Walker	1958–64
Barbra Streisand	1964–67	Jerry Wallace	1965–
Supremes	1962–	Dee Dee Warwick	1965–
Tams	1962–68	Dionne Warwick	1962–
Johnnie Taylor	1963–65	Baby Washington	1961–65
Nino Tempo and April	1962–67	Dinah Washington	1959–63
Stevens		Lenny Welch	1960–65
Temptations	1964–	Lawrence Welk	1956–65
Joe Tex	1964–	Mary Wells	1961–68
B.J. Thomas	1966–	Margaret Whiting	1956–67
Carla Thomas	1961–	Who **(British)**	1965–
Sue Thompson	1961–65	Andy Williams	1956–
Johnny Tillotson	1958–65	Billy Williams	1956–59
Tokens	1961–	Roger Williams	1955–
Ike and Tina Turner	1960–	Jackie Wilson	1957–68
Turtles	1965–	Nancy Wilson	1963–
Conway Twitty	1957–62	Stevie Wonder	1963–
Tymes	1963–68	Yardbirds **(British)**	1965–67
Jerry Vale	1956–65	Young Rascals	1965–
Frankie Valli	1966–	Timi Yuro	1961–65
Vanilla Fudge	1967–	Zombies **(British)**	1964–
Billy Vaughan	1955–65		

Many of the artists listed have no ending date for their hits. An example is the Zombies. This is because these artists were still having hits after 1969, and this survey is only of the artists and hits of the '50s and '60s.

In addition, no new artists are listed after 1967. The data collection of new artists stops at 1967, since the survey was only of the major acts having at least five hits and lasting for at least three calendar years. To continue to list major artists after 1967 would require including hits of the 1970s, which this survey does not include. For instance, Oliver had his first hit, "Good Morning Starshine," in 1969. To learn if Oliver became a major artist (three years or more) would mean looking to see if he had hits in the '70s. Oliver and any other new artists after 1967 are not listed.

This does not bias the survey however. The authors quoted before said nothing about who was still having hits after 1969 or even after 1967. The thesis those writers established was that the pre-1964 American artists had precious few hits after the British arrived in 1964. Considering new artists who had hits starting after 1967 would be irrelevant to their thesis and this discussion.

Except in cases where it is clearly stated, only the major artists listed above are included in the following discussion, data and graphs. There were other artists, of course. The Randells, for instance, had a hit with "The Martian Hop" in 1963, and the High Keys had "Que Sera, Sera." These artists are not included, since no one ever claimed that the careers of these one-shot artists were especially hurt by the British invasion. A one-shot artist is an artist who had just one record on the chart in his or her career, often a very big hit. The claim always made is that the careers of artists such as Bobby Vee, Bobby Rydell, and Bobby Darin were stomped out by the British Rockers who dominated the charts from 1964 onward.

NUMBER OF ARTISTS PER YEAR

In order to determine whether the British acts dominated U.S. charts, it is necessary to look closely at the major artists of each year of rock 'n' roll and look for trends over time. For example, was there a massive, drastic change in the number of American artists having hits after the Beatles and the other British acts arrived? Did many established U.S. artists stop having hits once the invasion took place? Did the Beatles and the British dominate the charts in 1964 and the following years? And did the number, and therefore the variety, of artists having hits increase as a result of the influx of the Beatles and their musical countrymen?

The line with solid black circles on Graph 1 shows the total number of major rock 'n' roll artists (as defined above) each year from 1955 through 1967. All artists, both U.S. and British, are included in this measure.

In 1955, generally acknowledged as the first year of rock 'n' roll, there were not quite 50 major rock 'n' roll acts — artists who would eventually have at least five hits over a span of three or more calendar years. As rock 'n' roll caught on, the number of acts then grew rapidly through the second half of the '50s, as one would expect. After all, there was a lot of room on the charts to accommodate new artists when the music was so new.

By 1956, there were about 85 major acts — the original 50, plus some 35 more. The number grew steadily for the first four years of rock 'n' roll, until there were 155 major rock 'n' roll artists by 1959, the end of the first half-decade of the new music.

About this time, there was an indication that perhaps the charts had begun to fill up and the number of major popular acts had reached a maximum (about three times the number of artists on the charts in the first year of rock 'n' roll). In 1960 less than five new artists joined the ranks of "major acts," whereas from 1955 through 1959, some 20 to 30 new acts were added to the list of major artists each year. The graph clearly seems to be leveling off in 1960. Were the charts full?

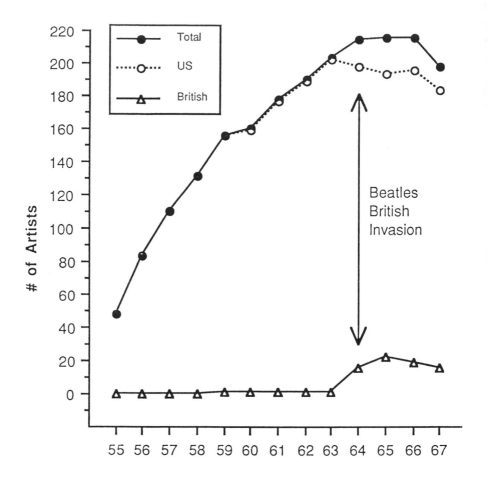

Graph #1, number of artists per year. Vertical figures denote number of artists; horizontal numbers refer to calendar years.

No, the decrease in the number of new acts was only temporary. The increase resumed in 1961, with about 20 new artists that year for a new total of over 175 acts. In 1962 the number again increased, reaching nearly 190 major artists on Billboard's Top 100 over the course of the year.

Then came 1963, the last year before the British invasion. The popular wisdom holds that 1963 was the doldrums in rock 'n' roll, old established acts wheezing out lame records, nothing new happening, a time of stagnation from which only new artists, such as those from the next year's invasion records, could uplift the hapless American rock 'n' roll fan.

Stagnation? As shown on Graph 1, 1963 was the first time that the number of major rock 'n' roll artists exceeded 200. The year of the girl groups invasion and the surf and drag invasion was 1963. Far from bringing stagnation, 1963 had the greatest number of major artists ever in the history of rock 'n' roll. The kids were not "looking around" for something new. Instead, they were accepting an increasingly wide spectrum of new major acts.

The next year was 1964, the year of the Beatles British invasion — the year the rock historians report that the old was overturned and the new took over — shown on the graph by an arrow. What was the effect of this invasion on the number of acts on the American charts?

As seen by following the line with solid black circles, the first year there was virtually no effect. The number of acts continued its climb, but just barely, to a total of just over 210. Even though many new British artists came onto the scene in 1964, the total number of major artists in the United States went up less than 10. What does this relatively small increase in the number of new artists indicate? Either many major established U.S. acts bit the dust, as many claim, and were replaced by British acts. Or else the majority of the British groups had a few hits for a couple of years, but lacked the staying power to qualify under the present definition of major artists having five or more hits over three years. This graph does not answer that question.

Next, a unique thing happened in 1965, the second year of the Beatles British invasion. Staying with the black circles, for the first time in the history of rock 'n' roll, the number of major acts actually leveled off. The Beatles invasion was the first time that the number of new major artists ever failed to increase substantially over the previous year! With an increase of only one in the number of major acts in 1965, if there was a period of stagnation in rock 'n' roll, the stagnation was not in 1963 and relieved by the Beatles invasion. This graph would indicate that stagnation did happen. But it did not happen before the Beatles; the stagnation occurred after them. Keep in mind that these data do not include minor aritsts with just a couple of hits over a couple of years, but only major artists who were the backbone of the music industry.

The situation stayed exactly the same in 1966. There was no change at all in the number of major acts. The British invasion produced complete stagnation, halting the growth in the number and therefore in the variety of the acts having hits in the United States.

Then, in 1967, the number of acts did something that was unprecedented — it actually fell. And it fell to a level below that of 1963, to only 197 major artists.

Myth: American rock 'n' roll had stagnated between 1960 and 1963, but was revitalized by the Beatles British invasion.

Reality: Far from rescuing American kids from stagnation in music, the first effect the British invasion had was to stifle, not energize, the rock 'n' roll charts. Up until the time of the Beatles British invasion, the number of major artists had increased every year. After the invasion, it not only stopped increasing, but the number actually fell. It's possible that the maximum number of acts, which had almost seemed to have been reached in 1959, was actually reached in 1963. But if that were the case, the number would have merely leveled off. Instead, the number actually decreased. The only possible explanation is that the Beatles British invasion caused the leveling off, stifling rock 'n' roll, and for the first time putting a limit on and even reducing the number and therefore diversity of rock 'n' roll artists and types of music.

At the 1963 point on Graph 1, the line of solid black circles starts to branch. This branch, marked with open circles, represents the number of major American rock 'n' roll artists still having hits each year. As can be seen, the number of artists represented by this line drops somewhat. In fact, the drop is similar in pattern to the overall drop of the solid line. In short, the dashed line shows that after 1964, the number of major U.S. artists leveled off and decreased. Were they replaced by the new major British artists?

Yes and no. At the bottom of the graph, there is another data line. This line, marked with triangles, represents the number of British artists having hits in the U.S. after 1964. The number jumps from near zero in 1963 to over 15 in 1964 and nearly 25 in 1965. The total number of major British rock 'n' roll artists to emerge from the Battle of the British Invasion over a two year period was just 25. After two years, the number surviving the battle begins to drop off and continues to drop through 1967. In the long run of the '60s, less than two dozen British acts survived.

The comparison here with the open-circle line is interesting. Both drop off in the later '60s; the number of British artists drops off beginning in 1966, but the number of American artists goes up in that same year. So, the American artists did not lose much of the U.S. chart action. However, in 1967, the number of American major artists took another drop, just as the number of British artists was already doing.

Myth: The groups of the British invasion dominated the U.S. charts in 1964.

Reality: Only about two dozen major British invasion artists had hits in the United States following the Beatles British invasion, and their staying power was not great. By 1967, there were only about 16 left. This compares to almost 185 major U.S. artists still having hits in 1967. The British acts *did not* greatly reduce the number of major American artists having hits in the United States. Moreover, very few British acts became major artists in the United States.

Myth: The influx of so many new British acts revitalized American music.

Reality: After the invasion, stagnation, defined as the same artists having hits with no new blood being introduced, continued. In 1967, the number of major U.S. artists, major British artists, and overall artists fell to a new low.

Graph 1 can be a little obscure. Because the number of major artists increased so dramatically for the first 10 years of the rock 'n' roll era, a change in the graph's main line near the end could be confused as a result of the chart's filling up instead of a result of the Beatles British invasion. A way to control for changing numbers is to convert data to percentages.

Graph 2 shows the same American artist data as Graph 1, expressed as a percentage of all major artists on the U.S. charts who were American. From 1955 to 1958, the percent was 100. However, 1958 was the last year that 100 percent of the major rock 'n' rollers popular in the states were American. A few British artists began having hits in the United States beginning in 1959, but 99 percent of the major acts were still American.

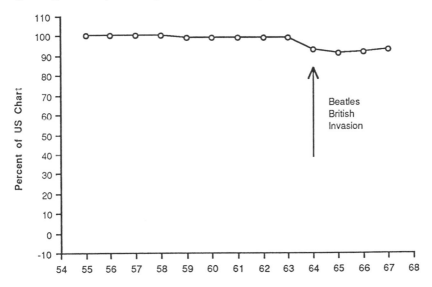

Graph 2. Percent of U.S. charts held by U.S. artists.

The arrow on Graph 2 shows the year of the Beatles British invasion, 1964. Here the effect of the invasion is shown by a drop in the line. As British artists became popular, true to the common conception, American artists were displaced. But was the effect "devastating," as reported? Were "countless" U.S. artists displaced, as the rock writers assert? We can answer that by specifying the percent of American artists displaced year by year: 1963, 1 percent; 1964, 7 percent; 1965, 9 percent. After that time the U.S. acts recovered, and began edging the line back up toward 100 percent, although that point is never again reached.

Myth: The U.S. charts were dominated by invasion acts during the Beatles British invasion.

Reality: The biggest effect that the invasion had on U.S. artists came in 1965, the second year of the invasion. At that time, 91 percent of the artists were American, and only 9 percent were British. Far from dominating the U.S. record market, only one in ten major rock 'n' roll artists in the states at the peak of the invasion was British. Nine out of ten were still American.

Graphs 1 and 2 show that the British invasion artists, far from dominating or devastating U.S. rock 'n' roll, made only a minor dent in the number and proportion of major American artists popular in the states. This answers one half of the question of the effect of the invasion: No, the British did not dominate the U.S. charts.

The second part of the question was, did the British invasion, as claimed, actually serve to end the careers of many major U.S. artists? This question is answered by Graph 3.

This graph shows the number of major artists whose careers ended per year, when their records were no longer making it onto the Top 100. An artist first had to be a major one to be included; that is, have five hits and be popular over three calendar years. Obviously, no artist could have died during 1955 or 1956, since that would mean they had lasted only one or two years, and could not have had time to become major artists.

Therefore, the data in Graph 3 begin with 1957. As shown by the line marked with open circles, in that year, less than ten major American artists' careers ended. In 1958, even fewer died off, less than five. In 1959 the number approached 15, then in 1960, it fell to 12.

In 1961, the number of major artists whose careers ended exceeded 20 for the first time. Then, beginning in 1962, the number of artists whose careers ended fell for two consecutive years, as it had in 1957–58. In 1963, the number was back to 15, near the 1959 level.

In other words, from 1957 to 1963, a stairstep pattern developed, with the number of artists whose careers ended going up, then down a bit, then up again from year to year. The variation was slight. On average, 15 to 20 major U.S. artists had their careers end each year up through 1963, the eve of the Beatles British invasion.

The number of artists with careers ending increased again, to 20 during the invasion year of 1964 (marked with an arrow). Were these 20 artists who

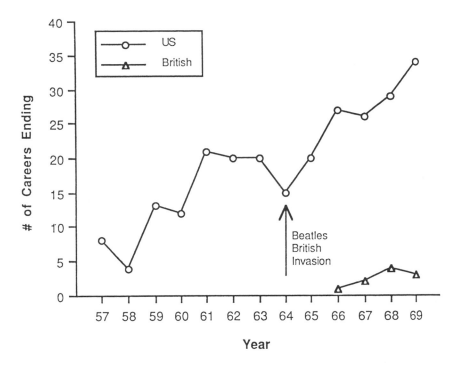

Graph 3. Number of careers ending per year.

died part of the "devastating killing off of the major American artists" the critics write of? Well, 20 was the same number of artists that died in 1962, and slightly fewer than the number of major U.S. artists who had died back in 1961. If there was a killing off of American artists as a result of the invasion, the slaughter was not particularly big. A similar killing off, or perhaps a better term would be dying off of American artists had taken place twice already in the early 1960s, with no Beatles or British invasion required.

The number of major artists with careers ending rose to new heights in 1965, reaching over 25 for the first time. But even this was only slightly greater than the 1961 rate or even the average. From then on to 1968, the rate tended to increase, although it never reached as high as 35.

(The data on this graph go to 1968, since we are marking the end of major careers, and careers did end prior to 1970.)

Myth: When the Beatles and other British artists invaded the U.S. in 1964, they displaced many long-reigning American stars.

Reality: The Beatles invasion did not have a substantial effect on the number of major American artists whose careers ended in 1964. If you lay a pencil on the line of Graph 3, you see that in the long run from 1955 to

1969, the increase was constant, a straight line. The number of major artists whose careers ended increased steadily from the 1950s on, with no important change in the upward trend because of the Beatles and other British acts. The overall rise was due to the increasing number of artists. The more artists, the more there are to die off. There is no indication of an increase in established American artists' careers ending as a result of the 1964 British invasion.

There is another line on the bottom of Graph 3, marked with triangles. This line shows the number of British artists whose U.S. popularity ended each year. Through 1964, the number of "dying" British rock 'n' rollers was zero for two reasons: there were virtually no major British artists in the U.S., and until an artist had five hits over three years, that person could not qualify as a major artist. The first year an invasion artist could have his career end was 1966: If any British act had at least one hit in 1964, at least one other hit in 1966, an overall total of five hits, and its last hit in 1966, then it would be recorded as having its career end in 1966. Beginning in 1966, invasion artists began dying off. The number increased for two years, then it topped out in 1967. There were so many fewer British acts in the U.S. in the '60s than American acts (as shown in Graph 1), however, that this line is hard to interpret. You will recall that big differences in numbers can be handled by converting data to percentages. The same data shown on Graph 3 are shown again on Graph 4, but as percentage data.

But set aside the graphs for a moment. A long list of all of the major artists of the 1950s and '60s was presented earlier. From this list, a shorter list of all of the major artists whose careers ended in 1964 was made and is presented here. By looking at this shorter list, we can see what type of artists' careers ended during the British invasion.

U.S. Artists' Careers Ending in 1964

Anita Bryant	Burl Ives
Ace Cannon	Sandy Nelson
Coasters	Orlons
Johnny Crawford	Little Junior Parker
Crystals	Lloyd Price
Duane Eddy	Santo and Johnny
Four Preps	Linda Scott
Bobby Freeman	Junior Walker

What kinds of artists were killed off (or just died off) in 1964? Out of 16 acts, there were four instrumentalists—saxophonist Ace Cannon, drummer Sandy Nelson and guitarists Duane Eddy, and Santo and Johnny; there was one folk singer—Burl Ives; and two male groups—the Coasters and the Four Preps.

The usual allegation is that the British acts most damaged certain types of American artists' careers in 1964. These types included white male teen idols, female solo artists, surf groups, and girl groups. This list of major American artists whose careers were ended in 1964 shows that only two solo female artists, Anita Bryant and Linda Scott, ended careers in 1964. Only one white solo ("Teen Idol") vocalist, Johnny Crawford, ended in 1964. Only two girl groups, the Orlons (who had one male member) and the Crystals, a Phil Spector group, ended hit careers in 1964. However, what kind of music was most affected by the invasion? Teen idols? Surf? Girl groups? *Seven* of the 16 artists whose hits stopped coming in 1964 were black, something which rock writers never mention as being hurt by the Beatles and their invasion.

Meanwhile, as shown by the triangle line, British artists started dying off almost immediately after the invasion got established.

Myth: The invasion eliminated an unprecedented number of important if unsubstantial U.S. artists, such as teen idols and surfers. These were replaced with important, long-lived British acts.

Reality: Besides there being no particular upswing in the number of American artists going down the tubes as a result of the Beatles and their invasion, there were no particular types of artists whose careers ended in 1964. Categories of artists who had relatively few members disappear in 1964 included male singers and girl groups. No major surf artists' hit runs ended in 1964. The biggest categorical impact of the invasion was felt by black artists.

Remembering the increase shown in Graph 1 of the number of major artists in existence during the first years of rock 'n' roll, it is no wonder that the number of artists whose careers ended each year in Graph 3 went up each year. Each year there were more and more rock 'n' roll artists. The more there were on the charts, the more there were to die off.

Graph 4 is in some ways clearer than Graph 3. It shows the "dying" artists as a percentage of the total number of major artists, which is fairer since it allows for the fact that there were almost 10 times more American than British artists. The open circle line shows the percent of U.S. artists' careers dying each year. The trend is only slightly up over time. Lay a pencil on this line, and you will see that the slant is not steep, but it is pretty stable. When the invasion hit, shown by the arrow at 1964, there was not a big blip in the line. Contrary to the accepted view, the rate of U.S. artists whose careers ended each year did not increase suddenly in 1964 or 1965.

Beginning in 1966, British artists who began in 1964 had now been around for three calendar years and were starting to die off. By 1967, the rate that British artists' careers were ending had gone higher in three years than

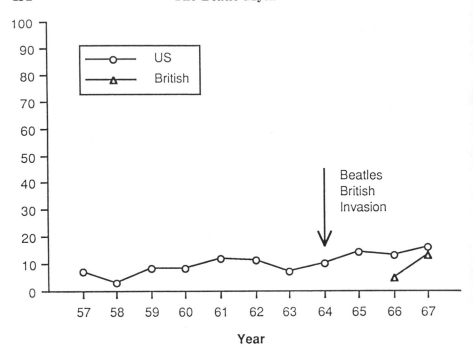

Graph 4. Percent of artists' careers ending per year.

the U.S. rate had in ten years, reaching pretty much the same percentage. The British invasion troops were not as hardy as the established, but supposedly endangered, U.S. artists! Common opinion notwithstanding, it was the British whose careers ended en masse, in the postinvasion years, not the Americans.

Myth: American artists dropped like flies after the British invasion, unable to compete with the more substantive British groups.

Reality: There was no substantive effect of the British invasion on the careers of established major U.S. artists. Contrary to the popular concept, established U.S. artists continued to survive, and to die off, at about the same rate they always had, prior to the British invasion. Major British artists began dying off very quickly, however, after the first two years of the invasion.

Neil Sedaka talked about rock 'n' roll artists' careers and the reasons they ended in an interview he did on television in the mid-1980s:

Most of the rock 'n' rollers in those days—Brenda Lee, the Everly Brothers, Fats Domino—had a five-year run. My brother-in-law, Eddie, who is kind of an intuitive person, said, "You know, you're only going to have a five-year run." And I knew it in the back of my mind that that was what it was going to be. In 1963 it was over, after selling 25 million records.

The same opinion is held by Phil Everly, speaking in Bruce Pollock's 1981 book *When Rock Was Young*. Phil Everly discusses the end of the hit trail of the Everly Brothers: "Being hot on records lasts about five to six years for most acts. It's true of Elton John, it's true even of the Beatles. Then, it peaks out, and the next thing comes along."

Don and Phil Everly's last Top-10 hit was "That's Old Fashioned" in 1962, two years before the invasion. Their last Top-40 hit was 1967, three years after. For them the thing that came next was not the invasion, but either surf music or acid rock, depending on when you feel their hits ended, 1962 or '67. But it was not the Beatles invasion of 1964.

We have seen in Graph 1 that the total number of major artists increased each year up until the Beatles British invasion. Also, Graph 3 revealed that the number of major artists whose careers ended each year was about the same before and after the invasion. But what about the number of new major artists? How did that change from year to year? Did the new British acts have any influence on the rate at which new U.S. artists became successful, major artists? Graph 5 addresses this question.

In 1955, as shown by the solid circle line on Graph 5, the number of new artists was the same as the total number of artists shown back on Graph 1, almost 50. This was the first year of rock 'n' roll, so any artist was by definition going to be a new artist.

In 1956, the number of new artists declined to 35, and stayed there for two years. Then the number decreased by ten, to 25 in 1958. A slight recovery was made in 1959, but an all-time low number of new major artists was achieved in 1960, only 15. In other words, the number of new major artists in the U.S. per year declined though the 1950s as the rock 'n' roll bandwagon began filling up.

Myth: Many rock 'n' roll writers and critics cite the era from 1960 to 1963 as a dead spot in rock 'n' roll, a dead spot incidentally brought back to life only by the British invasion of 1964.

Reality: There was a recovery in the number of new artists in 1961, comparable to the levels of 1956, the second year of rock 'n' roll. The early 1960s were clearly alive with new major artists breathing new life into the rock 'n' roll of the preinvasion period.

In 1962 and 1963, the number of new artists did decline somewhat once again. However, the rate of decline was less than the rate had been during the '50s.

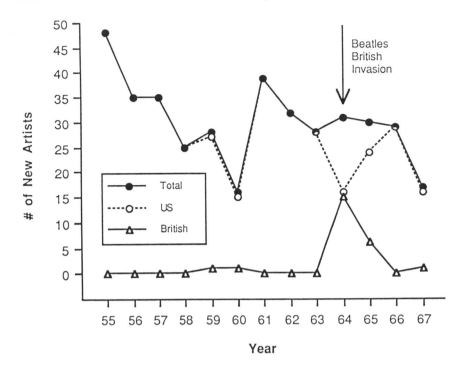

Graph 5. Number of new artists per year.

Then we hit 1964, where the arrow marks the Beatles British invasion. Here is where new life is breathed into rock 'n' roll, right? Lots of new artists and new music, an era of unprecedented musical dynamism and competition, right?

Wrong. While it is true that the black circle line shows that there was a slight increase in the total number of new major artists, both U.S. and British, in the invasion year 1964, the increase was the smallest of any of the increases ever seen, and did not reach the level of 1962.

And after 1964, the trend in new artists was down. Each year—1965, 1966, and 1967—the number of new major artists declined.

Myth: With the Beatles British invasion, an unprecedented number of new faces, in this case British groups, graced the American rock 'n' roll charts.

Reality: In reality, the time of the Beatles British invasion was a period of a steady decrease in the number of new faces on the charts.

The dotted, open-circle line branching off the main line in Graph 5 is the number of new U.S. artists each year. Here we finally see a potentially major effect of the Beatles and the British invasion on American artists. The number of new, major U.S. artists drops suddenly to only 16. Still, this is hardly a huge, unprecedented blow to U.S. music. Back in 1962, with no Beatles or invasion, there were only 15 new artists, so the 1964 number is still within the normal range of variability.

The number of new major Americans begins to recover and returns to about the pre–Beatles level after 1965. But finally, by 1967, the number for American artists falls once again.

At the bottom of Graph 5, another British line marked by triangles shows the number of major British artists on the U.S. Top 100. What does this line reveal about the year of the Beatles, 1964?

In 1964, only 15 new major British artists came from the British invasion. Compared to the number of British artists up to that time, 15 is an impressive figure. But compared to the 200 or so major U.S. artists still having hits that year, and the 16 new major U.S. artists starting their hit careers the same year — well, the British invasion becomes less impressive than rhetoric would have us believe.

Myth: The Beatles invasion injected a huge number of British groups into American music, stifling lesser quality, less talented, American artists.

Reality: The Beatles British invasion did not add a huge number of new British artists to the U.S. charts — only 15. While impressive to be sure, it was not as many as new U.S. artists.

Myth: Established U.S. artists were killed off by the Beatles invasion.

Reality: It was not *established* U.S. artists who felt the impact of the Beatles British invasion. It was the *new* U.S. artists.

In 1964, the number of new major artists was roughly the same as usual. Due to the British invasion, however, almost half of those new artists were British. Thus, instead of killing off established U.S. artists as so often claimed, the true effect of the infamous Beatles British invasion was evidenced by a suppression in the number of new American artists in 1964. Half of the new major U.S. artists we would normally have heard from in 1964 were displaced by the new British acts.

It was not Bobby Vee or Bobby Rydell or Bobby Darin or Bobby Vinton or Bobby Anybody who suffered at the hands of the British. The careers of people we never heard of were stopped aborning by the British, and perhaps some minor acts like Bob Kuban or Tommy Tucker were kept minor by the competition of the British for American teens' record dollar, and were not allowed to become major artists. But either way, the established U.S. biggies were not hurt by the British invasion. Moreover, one-half of the new major artists in the states in 1964 were American, and in 1965 84 percent of the new artists were.

Continuing with Graph 5, the British new artist line drops dramatically each year after 1964, from 15 in 1964 to six in 1965 to only one in 1967. Who says it was a big advantage to be British after 1964? The kiss of death, more like. The honeymoon was over for the British rock 'n' rollers by 1966: that year, the number of new major British artists was, for all practical purposes, zero.

The number of new American artists had been pretty stable, on the average, since 1956. After 1964, the stifling effect of the British artists kept the number of new American artists low. By 1967, it had dropped to nearly the all-time low of 15, a record set in 1960.

Myth: After the Beatles British invasion, an artist had a much better chance of success if he or she were British, and American acts had it tough.

Reality: After 1964, almost no new major British artists were forthcoming. On the American side, not being British was a liability only in 1964. In '65 and '66, as shown by the open-circle line, being American was an advantage, while as shown by the triangle line, being British was not.

Everything declined for some reason in 1967. It was as if the British said, "If we can't have new major artists, neither can you."

Graph 5, showing the number of new artists each year, almost hides the effects of the Beatles British invasion, because much of the up and down variation was American as shown by the open circle line.

Then in 1964, the new artist tally was suddenly split 50/50 between the U.S. and Britain. This confirms the findings of Graph 5 — the important effect of the British invasion on major U.S. artists' popularity was to reduce the number of new artists for the year 1964; it was not a wiping out of the established artists as purported by many. But even this effect of the invasion was short-lived. By 1966, just two short years later, the new major artists were once again 100 percent American.

Myth: American acts could not compete with the Beatles British invasion artists.

Reality: The only effect on major U.S. artists' popularity of the British invasion was a temporary reduction in the number of new U.S. artists to become major successes, which quickly recovered to near 100 percent by 1966.

All of the hit data reported so far have been on major artists, and were based on *Billboard* magazine popularity charts. Now we look at the question of how much the U.S. rock 'n' roll scene was taken over by the British

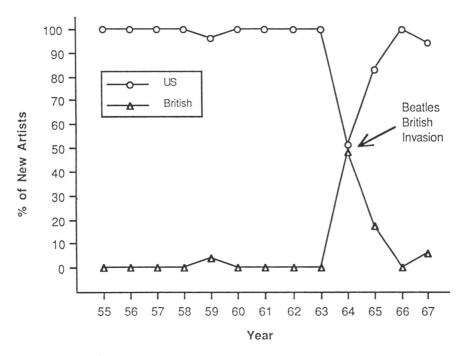

Graph 6. Percent of new artists — U.S. versus British.

invasion, according to the charts in *Cashbox* magazine. Each year, *Cashbox* publishes a list of the Top 50 songs for the entire year. This yearly list provides another way to measure the impact of the British invasion on the U.S. pop scene.

Graph 7 is a bar graph. For each year, there are two bars. The first bar shows the number of U.S. artists, major or otherwise, on the *Cashbox* Top 50 for that year, and the second bar shows the number of British artists on the Top 50 of the same year. For the year 1956, all of the songs on the yearly Top 50 were American. There was one British record each year in 1957 and 1958. Russ Hamilton had "Rainbow" in '57, and Laurie London had "He's Got the Whole World in His Hands" in '58.

In 1959, 1960, and 1961, *Cashbox* showed no British hits in the Top 50. There were two in 1962, instrumentals by Kenny Ball and Mr. Acker Bilk. In 1963, there were 49 American records and one British record, another instrumental, "Telstar" by the Tornadoes.

Then, 1964. The year the revisionist writers tell tales of the "devastation of the U.S. music scene," "the most difficult period for American artists to survive," when U.S. artists "took a back seat to the British invasion," and when, "with the coming of the British invasion, American artists fell behind." Right?

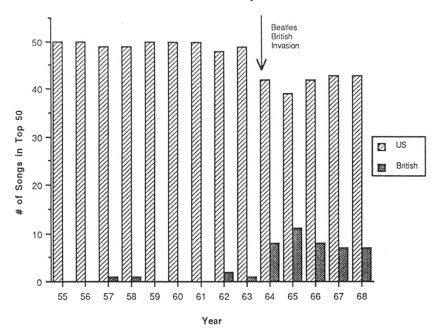

Graph 7. Number of Top 50 songs per year, U.S. versus British.

Wrong. In 1964, out of the Top-50 songs on the *Cashbox* list, 42 were American, and only eight were British. Of those, only three made the year's Top 10, and only *three* of the total were by British groups other than the Beatles. Only four British invasion acts, major or minor, made the Top 50 in 1964.

The invasion did a little better in 1965, with 39 American records versus 11 for the English. But only two English records made the yearly Top 10 for '65.

By 1966, the British were on the decline, with only eight songs in the Top 50. Why, in '66, the British got *only one* record in the year's Top 10. In 1967, the British scored only seven Top-50 hits, and the only one to make the Top 10 was Lulu's "To Sir, with Love," not exactly brash British invasion rock.

In 1968, the last year of the real invasion, there were again only seven British records versus 43 U.S. records in *Cashbox*'s list, and only one— "Hey, Jude"—in the Top 10.

Myth: The Beatles British invasion acts dominated the U.S. charts.

Reality: The British share of the annual Top-50 hits peaked at 11 songs in 1965, which was impressive, but the Americans never lost dominance of the Top 50.

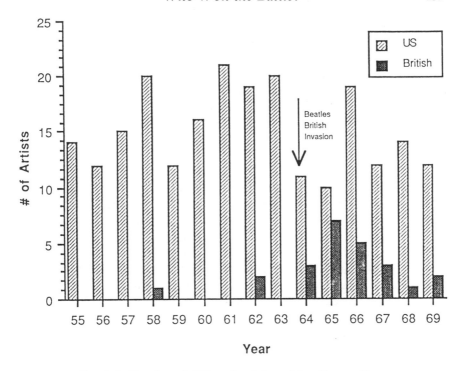

Graph 8. Number of different artists making #1 recordings.

Graph 8 shows artist popularity as reported by *Billboard* magazine, week by week, in terms of national #1 hits. From 1955 to 1963, the number of different U.S. artists making #1 varied between 12 and 21 per year. Then, in 1964, the British invasion reduced that to a new low of 11, just one less than the previous low of 12. In 1965, the British effect on the number of #1 hits that were by American artists was dropped by one more to 10.

Myth: U.S. artists could not get to #1 because the Beatles invasion groups monopolized the top of the charts.

Reality: American groups did have to share the #1 spot with the British and especially the Beatles, who accounted for two-thirds of the British #1s in 1964 and one-third in 1965. But nearly as many U.S. artists still had #1 hits in the Beatles British invasion years as in some '50s years.

The solid bars on Graph 8 show how many British acts had #1 hits each year. The number rose impressively in 1965, but never exceeded or even approached the number of American artists who made #1.

Myth: The British had all the big hits in the years of the Beatles British invasion.

Reality: Many British acts had #1 songs in the United States during the invasion, but they never outnumbered the U.S. acts making #1. Clearly, one of the biggest impacts the British artists had was here, in the weekly national #1 tally in 1965. People heard a lot of British music on the radio, because the #1 song was played every hour on most stations. This would magnify the impact of the invasion to the listeners' ears, especially the casual listener, like older people. But the Americans still had their share of #1 hits.

Graph 9 looks at *Billboard*'s Top-20 artists for each decade. This is a good overall gauge of whether or not the invasion brought about the "devastation of the U.S. music scene," "the most difficult period for American artists to survive," when U.S. artists "took a back seat to the British invasion," and whether, "with the coming of the British invasion, American artists fell behind."

The graph shows that in the decade of the '50s, all 20 of the Top-20 artists for the decade were American. In the '60s, the decade of the British invasion, 19 of the 20 were American. Only one British act, the Beatles (of course) made the U.S. Top 20. True, American artists have an advantage on the 1960s measure—the Americans had the full 10 years to impact the charts whereas the British acts had only six. But if it were true that the Beatles invasion wiped out the older U.S. artists, then they would have only four years to have hits, two less than the British acts' six years! In any case, of all the British acts only the Beatles made the Top 20 for the 1960s.

Myth: The Beatles British invasion groups were bigger than anything America had to offer in the '60s.
Reality: The only British act to successfully challenge U.S. chart supremacy for the decade of the '60s was the Beatles.

So, we move on to the '70s, when everyone had the full decade to flower. Still, only two British acts made the U.S. Top 20 in the 1970s— ex–Beatle Paul McCartney and post-invasion latecomer Elton John.

The entire discussion to this point has been about hit 45 rpm single records, because that is the arena in which the revisionsist rock writers claim overwhelming British victory over U.S. artists. Many fans may feel this is the wrong approach. It is a widely held view that the British acts, as popular as they were on the singles charts, showed their real strength with the popularity of their LPs.

Graph 10 therefore shows how well the British invasion forces scored on the *Billboard* LP charts between 1955 and 1972, compared to American Top-40 artists.

Most #1 albums: Obviously, while U.S. artists prevailed, 25 percent for

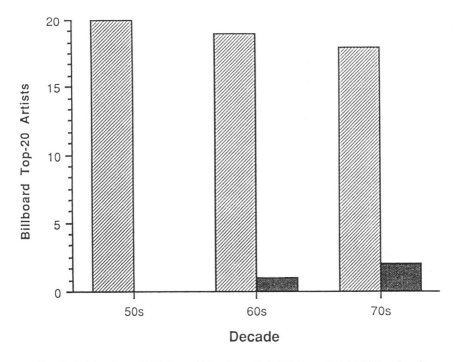

Graph 9. Number of *Billboard* Top 20 artists (U.S. and British) by decade.

the British sounds impressive, until you learn that the only British act to make the Top-10 LP list was the Beatles. Of the artists with the most Top-10 LPs, over 80 percent were American, and only two British acts, the Beatles and the Rolling Stones, made the list. Of the artists with the most LPs overall, nearly 100 percent were American, and the only invasion artist to make the list was the Beatles!

Myth: The place where the Beatles British invasion acts really beat the U.S. artists was in the LP arena.
Reality: The British invasion acts did no better with their LPs than with their singles—each made a fairly minor impact on the U.S. charts.

Graph 11 takes another look at the impact the British invasion artists had on the LP charts in America. It shows the percentage of all artists who were British having Top-10 LPs. The maximum was 20 percent.

Myth: Beatles British invasion artists took over the U.S. LP charts.
Reality: They accounted for one-fifth of the artists having Top-10 LPs for two years, which is very impressive but not overwhelming.

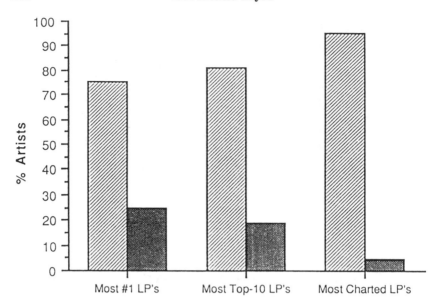

Graph 10. Comparison of U.S. and British artists with the most LPs by category, 1955–1972.

Once and for all, based on actual facts rather than personal opinion, the following questions are answered:

Did the British invasion of 1964 take over the U.S. charts? No, only *9 percent* were British in 1965, and *less* the following years.

Did the British invasion end the careers of many long-time U.S. acts? No, the number of U.S. acts dying off stayed the same following the British invasion.

Did the British artists excel in LPs more than in 45s? No, the British invasion did not even impact greatly on the LP charts in the states.

It is true that music lovers are apt to judge both the music they like, and the music they do not like, on "artistic" merit rather than chart success. Of course, artistic merit is not only undefinable, but will vary from individual to individual. That is why this book in general and this chapter in particular has not addressed these issues. Anyone who wants to say that the Beatles' music is "better" than Elvis' or Roy Orbison's or Fabian's is free to do so. Issue is taken only when the claim is made so often that certain types of music or certain artists' popularity with the public was ended in the Beatles British invasion. Anyone who was there and paying attention at the time knows it is not true, and the charts bear that out.

Just as the chart surveys in this chapter have shown, new acts may have been stifled by the Beatles British invasion, but the established artists' American music flourished.

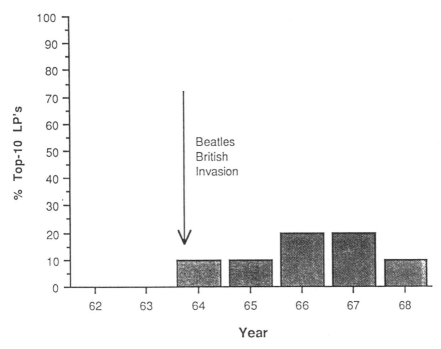

Graph 11. British artists' percentage of *Cashbox's* annual Top-10 LP list.

A Modern Look at the 1950s, '60s and the Beatles British Invasion

No matter what an individual thinks is good or bad, artistic and deserving of praise or hack work unworthy of approval, the children of the 1950s and the '60s still like their music and enjoy listening to it. So do their little brothers, their nieces and nephews, and their own kids! Three manifestations of this are the proliferation of television ads for oldies albums, the many local and satellite oldies radio stations and programs, and the reissue on compact discs of much of the '50s and '60s music.

Another interesting and unexpected area of oldies activity is the pervasive concentration of interest and activity pertaining to '50s and '60s music in national television commercials. Beginning in the late 1970s, oldies began turning up with increasing regularity on one television commercial after another. Everything from toothpaste and toilet cleaner to dolls and dog food has been sold with oldies. Some of the ads used the original record, some used a rerecording. Sometimes the rerecordings used the original artists, but not always. And sometimes the rerecordings used the original lyrics, but other times they used new lyrics to tie in to the product better. But in every form, the tunes were always instantly recognizable.

As a rock 'n' roll historian who is dedicated to facts and not opinion, this writer kept a log for many years of every oldies ad that came on television, including the song, the year it was popular, and the product or company it was used to advertise.

As time went by, and the oldies commercials became more and more frequently heard, a few comments in the media or on the street corner on this advertising gimmick began to appear. This was all very low key, however, and no one paid a great deal of attention to it, *until* the Beatles' song "Revolution" was used on a Nike television ad. Suddenly it seemed there was a new, mini–Beatles invasion, with a flurry of media attention. Just as "Yeah Yeah Yeah" had been around for years but was suddenly discovered when it was Beatle-ized, the oldies ads had been around for about a decade, but were suddenly "discovered" when a Beatles song was used.

Next thing you know, people were talking about all the '60s music being used to advertise products, and by '60s music, they meant Beatles, British, and post–British invasion music. Immediately the question occurred: Just as the minority of Beatles and British songs heard on the radio were exaggerated into a force that supposedly dominated popular music, could the feeling that the invasion and postinvasion music dominates the ads really be true, or is once again a minority of music being magnified by media attention?

Following is the log of oldies ads broadcast from 1980 to 1990. This list is provided to answer two questions concerning the Beatles and the British invasion. Are most songs used in commercials preinvasion versus postinvasion, and how many Beatles British invasion songs have been used?

Song Title	*Product or Company*

1955 — 4 Songs

"Love and Marriage"	Campbell's Combo
"Only You"	Red Lobster
"Rock Around the Clock"	Shield Soap
"Shake, Rattle, and Roll"	Frigidaire

1956 — 5 Songs

"The Great Pretender"	Red Lobster
"He's Got the Whole World in His Hands"	Radio Shack Phones
"Roll Over Beethoven"	Bolens Mowers
"That Magic Touch"	Hyatt Hotels
"Tutti-Frutti"	California Cooler

Song Title	*Product or Company*

1957 — 8 Songs

Song Title	Product or Company
"At the Hop"	WTBS-TV
"At the Hop"	Snapper Mowers
"At the Hop"	Fisher-Price Smooshies Dolls
"Come Go with Me"	Kentucky Fried Chicken
"I Feel Good"	Autolite
"I'm Walkin'"	Fisher-Price
"Let Me Be Your Teddy Bear"	Teddy Grahams (Nabisco)
"Wake Up Little Susie"	Teddy Grahams (Nabisco)
"The Way You Look Tonight" (also '61)	Michelob
"Whole Lotta Shakin' Goin' On"	Burger King Bagels
"Whole Lotta Shakin' Goin' On"	Glidden Paint
"Whole Lotta Shakin' Goin' On"	Missouri Lottery
"Whole Lotta Shakin' Goin' On"	Toyota

1958 — 13 Songs

Song Title	Product or Company
"Betty Lou Got a New Pair of Shoes"	Deer Foams
"Breathless"	Sunlight Dish Liquid
"Chantilly Lace"	Pizza Hut
"Chantilly Lace"	Velveeta
"For Your Love" (also '68)	Cable Value Network
"I Can't Stop Loving You" (also '62–'63)	Hershey Graham Bars
"It's All in the Game"	Hardees
"It's So Easy"	Toyota Tercel
"Splish Splash"	Drano
"Summertime Blues" (also '68)	Kawasaki
"Summertime Blues"	Sale of the Century
"Summertime Blues"	Toyota Tercel
"Summertime, Summertime"	Pizza Hut
"Tequila"	Velveeta
"Tequila"	The Weather Channel
"Twilight Time"	Red Lobster
"Yakitty Yak"	Coppertone

1959 — 11 Songs

Song Title	Product or Company
"Dedicated to the One I Love" (also '61 & '67)	Nutri-Grain
"I Only Have Eyes for You"	Amana
"I Only Have Eyes for You"	BMW
"I Only Have Eyes for You"	Totts
"La Bamba"	Pop Secret
"Mack the Knife"	McDonalds
"Shout" (also '62, '64, '67, & '69)	Kansas Lottery
"Shout"	Win, Lose or Draw
"Sea Cruise"	Diet Coke
"Sea of Love"	Chanel No. 5

Song Title	*Product or Company*
"Sleepwalk"	Mazda
"Unforgettable"	Revlon
"What'd I Say"	Stouffer Foods
"What'd I Say"	Water Pic Shower Massage
"You're 16"	Weight Watchers

1960 — 9 Songs

"Finger Poppin' Time"	Kentucky Fried Chicken
"Finger Poppin' Time"	Toyota
"I'm Sorry"	Bounty
"Itsy Bitsy Teenie Weenie Yellow Polka Dot Bikini"	Van Camp Beanie Weenies
"Mule Skinner Blues"	Kawasaki
"Peter Gunn"	Ford
"Stay"	Bennigan's
"This Magic Moment" (also '68)	Hyatt Hotels
"Twist"	Oreos
"You're 16"	Dole

1961 — 10 Songs

"Barbara Ann" (also '65)	Goodyear
"Barbara Ann" (also '65)	Quaker Granola Dipps
"Hit the Road, Jack"	Kentucky Fried Chicken
"Hit the Road, Jack"	Sears Tires
"Hit the Road, Jack"	Volkswagen
"I Fall to Pieces"	Mazda
"Let's Twist Again"	Pollenex Massager
"Mama Said"	Granola Dips
"Mama Said"	Mercury
"Peanut Butter"	Peter Pan
"Please Mr. Postman"	HBO/Cinemax
"Stand By Me"	Alzheimers Foundation
"Tossin' & Turnin'"	Almond Delight
"Who Put the Bomp"	Hi-C

1962 — 13 Songs

"Do You Love Me" (also '64)	Chew-eez Dog Food
"Do You Love Me"	Pizza Hut
"Don't Hang Up"	Teflon
"Duke of Earl"	Vanish
"Green Onions"	Miller Beer
"I Remember You"	Republican National Committee
"Locomotion"	Crest
"Make It Easy on Yourself" (also '65)	Easy Off
"My Boomerang Won't Come Back"	Matilda Bay
"Remember Then"	Subaru
"Sealed with a Kiss"	Zip Lock
"Surfin'"	Bally Fitness Centers
"Surfin' Safari"	Coastal Mart
"Twist and Shout"	Shout Cleaner

Song Title	*Product or Company*

1963 — 11 Songs

Song Title	Product or Company
"Be My Baby"	American Express
"The Bird's the Word"	Nintendo
"Call Me Irresponsible"	Subaru
"Danke Shoen"	Friskies
"Do-Wah-Diddy" (also '64)	Kentucky Fried Chicken
"Hello Muddah, Hello Faddah"	Downey Fabric Softener
"Hello Muddah, Hello Faddah"	Velveeta
"He's So Fine"	Hi-C
"Just One Look"	Toyota
"Louie, Louie" (also '66)	Chex Mix
"September Song"	Prudential
"September Song"	Retirement Home
"Wipe Out"	Pepsi
"Wipe Out"	Stridex

1964 — 15 Songs

Song Title	Product or Company
"Bread and Butter"	Friskies
"Bread and Butter"	Quaker Rice Cakes
"Dance, Dance, Dance"	General Motors
"Dancin' in the Streets"	Entertainment Tonight
"Dang Me"	McDonalds
"Everybody Loves Somebody"	Western Union
"Fun, Fun, Fun"	Bonanza Restaurants
"Fun, Fun, Fun"	Kentucky Fried Chicken
"Glad All Over"	Pampers
"Hi-Heel Sneakers"	Fresh Start
"Little GTO"	Volkswagen
"Oh! Pretty Woman"	Diet Center
"Please, Please, Please"	Burger King
"Somewhere"	Chrysler
"Surfin' Bird"	California Cooler
"The Name Game"	AT&T
"The Name Game"	Crest
"The Name Game"	Fisher-Price Jammers Sunglasses
"The Way You Do the Things You Do"	Lifetime Cable
"The Way You Do the Things You Do"	Pearl Vision

1965 — 13 Songs

Song Title	Product or Company
"Action"	Showtime
"Baby I'm Yours"	New Life Center, Topeka
"California Girls"	Clairol Herbal Essence
"Help Me, Rhonda"	Oster
"Hurts So Bad"	Gillette
"I Can't Help Myself"	Duncan Heinz
"Keep on Dancin'"	Boppers Dolls

Song Title	*Product or Company*
"Make Me Your Baby"	Johnson Baby Oil
"My Girl" (also '68)	American Express
"My Girl"	Sun Maid
"Papa's Got a Brand New Bag"	Success Rice
"Rescue Me"	American Express
"Satisfaction (I Can't Get No)"	Snickers
"Tell Her No"	Mita Copiers

1966 — 6 Songs

"Devil with a Blue Dress"	Mercury
"Hello, Dolly"	Oscar Meyer
"I've Got You Under My Skin"	Vanish
"Monday, Monday"	Sheraton
"Summer in the City"	7-Up
"When a Man Loves a Woman"	Levis
"When a Man Loves a Woman"	Subaru

1967 — 13 Songs

"The Beat Goes On"	Weather Channel
"Gimme Some Lovin'"	California Cooler
"Go Where You Wanna Go"	Mazda
"Groovin'"	Western Union
"Happy Together"	Golden Grahams
"I Can See for Miles"	Jiffy Lube
"I Heard It Through the Grapevine"	California Raisin Council
"I Heard It Through the Grapevine"	Levis
"I'm a Believer"	Plymouth
"I'm a Man"	Apple Mac Computer
"Little Bit o' Soul"	Le Mans
"Natural Woman"	Chic Jeans
"Nobody But Me"	Dominos Pizza
"Nobody But Me"	Friskies
"Nobody But Me"	Mita Copiers
"Rescue Me"	Slim Mint Diet Gum

1968 — 9 Songs

"Ain't Nothin' Like the Real Thing"	Burger King
"Born to Be Wild"	Suzuki
"Born to Be Wild"	Volkswagen
"Chewy, Chewy"	Duncan Hines
"Dream a Little Dream of Me"	Hot Springs, Arkansas
"Girl Watcher"	Wheel of Fortune
"It's a Beautiful Morning"	McDonalds Breakfast
"Mission Impossible Theme"	Spray & Wash
"Mission Impossible Theme"	Stain Stick
"Revolution"	Nike

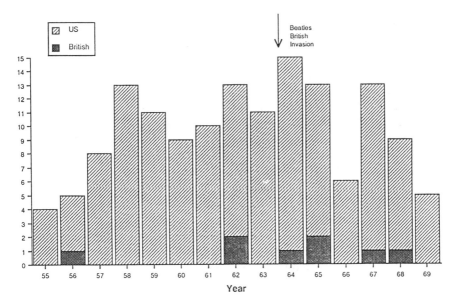

Chart 12. Number of songs from the years 1955–1969 used in television commercials.

Song Title and Year	*Product or Company*
"Yummy Yummy Yummy"	Skittles
"Yummy Yummy Yummy"	Yum Yums Dolls

1969 — 5 Songs

"It's Your Thing"	Pearl Vision
"Let the Sunshine In"	French's Mustard
"Put a Little Love in Your Heart"	Promise
"Sugar, Sugar"	Equal
"Who Do You Love"	HBO

Graph 12 shows how many different oldies from the years 1955–1969 were used in television commercials. If a song was used by more than one advertiser, it was counted only once, because the analysis is of the number of songs used, not the number of commercials. There were 180 commercials using 145 different oldies.

This graph reveals four peak periods from which old rock 'n' roll songs were used in commercials from 1980 to 1990 — 1958, 1962, 1964–65, and 1967.

The first peak period, 1958, should be no surprise, since 1958 is considered by many (not including this author) to be the end of the golden age of rock 'n' roll.

The fact that the second peak is 1962 will surprise many. This is because 1962 is commonly criticized as the core of the early-'60s wasteland. Of course, now that it has been illustrated that 1962 was a period of growth and variety in rock 'n' roll, it should really come as no surprise that 1962 is so popular in commercials.

It is probably expected that 1964–65 has so many oldie commercials, since that is the prime Beatles British invasion period. Yet, surprisingly, there was only one, single, solitary invasion record to be found in the 1964 commercials and only two from 1965. For 1964–65 to have so many commercials with non–British oldies, U.S. music must have been quite alive and well at the peak of the British invasion.

The fact that the third peak year, 1967, had only one British record is also interesting. Normally, 1967 is considered the end of the golden age of Beatles invasion music.

The two lowest points are 1955, and 1969. Clearly those years are at not just the chronological edge of the '50s and '60s music scene, but at the edge in the ears of Madison Avenue, too.

The number of songs from the nine-year pre–Beatles period was 84, for an average of 9.3 songs per year.

The number of songs from the invasion year of 1964 was 15.

The number of songs from the five-year post–Beatles period was 46, for an average of 9.2 per year.

It is absolutely amazing that the average number of oldies per year from the pre- and post-invasion era is virtually identical. Advertisers show no preference at all for one era over another.

Myth: Once the American public heard the Beatles British invasion songs and the American music that followed, 1950s and early '60s music was considered passe.

Reality: At least according to the market research done by Madison Avenue, the pre-invasion music is just as attractive to the public as post-'64 oldies.

Equally amazing is the fact that the number of songs selected for commercials from 1964, the year of the Beatles British invasion, was almost twice that for the average year. This bears out the contention that the year of the Beatles invasion was a special one for music. However, this was not due to the invasion, because only one invasion song, the Dave Clark Five's "Glad All Over" was used in an ad. In fact, only five of the 134 songs used from all the years were British invasion, less than 4 percent of all the songs used. The other four British songs were the Zombies' "Tell Her No," the Rolling Stones' "Satisfaction" from 1965, the Who's "I Can See for Miles" from 1967, and the Beatles' "Revolution," which was from 1968, not from the prime invasion period of 1964–65. (One other invasion song, "Do-Wah-

Diddy," was also used. But since it was originally an American girl group hit by the Exciters, calling it British would be stretching things.)

What is really interesting is that British songs from the preinvasion years were also used from time to time. "He's Got the Whole World in His Hands" from 1956, and "I Remember You" and "My Boomerang Won't Come Back," both from 1962, were used in commericals. To have three British songs from the pre-'64 period, just one from the big British year of 1964, and just four in the postinvasion era as in the preinvasion era is telling.

Myth: Because of its special nature, popularity, and the place it has in people's hearts, Beatles British invasion music is used in many television commercials.

Reality: Less than 4 percent of all the oldies used in television ads are from the Beatles British invasion.

The one thing these data show is that Madison Avenue pretty much ignores the British invasion. Why is this worth knowing? It is a measure of the endurance of artists' music. Advertisers conduct extensive market research before they air ads nationwide. They would never use music in an ad if that music were unpopular or unremembered, nor overlook especially well-appreciated songs.

Some 22 songs were used in more than one commercial. Three songs were used three times: 1957's "At the Hop"; 1961's "Hit the Road, Jack"; and 1964's "The Name Game." Two songs were used on four different commercials: 1957's "Whole Lotta Shakin' Goin' On," and 1967's "Nobody But Me."

Of all the multiple-use oldies, of the ones used three or more times, three were pre-Beatles British invasion, and only one postinvasion. Not one was British. (A few British artists, such as the Beatles, have taken legal steps to prevent their songs from being used in commercials. However, this is not an important factor, as many other British artists have not taken such action. Plus, American artists often take steps to protect their songs from commercial exploitation, as well.)

The data from the ads jibe with the data from the 45 and LP music charts of the '50s and '60s.

American rock 'n' roll, while no doubt influenced musically by the British acts, was not killed off by the British invasion as the rock 'n' roll history revisionists try to tell everyone. When the facts of American rock 'n' roll are finally uncovered, it turns out that the reports of its death have for years been greatly exaggerated!

Sure, the British invasion was a success, in the sense that it got quite a few British artists and songs on the U.S. charts for the first time. In fact, there were probably almost as many British on the U.S. charts as there were surfers or girl groups. And it is amazing that such a small country could produce so many good songs and stars all at once. It reminds one of the many acts to come out of New York in the 1950s, out of Philadelphia in the early '60s, out of Los Angeles in the mid-'60s, and out of San Francisco in the late '60s.

And, yes, the British invasion songs, and especially the records of the Beatles, were wonderful. But the Beatles British invasion music did not squash American music.

All of the oldie DJs, oldies satellite services and oldie stations which routinely program up to 50 percent of their music from the Beatles British invasion songs of the period 1964–1966 should be rethinking their programming policies. Few of them have done half the market research that national television sponsors do. Clearly, the ad makers' research has shown them that American rock 'n' roll oldies still have widespread appeal, and evidently help keep people from changing stations during commercials. And if you think about it, that is all records are — commercials. But instead of "buy this toothpaste or car," they say "buy this record or CD!"

Chapter 6

Summary

The basic Beatle myth has continued up to the present. Rhino Records is a well-respected company which presses high-quality reissues of '50s and '60s music. On the liner notes to their LP *Frat Rock Volume 4* (Rhino #70190), the Rhino staff, as usual, gave a bit of trivia about each selection. I think this is great. I respect the Rhino catalog. As a collector, rock historian, fan, and DJ, I appreciate the service Rhino provides with quality LP releases.

But I expect better from Rhino than the liners on *Frat Rock Volume 4*. The writer of those notes, when writing about Roger Miller's hit drinking song "Chug-a-Lug" asserts, "The toast to grade wine in a mason jar was one of the few non–Brit hits of late 1964."

A quick look at a few 1964 music charts shows how absurd this claim is. Radio station KEWI, a typical Top-40 screamer in 1964, published a "Good Guy Tundex" hit music survey on October 25 of that year showing "Chug-a-Lug" at #5. How many "Brit" records versus "non–Brit" records made this late '64 KEWI chart? Just one lonely Brit hit was on KEWI's Top 10, and this wasn't even a Beatle song. It was a British version of American composer/performer John D. Loudermilk's song, "Tobacco Road," here by the one-hit British group, the Nashville Teens. Only four more British records made KEWI's entire Top 40 on October 25, 1964. Out of 40 records, only five were British, just 12.5 percent. Even the "Pick to Click" for the week is American! The author of the revisionist liner notes on the Frat Rock LP perpetuated the Beatle myth by writing that Roger Miller was one of the few non–Brits to chart in late 1964.

While this station's playlist showed Americans dominating the late '64 charts, perhaps it was a local aberration. Maybe KEWI was out of step with the rest of America. To test this possibility, Lillian Roxon's widely distributed *Rock Encyclopedia* was checked. The late Roxon's reference book shows that only eight of the *Cashbox* Top-50 songs for the entire year of 1964 were British, a slim 16 percent.

Billboard's national chart for the week of December 19, 1964, was used as another check against KEWI's Tunedex. Including British female singers

Week of October 25, 1964

1.	Last Kiss	J.F. Wilson
2.	Ain't That Loving You	E. Presley
3.	Pretty Woman	R. Orbison
4.	Mercy Mercy	D. Covay
5.	Chug-A-Lug	R. Miller
6.	Baby Love	Supremes
7.	Tobacco Road	N. Teens
8.	You Must Believe Me	Impressions
9.	Death of an Angel	Kingsmen
10.	Bread and Butter	Newbeats
11.	Sing in the Sunshine	G. Garnett
12.	Baby Don't You Do It	M. Gaye
13.	Do Wah Diddy Diddy	M. Mann
14.	Reach Out for Me*	D. Warwick
15.	Wendy	Beach Boys
16.	Is It True	B. Lee
17.	The Door Is Still Open	D. Martin
18.	Out of Sight	J. Brown
19.	Let It Be Me	Everett/Butler
20.	Ain't Doing Too Bad	B. Bland
21.	Jump Back	R. Thomas
22.	Gone, Gone, Gone*	Everly Bros.
23.	She's Not There	Zombies
24.	Have I the Right?	Honeycombs
25.	Come a Little Closer	Jay/Americans
26.	I See You*	Cathy & Joe
27.	I Need Your Loving	Four Tops
28.	Dancing in the Street	Vandellas
29.	Talk with My Man	M. Collier
30.	Leader of the Pack	Shangri-Las
31.	I Guess I'm Crazy*	J. Reeves
32.	Smack Dab in Middle*	R. Charles
33.	It Ain't Me, Babe*	J. Cash
34.	Sand in My Shoes	Drifters
35.	Ride the Wild Surf	Jan & Dean
36.	Slow Down/Match Box	Beatles
37.	Young and In Love	Romantics
38.	Look Away	G. Mimms
39.	Four Strong Winds*	B. Bare
40.	I'm Crying	Animals

* — Indicates former KEWI Pick

KEWI Tunedex, October 25, 1964.

Pet Clark and Sandie Shaw, only 14 of the 100 songs on *Billboard*'s popularity poll were British, a mere 14 percent.

In short, roughly 15 percent of all the popular records in America late in 1964 were British. And those were not clustered in the Top 10 or the Top 40.

Finally, of the #1 songs in America in 1964, a review showed only four British invasion artists had #1 hits in that year — the Beatles, Peter and Gordon, Manfred Mann, and the Animals. And except for the Fab Four, each of those invasion artists had only one #1.

The Beatles were the best. A list of their achievements is impressive:

The number 1 record for 1964 — "I Want to Hold Your Hand."

The Number 1 record for 1968 — "Hey Jude."

The Beatles were the only artists to hold positions #1, #2, #3, #4, and #5 on the Top 100 at the same time.

The Beatles set the pattern for long singles with "Hey Jude."

The Beatles outsold every other artist in the mid-'60s.

The Beatles were the catalyst for the British invasion.

The Beatles' movies, *A Hard Day's Night* and *Help!* are classic hits.

The Beatles helped set trends in dress, speech, attitudes and music.

The Beatles' "Hey Jude" was the #1 record of the '60s.

The Beatles' "Hey Jude" was the #10 record of the rock era.

The Beatles were the second biggest artists of the '60s, after Elvis.

The Beatles' Paul McCartney was the second biggest artist of the '70s.

The Beatles were the second most popular artists of all time.

The Beatles rank fourth in the number of hit records overall.

The Beatles had the most #1 records of any artist.

The Beatles rank second after Elvis for most weeks with a #1 record.

The Beatles had 21 records make #1.

The Beatles ran second in the most consecutive Top-10 and Top-40 records.

The Beatles had the most #1 LPs.

The Beatles had the fourth most Top-10 LPs.

The Beatles had 26 two-sided hits.

The Beatles had hits simultaneously on more record labels than anyone.

The Beatles had the most #1 records in England.

The Beatles' huge number of hit records in England was exceeded only by Elvis Presley and Cliff Richard.

The Beatles had 17 #1 hits in England.

The Beatles and Elvis are the only artists to have radio stations with formats consisting of only their records 24 hours a day.

Everyone knows the Beatles were fabulous. The British invasion was fantastic; I love that music. The Beatles are the greatest. I have hundreds of records from that genre. But ... why gild the lily? Revisionist rock 'n' roll history is rampant enough without a reputable company like Rhino jumping in as well!

Beatles and British Invasion "Myths"

The Beatles started the so-called Beatle haircut.

The Beatles started the so-called Beatle boots.

The Beatles started the so-called Beatle collarless suit coat.

The Beatles created and popularized the phrase "Yeah Yeah Yeah."

The Beatles and the British invasion devastated, decimated, took over, hijacked, and otherwise dominated the U.S. music charts in the mid-'60s.

The Beatles British invasion music repudiated the American music of the period 1959–1963.

Many long-established U.S. artists, particularly teen idols and other singers like the Everly Brothers, the Shirelles, Lesley Gore, Johnny Tillotson, and the "Bobby-singers" (Rydell, Vee, Vinton, and Darin) were eliminated by the Beatles and the British invasion.

Many U.S. music movements like folk, surf, and girl groups were eliminated by the Beatles and the British invasion.

By the end of the '60s, the British invasion's overall impact on the U.S. singles charts had for all practical purposes been total.

The British invasion artists dominated the U.S. LP charts.

Roger Miller was one of the few non–Brits to have a hit in late 1964!

Beatles and British Invasion Realities

The Beatles did not originate the so-called Beatle haircut.

The Beatles did not start the so-called Beatle boots.

The Beatles did not popularize the phrase "Yeah Yeah Yeah."

The Beatles and the British invasion did not devastate, decimate, take over, hijack, or otherwise dominate the U.S. music charts in the mid-'60s.

The Beatles British invasion did not repudiate the American music of the period 1959–1963 — a substantial percent of the British invasion records were remakes or covers of American hits from the late-'50s and early '60s.

Not one long-established U.S. artist, such as teen idols and other singers like the Everly Brothers, the Shirelles, Lesley Gore, Johnny Tillotson, and the "Bobby-singers" (Rydell, Vee, Vinton, and Darin) was eliminated by the Beatles and the British invasion.

By the end of the '60s, when the Beatles (still at the top) were breaking up, the British invasion's overall impact on U.S. singles charts had for all practical purposes ended.

The British invasion artists did not dominate the U.S. LP charts.

In late 1964, over 85 percent of the United States hits were by non–Brit artists like Roger Miller and his hit "Chug-a-Lug."

A little more research on the part of Rhino as well as other rock writers, and a lot less opinion, would be more appropriate than the revisionist writings so commonly published. Beatles and British invasion music can stand on its own without inaccurate glorification.

In case the reader missed the explanations in the text, here are the answers to "The Beatle Myth True/False Quiz" from the Introduction.

Answers to the Beatle Myth True/False Quiz

1. The "Beatle haircut" was responsible for U.S. males wearing long hair.

False. John John Kennedy, son of the president, and Theodore "Beaver" Cleaver of television fame, along with millions of other U.S. kids, wore the same haircut in 1960 and 1957, respectively. It was the coming thing for years before the Beatles.

On the West Coast in 1963, the surfers wore the same style on the beach where Brylcream was not an option. It was a natural way to wear your hair.

On the other hand, the style was slow to catch on, and the Beatles did little if anything to speed up its adoption. A look through any high school yearbook from the mid- to late '60s shows that short, combed, slicked back hair was still the norm through the '60s, and long hair was not really worn until the 1970s, after the Beatles had broken up!

2. The Beatles introduced American kids to "Beatle boots."

False. Most American teen artists, and many teenagers, were already wearing the boots before 1964. For instance, see the 1962 Jan and Dean *Golden Hits* LP cover photo on Liberty Records. It was the Beatles who emulated the Americans.

3. The Beatles popularized the musical lyric "Yeah Yeah Yeah!"

False. A survey of pre-1964 rock 'n' roll records reveals 144 songs featuring "Yeah Yeah Yeah." Many of these were American recordings which were also popular in England in the 12 months just before the Beatles' "She Loves You" was recorded. The term "Yeah Yeah Yeah" became associated with the Beatles, but association should not be transformed into their introduction or popularization of it.

4a. In 1964, the Beatles and the rest of the British invasion groups eliminated the established American artists (Roy Orbison, Bobby Vee, Tommy Roe, the Everly Brothers, Neil Sedaka, etc.) from the American charts.

False. Roy Orbison's biggest hit, "Oh, Pretty Woman," was #1 in 1964. Bobby Vee's biggest hit, "Come Back When You Grow Up," was #1 in 1967. Tommy Roe's biggest hit, "Dizzy," was #1 in 1969. The Everly Brothers and Neil Sedaka did not have any more big '60s hits after the Beatles and British invaded America in 1964. However, their chart decline began in 1962, two years before the invasion.

4b. In 1964, the Beatles and the rest of the British invasion groups eliminated the established American musical styles (girl groups, surf and drag, teen idols) from the American charts.

False. Besides the teen idol hits named in 4a, the only car song to ever make #1 was in 1964, "I Get Around." And, combining styles, the girl group the Shangri-Las had the only female drag hit to ever make #1, "Leader of the Pack," in the winter of '64-'65. Furthermore, the Beatles and British invasion acts rerecorded so great a number of American songs from the period immediately preceding the Beatles' arrival as to constitute a tribute to and continuation of the American music, not the elimination of it.

5. British music dominated the U.S. charts in the mid-'60s.

False. At the height of the British invasion, 1965, the total percent of the American Top-100 chart held by British artists was less than 10 percent. Impressive, yes. Domination, no. And that was the peak. The percent declined after that.

6. The Beatles popularized the practice of artists writing their own songs.

False. American pre–Beatle aces who penned their own music included Tommy Roe, Roy Orbison, Buddy Holly, Paul Anka, Neil Sedaka, Jan and Dean, the Beach Boys, the Everly Brothers, and a host of others.

7. Anything and everything the Beatles released in the U.S. became a hit.

False. The following Beatle 45s failed to make the U.S. Top 40 when released. (Some later became hits on rerelease, or had hit flip sides.)

1963

"From Me to You"	"Please Please Me"
"She Loves You"	

1964

"Sie Liebt Dich"	"If I Fell"
"I'm Happy Just to Dance with You"	"From Me to You" (reissue)
	"All My Loving"
"Why"	"You Can't Do That"
"There's a Place"	"Roll Over Beethoven"
"I Should Have Known Better"	

1965

"I'm Down"   "Act Naturally"
"Yes It Is"   "Boys"

1966

What Goes On"

1967

"I Am the Walrus"

8. The Beatles and their music were popular naturally, unlike the manufactured images and popularity of early '60s American artists, and the British invasion artists in general were more successful than the U.S. teen idols.

False. Manager Brian Epstein manufactured the Beatles' image. He picked out their matching outfits including the collarless jackets and their boots; he made them wear their hair in the famous haircut; he made them smile; when no crowds came to their first London concert, he arranged for a small group of screaming girls to appear on the sidewalk and be photographed to represent a nonexistent screaming mass for the press. When the Beatles' first British release failed to catch on, Epstein personally purchased 10,000 copies to get it on the charts. When several 1963 American releases fizzled without cracking the Top 100, Epstein arranged an unprecedented, preinflationary $50,000 promotional campaign with Capitol Records which included free Beatle wigs for all the U.S. DJs. Teen idols on the average had longer careers, more hit 45s, and more chart LPs than the British invasion groups.

9. Beatle LP albums were the first played on AM radio, which had up to then played only hit 45s.

False. Many AM radio stations featured one or more LPs each week. These were often listed on the stations' popularity/playlist sheets given away at record counters. For an example, see the K-TOP 40 survey for July 1, 1963, and the others behind it, which show that each week there was a "Pick Album." A cut was played from the pick album each hour all week, so that the entire LP was played on the air 14 times during the week. (Two K-TOP Pick Albums this writer recalls hearing on K-TOP were Larry Verne's *Mister Custer* and *Bobby Vee Meets the Ventures*, both of which this writer subsequently purchased.)

10. American rock 'n' roll was unable to compete musically with the British sound.

False. Many British artists did not crack the top charts in America in the mid-'60s. Popular British and Beatle-esque rock groups who could not penetrate the U.S. music market included the Rockin' Berries, the Shadows,

Big 7 Picks of the Week

Certified

k·TOP 40

Silver Dollar Survey

Charlie Christian

6-8
Rock Me In The Cradle Of Love
Dee Dee Sharp

Bob Barber

8-12
Blowin' In The Wind
Peter Paul & Mary

Tom Grimes

12-4
Green, Green
New Christy Minstrels

Bob Harris

4-7
Will Power
Cookies

Johnny Ford

7-9
Detroit City
Bobby Bare

Rick Douglass

9-Midnight
I (Who Have Nothing)
Ben E King

Prof. J. Jazmo Bop

Midnight-6
I Wonder
Brenda Lee

Monday

RECORDS INTRODUCED AND HEARD FIRST ON K-TOP

Week of July 1, 1963

#	Song	Artist
1.	Surf City	Jan & Dean
2.	Tie Me Kangaroo Down, Sport	Rolf Harris
3.	Sukiyaki	Kyu Sakamoto
4.	Wipe Out	Surfaries
5.	It's My Party	Lesley Gore
6.	Easier Said Then Done	Essex
7.	Devil In Disguise	Elvis Presley
8.	Hello Stranger	Barbara Lewis
9.	No One/Without Love	Ray Charles
10.	Memphis	Lonnie Mack
11.	So Much In Love	Tymes
12.	Blue on Blue	Bobby Vinton
13.	Pushover	Etta James
14.	Surfin' USA/Shut Down	Beach Boys
15.	Pride and Joy	Marvin Gaye
16.	Don't Say Goodnight And Mean Goodbye	Shirrells
17.	Fingertips Pt. 1	Little Stevie Wonder
18.	Ring of Fire	Johnny Cash
19.	Goodnight My Love	Fleetwoods
20.	Hopeless	Andy Williams
21.	Harry The Hairy Ape	Ray Stevens
22.	Not Me	Orlons
23.	My True Confession	Brooke Benton
24.	Marlena	Four Seasons
25.	If You Need Me	Solomon Burke
26.	One Fine Day	Chiffons
27.	Don't Try to Fight It Baby	Eydie Gorme
28.	The Bounce	Olympics
29.	I'm Movin' On	Matt Lucas
30.	I Wish I Were A Princess	Little Peggy March
31.	Be True To Yourself	Bobby Vee
32.	Come Go With Me	Dion
33.	Don't You Forget It	Perry Como
34.	Old Smokey Locomotion	Little Eva
35.	Summer's Comin'	Kirby St. Romain
36.	Danke Schön	Wayne Newton
37.	Just One Look	Doris Troy
38.	Hello Jim	Paul Anka
39.	Topeka My Home Town	Terry Lee
40.	On Top of Spagetti	Tom Glazer

Pick Album
Looking Back --- Ace Cannon -- Hi

12-6
My True Confession
Brooke Benton

40. Easier Said Than Done

Tom Glazer
Essex

Pick Album
Wildwood Days
Bobby Rydell
Cameo

Pick Album
"My Boyfriend's Back" - - Angeles - - Smash

Rags To Riches
Sunny & Sunliners

Little Red Rooster
Same Cooke

12--6
Blue Winter
Connie Francis

Young Wings Can Fly

Ruby & Romantics

Surfer Girl   Pick Album
Gonna Send You Back to   Surfer Girl -- Beach Boys -- Capitol
          Georgia

40. Anyone Who Had a Heart

Stevens & Tempo

Timmy Shaw
Dionne Warwick

Pick Album
Mixed-Up Hearts --- Leslie Gore
-- Mercury

Sounds Unlimited, the FourMost, and the Four Pennies. There were many solo singers, women, and other non–Beatle-esque British artists who had #1 hits in England in 1963–67 but who never successfully competed on the U.S. Top 40 during the British invasion, including Jet Harris, Tony Meehan, Cilla Black, Sandie Shaw, Jackie Trent, Helen Shapiro, Cliff Richard, Ken Dodd, Frank Ifield, the Overlanders, Chris Farlow, and Long John Baldry. There were, of course, many more.

Opposite: **Note the weekly "Pick Album" selections at the bottom of each survey.**

Afterword
with Bobby Vee

One of the more curious aspects of the British invasion music was the singers' accents—or lack thereof. A few invasion groups capitalized on their accents in their overtly British records. The best example is Herman's Hermits' record "I'm Henry VIII, I Am." But the rest of the British acts, nearly unintelligible to Americans when interviewed because of their thick, usually working-class British accents, sang with scarcely a trace of an accent. In an interview, the Beatles said they learned early on that their music's sound was accepted better if they sang with American accents.

Of course, the Beatles, as well as the majority of other British acts, sang many American hits. The roots of the British invasion documented that. But the roots went even deeper than the obvious ones represented by the many British invasion acts who had U.S. hits with covers of U.S. oldies. For example, the Manchester group Wayne Fontana and the Mindbenders' big American hits may have been originals such as "Game of Love" and "A Groovy Kind of Love," but their original British releases included such American favorites as Fats Domino's "Hello, Josephine," Bo Diddley's "Road Runner," and Major Lance's "Um Um Um Um Um Um."

Some British artists who have never been known to American fans of the Beatles British invasion had roots in American hit records. Here is a brief list of American hits and the British and American artists who did them.

Title	American	British
"All My Love"	Jackie Wilson	Cliff Richard
"Alley Cat"	Bent Fabric	David Thorne
"Anyone Who Had a Heart"	Dionne Warwick	Mary May; Cilla Black
"Battle of New Orleans"	Johnny Horton	Bob Cort; Lonnie Donegon
"Bobby's Girl"	Marcie Blane	Susan Maughan

Title	American	British
"Bongo Rock"	Preston Epps	The Jet Streams
"Cindy's Birthday"	Johnny Crawford	Shane Fenton and the Fentones
"Donna"	Ritchie Valens	Marty Wilde
"Endless Sleep"	Jody Reynolds	Marty Wilde
"A Hundred Pounds of Clay"	Gene McDaniels	Craig Douglas
"I Saw Linda Yesterday"	Dickie Lee	Doug Sheldon
"I'm Gonna Get Married"	Lloyd Price	Bob Cort
"Makin' Love"	Floyd Robinson	Hylda Baker
"Only Sixteen"	Sam Cooke	Craig Douglas
"Personality"	Lloyd Price	Anthony Newley
"Pretty Blue Eyes"	Steve Lawrence	Craig Douglas
"Rubber Ball"	Bobby Vee	Marty Wilde
"Runaround Sue"	Dion	Doug Sheldon
"Sea of Love"	Phil Phillips	Marty Wilde
"Sleep Walk"	Santo and Johnny	Johnny Douglas
"Tallahassee Lassie"	Freddie Cannon	Tommy Steele
"A Teenager in Love"	Dion and the Belmonts	Marty Wilde; Craig Douglas
"Tiger"	Fabian	The Jet Streams
"When My Little Girl Is Smiling"	The Drifters	Craig Douglas
"Why"	Frankie Avalon	Anthony Newley
"Willie and the Hand Jive"	The Johnny Otis Show	Cliff Richard
"Your Ma Said You Cried in Your Sleep Last Night"	James Ray	Doug Sheldon

These are just a few of the uncounted British hit records that were originally bestsellers in America, then were adapted or covered in England during the early years of rock 'n' roll by artists who were largely unknown in America even during the height of the Beatles British invasion.

Some North American singers responded to the invasion by adopting the "new" British style of music, much as the British had been adapting American music for ten years. Canadian Terry Black released many 1964 singles like "Unless You Care" and "Say It Again" on Tollie, one of the Beatles' labels, with minimal success. A Texas band, pretentiously calling themselves the "Sir" Douglas Quintet, pretended to be British and scored with several singles including 1965's hit "She's About a Mover." Three other Americans pretended to be Australian and had hits like "I Want Candy" and "Night Time." A group of Californians calling themselves the "Beau Brummels" picked their name because it sounded British and alphabetically, they knew that their records would be filed in record stores' racks right after

"Beatles." "Laugh Laugh" and "Just a Little" in 1965 were two of their six hits.

There are many more examples, but two deserve special notice. Bobby Rydell was a male mainstay who had over 30 hits in his career and who still tours.

In 1965, he recorded an excellent American version of Peter and Gordon's "World Without Love." Both versions, English and American, entered the U.S. charts simultaneously. In the same way that the Beatles sang their records using fake American accents, Bobby Rydell and his background singers sang "World Without Love" with British accents. Needless to say, Rydell was roundly criticized for his recording, which was seen as a direct rip-off of the British invasion movement. Yet what he did was in no way different from what all the British acts were doing with their roots of the British invasion "cover" records, sung with fake American accents.

Was he being any less original than Peter and Gordon themselves, who got not only "World Without Love" from John Lennon and Paul McCartney, but their two followups, "Nobody I Know" and "I Don't Want to See You Again," from the Beatles as well? For their three subsequent releases, Peter and Gordon even recorded, in turn, songs written by Americans Del Shannon, Buddy Holly, and Phil Spector. And Bobby Rydell was wrong to do one little number composed and sung by British citizens?

Bobby Rydell, whose career had been on the wane anyway, saw his recording of "World Without Love" peak at #80, while Peter and Gordon's went to #1, perhaps due to prejudices of nationality, perhaps to prejudices of musical preference.

Bobby Vee was another male mainstay. A singer in the Buddy Holly vein, his career was even bigger than Bobby Rydell's, with nearly 40 hits in ten years. In 1964, Bobby Vee released a 45 with two British-sound records, and an LP titled, *The New Sound from England*. The records were great. The 45 was "I'll Make You Mine" with a falsetto "Ooooh!" which was inspired by the Beatles' "Ooooooh" on "She Loves You," which in turn they got from Little Richard's 1957 single, "Jenny Jenny." Vee's flip side was "She's Sorry," patterned openly after "She Loves You," right down to the "Yeahs." These efforts were greeted with total disdain by many people, as if keeping up with the times were not essential to anyone's career. I interviewed Bobby Vee about the Beatles and about his "English sound" records (my questions in italics):

I read an article in 1964 saying that George Harrison had heard your singles "I'll Make You Mine" and "She's Sorry" before you released them, and that he approved of them. Is that true?

Right. Yes, that was true, as a matter of fact. The album *The New Sound from England* came from my touring in England. This was before the Beatles were popular in the United States. But I saw this tremendous energy happening in England and it was all centered around the Beatles, and their four-piece rock 'n' roll sound that was very exciting to me. I guess they reminded me, name-wise of the Crickets, who I had done an album with, and style-wise they reminded me of the rockin' fifties. It was raw, it was like the old music that wasn't so polished, that still had some rough edges. That was something that I had always enjoyed about the fifties, the music that was so raw.

So I was over in England with Snuffy, Snuff Garrett, my producer. We heard this music, and we both felt that this was going to be something to contend with, a major force. As a result, I put out what was probably the first tribute album to the English invasion. Soon, everyone was swept up in it. But my album was called *The New Sound from England*. At that time, there were only a few Beatle songs that were popular. Some of the Beatles' things had been released in 1963, but the first time around they didn't mean much, the stations didn't play them. So we did a couple of those songs, and then I wrote the rest of the songs on the album.

After that album was done, I went over to England to tour some more. When I arrived, the press reviews of the album were just disastrous. They all thought that I was trying to jump on the band wagon and they hated me for it. It was so ironic then that one night, I was sitting in my hotel room and I got a phone call from my manager. He said to me, "You ought to come over here. There is a party going on at EMI, a lot of people are here, including the Beatles. You should come on over." He didn't have to twist my arm, because even though they weren't that big in the states, I knew of them.

So I went over to the party and met the guys. They all had nice things to say about my record, they took it as a compliment to them. They also talked about some of my old songs that they had always liked. It was very enjoyable. There is even a tape, it has been bootlegged on some LPs and cassettes, of the Beatles doing "Take Good Care of My Baby" [this song was #1 in 1961 by Bobby Vee in both the states and England]. The Beatles had recorded it when it was popular but didn't have a vehicle or a label to release it on at the time. But it has surfaced now.

In other words, the press and even the fans panned your effort, but the Beatles themselves liked it and liked you and your music. That is ironic. Why do you suppose many fans of the British music reject or put down the rock 'n' roll that preceded it, when the British groups they embraced actually liked the old music and were simply emulating it?

I think that there is a turnover of audience, a new younger audience that comes along and wants something else. I also think it is entirely possible for record artists to become caricatures of themselves. They have a certain sound and it sells and then all of a sudden, everything sort of sounds the same. Next, people get bored with it, or at least they look for something new, something they find more stimulating. And add to that the new audience that comes along who have got something else that is exciting to them, electronics or whatever.

I do believe that quality lasts. I don't think any less of "Peggy Sue" today just because it is old, and I don't think any less of "Wake Up Little Susie."

Like a Rembrandt painting in a museum. If it was great before, it is still going to be great today, even if no one is painting in that style today. So a song that was good then is still good today, though people are not singing that way today.

Right. I believe that is true. A few years ago, they had an album that was a collection of all my old songs that was released only in Great Britain. To my amazement, it went to #4 on the national album chart. It was a gold album. I think that the people who bought the album were probably people who bought those songs the first time around or they wanted to have bought them or bought them and lost them and wanted them again now, or it reminds them of a space and time in their life that is meaningful to them. It is hard to understand or explain. But then again, because there has been a lot of focus on the records of the fifties and the sixties, there are a lot of young people who collect now. The late fifties and early sixties took, I believe, unfair lumps by writers caught up in the English movement of the mid-sixties. I think part of it had to do with turning away from anything established in all areas of society...

Like the Vietnam war, racial discrimination, sexism, industrial pollution, and the generation gap. Musically, many writers have thrown out the baby with the bath water, so to speak. But now, it is time for that to change, isn't it?

Yes, and it is interesting to me the amount of airplay the early sixties is getting today on classic rock 'n' roll stations. Lots!

That was how Bobby Vee experienced the "English" invasion.

Many rock 'n' roll revisionists are young, too young to have lived through rock 'n' roll from its beginnings. Much of the inflation of the British and Beatles' music popularity had been at the expense of earlier, American music, implying that the earlier music was inherently less valuable. Perhaps the best way to close this book is by quoting Carl Belz' comments on the '50s revival group, Sha-Na-Na, in *The Story of Rock*:

Whatever their motivation, however, the group's interpretation of the fifties invariably seemed satirical; they seemed to view early rock and its life styles as inherently ridiculous. But that is a popular view, shared by those who did not experience the music's beginnings, or whose self-consciousness irretrievably distances them from an understanding of folk innocence (p. 214).

Appendix A: Chronologies

Phase I: Pre-1964 British Artists with U.S. Hits

Lonnie Donegan — "Rock Island Line," "Lost John," "Does Your Chewing Gum Lose Its Flavor on the Bed Post Overnight?"
Russ Hamilton — "Rainbow"
Laurie London — "He's Got the Whole World (in His Hands)"
Chas. McDivitt Skiffle Group with Nancy Whiskey — "Freight Train"
Chris Barber's Jazz Band — "Petite Fleur"
Cliff Richard — "Living Doll," "Lucky Lips," "It's All in the Game"
Gary Mills — "Look for a Star"
Charlie Drake — "My Boomerang Won't Come Back"
Kenny Ball — "Midnight in Moscow"
Mr. Acker Bilk — "Stranger on the Shore"
The Springfields — "Silver Threads and Golden Needles," "Dear Hearts and Gentle People"
Frank Ifield — "I Remember You," "Lovesick Blues," "I'm Confessin'," "Please"
The Tornadoes — "Telstar," "Ridin' the Wind"
The Beatles — "From Me to You"
The Caravelles — "You Don't Have to Be a Baby to Cry," "Have You Ever Been Lonely"

Phase II: 1964 Chronology of British Invasion Songs

"I Want to Hold Your Hand"
"She Loves You"
"I Only Want to Be with You"
"Please Please Me"
"I Saw Her Standing There"
"My Bonnie"
"Glad All Over"
"From Me to You"

"Hippy Hippy Shake"
"Twist and Shout"
"All My Loving"
"Roll Over Beethoven"
"Needles and Pins"
"Can't Buy Me Love"
"Do You Want to Know a Secret"
"Stay Awhile"

189

"You Can't Do That"
"Thank You Girl"
"Bits and Pieces"
"I Knew It All the Time"
"There's a Place"
"Love Me Do"
"Diane"
"I'm the Lonely One"
"Little Children"
"Why"
"Ain't That Just Like Me"
"Do You Love Me"
"Good Golly Miss Molly"
"World Without Love"
"P.S. I Love You"
"Not Fade Away"
"My Boy Lollipop"
"Sweet William"
"Sugar and Spice"
"Don't Let the Sun Catch You
  Crying"
"Yesterday's Gone"
"Yesterday's Gone"
"Just One Look"
"Can't You See That She's Mine"
"Nobody I Know"
"Four by the Beatles"
  "This Boy"
  "Roll Over Beethoven"
  "All My Loving"
  "Please Mr. Postman"
"Sie Liebt Dich"
"I Believe"
"A Hard Day's Night"
"Ain't She Sweet"
"I Should Have Known Better"
"And I Love Her"
"If I Fell"
"I'll Cry Instead"
"I'm Happy Just to Dance with You"
"I'll Keep You Satisfied"
"How Do You Do It"
"I'm the One"
"Tell Me"
"It's All Over Now"

"You're My World"
"Bachelor Boy"
"Because"
"From a Window"
"You're No Good"
"Some Day We're Gonna Love
  Again"
"A Summer Song"
"House of the Rising Sun"
"Matchbox"
"Slow Down"
"Have I the Right"
"I Like It"
"I Don't Want to See You Again"
"Do Wah Diddy Diddy"
"Tobacco Road"
"Find My Way Back Home"
"It's for You"
"Don't Throw Your Love Away"
"Gonna Send You Back to Walker
  (Gonna Send You Back to
  Georgia)"
"I'm Crying"
"Wouldn't Trade You for the World"
"You Really Got Me"
"Everybody Knows"
"Time Is on My Side"
"When You Walk in the Room"
"I'm Into Something Good"
"She's Not There"
"Anyway You Want It"
"Willow Weep for Me"
"Love Potion #9"
"Sha La La"
"As Tears Go By"
"(There's) Always Something There
  to Remind Me"
"Downtown"
"No Arms Can Ever Hold You"
"Boom Boom"
"All Day and All of the Night"
"I'll Be There"
"I Can't Stop"
"I Feel Fine"
"She's a Woman"

Phase III: Post–1964 British Invasion Artists

David and Jonathan
Freddie and the Dreamers

The Fortunes
The Yardbirds

Hedgehoppers Anonymous
Georgie Fame
Donovan
Tom Jones
The Troggs

The Spencer Davis Group
The Easybeats
Engelbert Humperdinck
The Who
Lulu

Appendix B: Roots of the Beatles British Invasion

American Songs Recorded by British Invasion Artists

Manfred Mann
"Do Wah Diddy Diddy"
  (Exciters)
"Sha La La"
  (Shirelles)
"Sweet Pea"*
  (Tommy Roe)

Peter and Gordon
"I Go to Pieces"
  (Del Shannon)
"True Love Ways"
  (Buddy Holly)
"To Know You Is to Love You"
  (Teddy Bears)

Gerry and the Pacemakers
"I'll Be There"
  (Bobby Darin)
"You'll Never Walk Alone"
  (Patti LaBelle and the Blue
  Belles/"Carousel")

The Hollies
"Just Like Me"*
  (Coasters)
"Searchin'"*
  (Coasters)
"Stay"*
  (Maurice Williams)
"Just One Look"

(Doris Troy)

The Rolling Stones
"Time Is on My Side"
  (Irma Thomas)
"Not Fade Away"
  (Buddy Holly)

The Swinging Blue Jeans
"Hippy Hippy Shake"
  (Chan Romero)
"Good Golly Miss Molly"
  (Little Richard)
"You're No Good"
  (Betty Everett)
"Don't Make Me Over"*
  (Dionne Warwick)

The Animals
"House of the Rising Sun"
  (traditional)
"Gonna Send You Back to Walker
  (Gonna Send You Back to Geor-
  gia)"
  (Timmy Shaw)
"Bring It on Home to Me"
  (Sam Cooke)
"See See Rider"
  (Chuck Willis)
  (Laverne Baker)
  (Bobby Powell)

The Dave Clark Five
"Do You Love Me"
(Contours)
"Reelin' and Rockin'"
(Chuck Berry)
"I Like It Like That"
(Chris Kenner)
"Over and Over"
(Bobby Day)
"You've Got What It Takes"
(Marv Johnson)
"A Little Bit Now"
(Majors)
"Put a Little Love in Your Heart"*
(Jackie DeShannon)
"Here Comes Summer"*
(Jerry Keller)

Herman's Hermits
"I'm Into Somethin' Good"
(Earl-Jean)
"Silhouettes"
(Rays)
(Steve Gibson & the Red Caps)
(Diamonds)
"Wonderful World"
(Sam Cooke)

Georgie Fame
"Yeh, Yeh"
(Mongo Santa Maria)

The Moody Blues
"Go Now"
(Bessie Banks)

The Searchers
"Sweets for My Sweet"
(Drifters)
"Sweet Nothin's"*
(Brenda Lee)
"Needles and Pins"
(Jackie DeShannon)
"Just Like Me"
(Coasters)
"When You Walk in the Room"
(Jackie DeShannon)
"Love Potion # 9"
(Clovers)

"Bumble Bee"
(LaVern Baker)
"Hi-Heel Sneakers"
(Tommy Tucker)
"Take Me for What I'm Worth"
(P.F. Sloan)

The Beatles
"Act Naturally"**
(Buck Owens)
"Anna (Go to Him)"
(Arthur Alexander)
"Baby, It's You"**
(Shirelles)
"Bad Boy"**
(Larry Williams)
"Boys"**
(Shirelles)
"Chains"**
(Cookies)
"Devil in His Heart"**
(The Donays)
"Dizzy Miss Lizzie"**
(Larry Williams)
"Everybody's Trying to Be My
Baby"**
(Carl Perkins)
"Honey Don't"**
(Carl Perkins)
"Kansas City/Hey Hey Hey"**
(Wilbert Harrison/Little
Richard)
"Long Tall Sally"**
(Little Richard)
"Match Box"**
(Carl Perkins)
"Misery"**
(Dynamics)
"Mr. Moonlight"**
(Dr. Feelgood and the Interns)
"Money"**
(Barrett Strong)
"Rock and Roll Music"**
(Chuck Berry)
"Roll Over Beethoven"
(Chuck Berry)
"Slow Down"
(Larry Williams)
"Till There Was You"**
(Anita Bryant) from *The Music
Man,* a Broadway musical

"Twist and Shout"   "Words of Love"**
(Isley Brothers)   (Buddy Holly)

  * British hit single by an invasion artist.
** Beatles' American LP cut.

Appendix C: A Chronological "Yeah Yeah Yeah" Discography

1951 — 1 recording	Artist	Rank	Year
"Sixty Minute Man"	Dominoes		1951

1957 — 6 recordings			
"Alone"	Brother Sisters		1957
"Whenever You're Ready"	Bob Luman		1957
"Steady"	Steve Lawrence		1957
"My Baby's Gone"	Johnnie and Joe		1957
"All Shook Up"	Elvis Presley	# 1	3-57
"Alone"	Shepherd Sisters	#20	9-57

1958 — 7 recordings			
"Sweet Baby Doll"	Johnny Burnette		1958
"Some Kind of Nut"	Danny and the Juniors		1958
"Do the Mashed Potatoes"	Danny and the Juniors		1958
"Yea Yea"	Kendall Sisters	#73	3-58
"Jeannie Jeannie Jeannie"	Eddie Cochran	#94	3-58
"Crazy Love"	Paul Anka	#15	4-58
"A Boy and a Girl"	Shepherd Sisters		5-58

1959 — 14 recordings			
"Heartaches of Sweet 16"	Kathy Linden		1959
"I Sympathize with You"	Conway Twitty		1959
"Fever"	Ray Peterson		1959
"These Lonely Tears"	Little Joe Cook		1959
"Boogie Woogie Feelin'"	Tony Casanova		1959
"The Switch"	Bobby Please and the Pleasers		1959
"Tall Paul"	Barry Sisters (British)		1-59
"I'm a Man"	Fabian	#31	1-59
"School Days"	(Flip side of "The Class") Chubby Checker	#38	5-59
"True True Happiness"	Johnny Tillotson	#54	8-59

1959 (con't)	Artist		Rank	Year
"Shout"	Isley Brothers		#47	9-59
"You've Got What It Takes"	Marv Johnson		#10	11-59
		UK	# 4	2-60
"First Name Initial"	Annette		#32	11-59
"A Year Ago Tonight"	Crests		#42	12-59

1960 — 14 recordings

"Poetry in Motion"	Bobby Vee			1960
"Got a Girl"	Four Preps		#24	4-60
		UK	#28	5-60
"Shortnin' Bread"	Paul Chaplain and His Emeralds		#82	8-60
"Volare"	Bobby Rydell		# 4	8-60
		UK	#22	8-60
"Twistin' USA"	Danny & the Juniors		#27	9-60
"If I Can't Have You"	Etta and Harvey		#12	9-60
"The Hucklebuck"	Chubby Checker		#14	10-60
"Whole Lotta Shakin' Goin' On"	Chubby Checker		#42	10-60
"Twistin' and Kissin'"	Fabian		#91	11-60
"Boys"	Shirelles (Flip side of "Will You Love Me Tomorrow")		# 1	11-60
"Robot Man"	Jamie Horton			1960
"Big John"	Carol and Anthony			1960
"Suzie Jane"	Ron Holden			1960
"Cutie Pie"	Johnny Tillotson			1960

1961 — 24 recordings

"Stewball"	Coasters			1961
"Patricia"	Ray Peterson			1961
"Tell Me Mama"	Janie Grant			1961
"Locomotion Twist"	Oliver and the Twisters			1961
"Vacation Time"	Johnny Maestro			1961
"Pin the Tail on the Donkey"	Paul Peek			1961
"Olds-Mo-Williams"	Paul Peek			1961
"Baggy Pants"	Jan and Dean			1-61
"Story of My Love"	Paul Anka		#16	1-61
"The Continental Walk"	The Rollers		#80	4-61
"Quarter to Three"	U.S. Bonds		# 1	5-61
		UK	# 7	7-61
"Little Devil"	Neil Sedaka		#11	6-61
		UK	#12	5-61
"Temptation"	Everly Brothers		#27	6-61
		UK	# 1	6-61
"Twist and Shout"	Top Notes (Flip side of "Always Late Why Lead Me On")			7-61
"Mr. Happiness"	Johnny Maestro		#57	7-61

1961	*Artist*		*Rank*	*Year*
"The Mountain's High"	Dick and Dee Dee		# 2	8-61
		UK	#37	10-61
"Let's Get Together"	Hayley Mills		#8	9-61
		UK	#11	10-61
"Walkin' Back to Happiness"	Helen Shapiro	UK	# 1	9-61
"Big John"	Shirelles		#21	10-61
"School Is In"	U.S. Bonds		#28	10-61
"Jeanie Jeanie Jeanie"	Eddie Cochran	UK	#31	11-61
"Everlovin'"	Ricky Nelson		#16	11-61
		UK	#20	12-61
"Multiplication"	Bobby Darin		#30	12-61
		UK	# 5	1-62
"Twisting USA"	Chubby Checker		#68	12-61

1962 — 31 recordings

"Daddy"	Debbie and the Darnels			1962
"I Want a Love I Can See"	Temptations			1962
"Counting Teardrops"	Barry Mann			1962
"Rabian, Teenage Idol"	Bobby "Boris" Pickett			1962
"The Duke of Earl"	Gene Chandler		# 1	1-62
"Do the New Continental"	Dovells		#37	1-62
"Her Royal Majesty"	James Darren		# 6	2-62
		UK	#26	3-62
"Good Luck Charm"	Elvis Presley		# 1	3-62
		UK	#1	5-62
"The Alvin Twist"	Chipmunks		#40	3-62
"Twistin' Matilda (and the channel)"	Jimmy Soul		#22	3-62
"Duchess of Earl"	Pearlettes		#96	3-62
"The One Who Really Loves You"	Mary Wells		# 8	3-62
"Thou Shalt Not Steal"	John D. Loudermilk		#73	4-62
"Walk on with the Duke"	Duke of Earl		#91	4-62
"Uptown"	Crystals		#13	5-62
"Hit Record"	Brook Benton		#45	5-62
"Party Lights"	Claudine Clark		# 5	6-62
"Dancin' Party"	Chubby Checker		#12	6-62
		UK	#19	8-62
"Locomotion"	Little Eva		# 1	6-62
		UK	# 2	9-62
"Little Diane"	Dion		# 8	7-62
"Lolita Ya-Ya"	Ventures		#61	8-62
"That Stranger Used to Be My Girl"	Trade Martin		#26	10-62
"The Conservative"	Orlons		# 4	10-62
	(Flip side of "Don't Hang Up")	UK	#39	12-62
"Stubborn Kind of Fellow"	Marvin Gaye (1st hit)		#46	10-62
"Love Came to Me"	Dion		#10	11-62
"I Dig This Station"	Gary U.S. Bonds			10-62

1962	*Artist*		*Rank*	*Year*
"Hotel Happiness"	Brook Benton		#13	11-62
"Zip-a-Dee Doo-Dah"	Bob B. Soxx and the Blue Jeans		# 8	11-62
"Comin' Home Baby"	Mel Torme		#36	11-62
		UK	#13	1-63
"Alone"	Four Seasons (Recorded in 1962)		#28	6-64
"Loop-De-Loop"	Johnny Thunder		# 4	12-62

1963 — 35 recordings				
"Puddin' 'n' Tain"	Alley Cats		#43	1-63
"He's Sure the Boy I Love"	Crystals		#11	1-63
"Call on Me"	Bobby "Blue" Bland		#22	1-63
"Let's Turkey Trot"	Little Eva		#20	2-63
		UK	#13	3-63
"He's Braggin'"	The Tip Tops			3-63
"Don't Say Nothin' Bad About My Baby"	Cookies		# 7	3-63
"Lover Boy"	Dee Dee Sharp (Flip side of "Do the Bird")		#10	3-63
"Locking Up My Heart"	Marvelettes		#44	3-63
"I Got a Woman"	Ricky Nelson		#49	3-63
"He's Got the Power"	Exciters		#57	3-63
"You Can't Sit Down"	Dovells		# 3	4-63
"(Today I Met) The Boy I'm Gonna Marry"	Darlene Love		#39	4-63
"Hot Pastrami"	Dartells		#11	4-63
"Come and Get These Memories"	Martha & the Vandellas		#29	4-63
"What a Guy"	Raindrops		#41	4-63
"Killer Joe"	Rocky Fellers		#16	5-63
"If My Pillow Could Talk"	Connie Francis		#23	5-63
"He's Braggin'"	Orlons			6-63
"Come Go with Me"	Dion		#48	6-63
"Fingertips"	Little Stevie Wonder		# 1	6-63
"Da Do Ron Ron"	Crystals		# 3	4-63
		UK	# 5	6-63
"Yeh-Yeh"	Mongo Santamaria		#92	6-63
"My Boyfriend's Back"	Angels		# 1	6-63
		UK	#50	10-63
"Mocking Bird"	Inez Foxx		# 7	6-63
		UK	#36	2-69
"If I Had a Hammer"	Trini Lopez		# 3	7-63
		UK	# 4	9-63
"A Breath Taking Guy"	Supremes		#75	7-63
"I Want a Boy for My Birthday"	Cookies (Flip side of "Will Power")		#72	7-63
"Wait 'Til My Bobby Gets Home"	Darlene Love		#26	7-63
"The Sweetest Boy"	Kittens			1963
"One Last Kiss"	Bobby Rydell		LP	1963

"When the Boy's Happy"	Raindrops	LP	1963
"The Ghoul in School"	Fortunes		1963
	(from the 1963 Italian-made movie *Werewolf in a Girls' Dormitory*).		

1963	*Artist*	*Rank*	*Year*
"What a Party"	Freddy Cannon		1963
"What's Happening"	Major Lance		1963
"She Loves You"	Beatles	Recorded on July 1, 1963	

The following 1963 records were recorded before 1964, when "She Loves You" became a hit in the USA, meaning that they were not inspired by "She Loves You." However, they were recorded after "She Loves You" was recorded on July 1, 1963, so they could not have helped inspire the Beatles to use "Yeah Yeah Yeah."

Song	*Artist*		*Rank*	*Year*
"The Kind of Boy You Can't Forget"	Raindrops		#17	8-63
"You Lost the Sweetest Boy"	Mary Wells		#22	9-63
"Sugar Shack"	Jimmy Gilmer and the		# 1	9-63
	Fireballs	UK	#45	11-63
"What I Gotta Do to Make You Jealous?"	Little Eva			9-63
"The Trouble with Boys"	Little Eva			9-63
"A Fine Fine Boy"	Darlene Love		#53	10-63
"Can I Get a Witness"	Marvin Gaye		#22	10-63
"Dear Abby"	Hearts		#94	10-63
"As Long As I Know He's Mine"	Marvelettes		#47	11-63
"Kansas City"	Trini Lopez		#23	11-63
		UK	#35	12-63
"Even Though You Can't Dance"	Raindrops		LP	1963
"That Boy John"	Raindrops		#64	11-63
"Over Yonder"	Appalachians			1963
"Do-Wah-Diddy"	Exciters		#78	12-63
"She Loves You"	Beatles		# 1	1-25-64

Bibliography

Belz, Carl. *The Story of Rock*. New York: Harper Colophon Books, 1972.

Berry, Peter E. *. . .And the Hits Just Keep on Comin'*. Syracuse: Syracuse University Press, 1977.

Betrock, Alan. *Girl Groups*. New York: Delilah Books, 1982.

_____. *Girl Groups: An Annotated Discography 1960–1965*. New York: Alan Betrock, circa 1975.

Blair, John. *The Illustrated Discography of Surf Music 1959–1965*. Riverside, Calif.: J. Bee Productions, 1981.

Burt, Rob. *Rockerama*. New York: Delilah, 1983.

_____. *Surf City Drag City*. Blandford Press, 1986.

Catres, Jim. *The Pictures Sleeve Guide*. Topeka, Kan., 1981.

Cohen, Nik. *Rock from the Beginning*. New York: Stein and Day, 1972.

Consumer Guide. *Rock 'n' Roll Trivia*. Skokie, Ill.: Publications International, Ltd., 1985.

Dachs, David. *Inside Pop America's Top Ten Groups*. New York: Scholastic Book Services, 1968.

Davis, Lloyd, Ron and Marvin. *Collectors Price Guide to 45 RPM Picture Sleeves*. Medford, Oregon: Winema Publications, 1977.

Dundy, Elaine. *Elvis and Gladys*. New York: Macmillan, 1985.

Escott, Colin, and Hawkins, Martin. *Sun Records*. New York: Quick Fox, 1975.

Gilbert, Bob, and Theroux, Gary. *The Top Ten*. New York: Fireside, 1982.

Goldstein, Stewart, and Jacobson, Alan. *Oldies But Goodies*. New York: Mason Charter, 1977.

Hardy, Phil, and Laing, Dave, editors. *The Encyclopedia of Rock, Volume Two — From Liverpool to San Francisco*. Great Britain: Panther, 1977.

Hopkins, Jerry. *Elvis*. New York: Simon and Schuster, 1971.

Lang, Dave. *Buddy Holly*. New York: Macmillan, 1971.

Leaf, Earl. *The Beatles Book Two*. Los Angeles: Peterson Publishing: 1964.

Liberty Records. *The Complete Catalog of Long Play Albums*. Los Angeles, 1968.

Lichter, Paul. *The Boy Who Dared to Rock*. Garden City, N.Y.: Galahad, 1978.

McColm, Bruce, and Payne, Doug. *Where Have They Gone?* New York: Tempo Books, 1979.

Macken, Bob, Forntale, Peter, and Ayres, Bill. *The Rock Music Source Book*. Garden City, N.Y.: Anchor, 1980.

McParland, Stephen J. *Beach Street and Strip — the Albums*. North Stratfield, Australia: Seagull, 1983.

_____, editor. *California Music Magazine*. Concord, Australia: 1976–1990.

Miller, Bill. *The Drifters*. New York: Macmillan, 1971.

Nite, Norm N. *Rock On.* New York: Thomas Y. Crowell, 1974.

————. *Rock On, Volume II.* New York: Thomas Y. Crowell, 1978.

Nugent, Stephen, and Gillett, Charlie. *Rock Almanac.* Garden City, N.Y.: Anchor, 1978.

Pollock, Bruce. *When Rock Was Young.* New York: Holt, Rinehart, Winston, 1981.

RCA Victor. *The Music America Loves Best.* New York: RCA, 1967.

Rolling Stone. *Rock Almanac.* New York: Collier, 1983.

Rolling Stone Press. *The Beatles.* New York: 1980.

Roxon, Lillian. *Rock Encyclopedia.* New York: Grosset & Dunlap, 1969.

Satkin, Marc. *The Official Rock and Roll Trivia Quiz Book.* New York: Signet, 1977.

Schaffner, Nicholas, and Elizabeth. *505 Rock 'n' Roll Questions Your Friends Can't Answer.* New York: Walker and Company, 1981.

Schwann. *Long Playing Record Catalog.* Boston: 1967–1968.

Shannon, Bob, and Javna, John. *Behind the Hits.* New York: Warner Books, 1986.

Shoire, Michael, with Dick Clark. *The History of American Bandstand.* New York: Ballantine Books, 1985.

Simon, George T. *The Big Bands.* New York: The Macmillan Company, 1967.

Solomon, Clive. *Record Hits the British Top 50 Charts 1954–1976.* London: Omnibus Press, 1977.

Spies, Jerry. *Phil and Don Home Again.* Shenandoah, Iowa: World, 1986.

Tobler, John. *Thirty Years of Rock.* New York: Exeter Books, 1985.

Uslan, Michael, and Solomon, Bruce. *Dick Clark's The First 25 Years of Rock & Roll.* New York: Greenwich House, 1981.

Wertheimer, Alfred. *Elvis in the Beginning.* New York: Collier, 1979.

Whitburn, Joel. *Bubbling Under the Hot 100 1959–1981.* Menomonee Falls, Wisc.: Record Research Inc., 1982.

————. *Pop Singles, 1955–1986.* Menomonee Falls, Wisc.: Record Research, Inc., 1987.

————. *Record Research.* Menomonee Falls, Wisc.: Record Research, 1970.

————. *Top LP's 1945–1972.* Menomonee Falls, Wisc.: Record Research, 1973.

————. *Top Pop Artists & Singles, 1955–1978.* Menomonee Falls, Wisc.: Record Research Inc., 1979.

————. *Top Pop Singles 1940–1955.* Menomonee Falls, Wisc.: Record Research, Inc., 1973.

————. *Top Pop Singles 1955–1986.* Menomonee Falls, Wisc.: Record Research Inc., 1987.

Magazines

The Rock Marketplace Magazine. Ed. Alan Betrock.

Who Put the Bomp Magazine. Ed. Greg Shaw.

Index

M